Prepositions Illustrated

Prepositions Illustrated

Gloria Wahlen

Illustrated by Toni Acock

Ann Arbor

THE UNIVERSITY OF MICHIGAN PRESS

Copyright © by the University of Michigan 1995
All rights reserved
ISBN 0-472-08289-2
Library of Congress Catalog Card No. 95-61197
Published in the United States of America by
The University of Michigan Press
Manufactured in the United States of America

2006   2005   2004   2003   8   7   6   5

To Hank Wahlen, my husband and sounding board, whose patience and humor helped me across, over, and beyond the Sea of Prepositions.

This book would not exist had it not been for Margaret Freitag, who saw the problems prepositions posed for ESL students and did something about them. Her original vision emanated from a paper she presented in Tokyo at the ESL convention in 1985. It was based on her years of experience teaching English to Japanese students and was restricted to the biggest preposition troublemakers: on, to, at, and by. She saw the antics of anthropomorphic eggplants as a non-ethnic, upbeat way to illustrate the various usages of these four words.

Margaret's editor at the University of Michigan Press, Mary Erwin, suggested she expand the concept to include all the prepositions, which she agreed to do. Her work on this version was under way and Margaret was researching the use of prepositions in other language families when she fell ill.

Margaret's death will not mean the end of her dream to make this contribution to the field she loved and excelled in. As her friend and fellow teacher, I feel privileged to have been asked to extend and complete *Prepositions Illustrated,* thereby bringing her dream to fruition.

To the Teacher

Prepositions rival articles in causing the most difficulty to both learners and teachers of English. This book aims to make the learning process easier and the teaching job more effective by introducing new slants on old methods, capturing interest through entertainment. Designed as a supplementary text for the specialized teaching or individual study of prepositions, it is intended principally for intermediate students. Beginning students, however, can gain much from the illustrations and from the simpler examples and passages. Advanced students should find it helpful for deep-rooting the correct usages of prepositions and for review of phrasal verbs.

Some of the teaching techniques included are saturation, illustrated examples and narrative passages, and exclusion. The first of these techniques focuses on a single preposition until the learner's mind is saturated with it. Such intense concentration eliminates the distraction and clutter of multiple input and minimizes error fossilization. In cases where the fossilization of incorrect usage has occurred or is occurring, it helps break this pattern of error.

The second reinforces each preposition with illustrated sentences and narrative passages. The meaning of a preposition often depends on the context in which it is used and, conversely, the context's meaning often depends on the correct usage of a preposition. While not always possessing inherent meaning, these elusive words become precise when presented in context. The impact of whimsical drawings clearly defining printed examples provides rich input.

The third technique uses the tactic of omission. When a preposition has been ingrained through frequent repetition in specific contexts, it is eventually missed if excluded from sentences in similar contexts. Its absence will be noted and cause the learner to feel a need to "fill in the gap."

Earl W. Stevick, (*Teaching and Learning Languages* [Cambridge: Cambridge University Press, 1982]), writes that getting an item from long-term memory into permanent memory depends mostly on intensity, which includes "vividness of exposure," and that its chances of receiving the necessary intensity increase with the total number of exposures. The three techniques used here work easily with each other, as well as with traditional exercises, to achieve this kind of intensity.

The Powerful Preposition

A parallel aim of this book is to upgrade prepositions in the consciousness of teachers and students alike to a more prominent position in the hierarchy of the English language. The application of the aforementioned techniques heighten awareness of the very existence as well as the strong influence of these powerful words. Like punctuation marks they are small and unobtrusive, but their misuse can muddy comprehension of the surrounding content. Incorrect placement, usage, or omission can bring misunderstandings and confusion, sometimes changing the intended gist of a phrase or a sentence:

He studied painting in/until 1989.
They jogged the park and exercised the gym.
She walked on the house and threw her purse in the table.
Drive the lake around and then go left the bridge across.

Prepositions serve many functions; the following are some of them:

As catalysts linking related words: Central Park lies between 110th Street on the north and 59th Street on the south.
As energizers creating distinct images: She poured boiling water from the kettle into the teapot.
As stabilizers, anchoring otherwise homeless words to a definite place in time or space: The sun hung high in the sky at noon.
As signals indicating direction and cause: Buffeted by the wind, we turned toward the ocean and walked along the shore.
As prefaces to comparison: That baby looks exactly like her sisters.
As signs of separation: Robin Hood took from the rich to help the poor.
As introducers of means: We heard the news via satellite.
As marks of manner: She pointed out the employee's error with great tact.

The Problem with Prepositions

Integral to the English idiom and crucial to the abstract and theoretical expressions that enrich the language, these little words carry a big load.

But as an ESL teacher you know they are big little problems too. The multiple personalities of prepositions often baffle students of English, and with very good reason. As they have evolved over the centuries, changes have occurred which cause many English prepositional usages to seem capricious and inconsistent.

To make the issue even more confusing, every language gives its own special twist to the way it regards and uses these bits of grammar—that is if it uses them at all!

Following are just a few examples of the use or absence of prepositions in other languages. They give some insight into language differences and into the difficulties involved in learning prepositions.

Russian is a highly inflected language that uses prefixes together with prepositions followed by designated cases. Different prepositions take six different case endings, each selected according to their desired meanings, e.g., the preposition K (KO) is always followed by the dative case. When used in reference to persons K (KO) generally means "to"; when used in reference to things it generally means "toward." And with some verbs "to" is rendered in Russian simply by the dative case without any preposition at all.

In German, data introduced by an inflected noun or an article would be introduced by a preposition in English: "eine Tasse Kaffee" does not require a preposition as "a cup of coffee" does. German uses prepositions as compounds of contractions, e.g., *ins Haus = in das Haus; dem* combines with *zu* to form *zum,* etc. A single German preposition can have a variety of meanings in various syntactical structures, rivaling English in its richness of use. But although they closely parallel English prepositions, because of inflections and distinctive compounds of words in idioms they do not always match up neatly.

Italian and English have some corresponding prepositions, but they are often used in different situations with very different meanings. Also, some verbs that take a direct object in Italian require a preposition in English, and vice versa. Only a few Italian verbs, which in English take a direct object, require a preposition. The most common are: *entrare* "in," *credere* "a" (when the object is a person), and *recordarse* "di." Some verbs require a preposition in both languages, but a different one. Italian also contracts five prepositions with the article, e.g., *a + gli = agli; con + il = col; a + le = alle.*

Among non-Indo-European language families, some have prepositions, some have postpositions, and some have no words indicating comparable usage. In the African language of Bantu, for instance, and in the languages of Southeast Asia (Burmese, Thai, etc.) there are no prepositions or postpositions. A Thai example would translate "Me go beach."

The Indian subcontinent has over two hundred dialects. In northern India some use prepositions; in southern India some use postpositions, and some use neither. Urdu, one of the official languages of India and one of two state languages of Pakistan, uses postpositions, e.g., "on the table" would translate directly as "table on." Also, a different preposition must be used when referring to a human being than is used before an inanimate object.

Turkish grammar also employs postpositions, which follow the word they govern, although some of the functions of English prepositions are performed in Turkish by case-suffixes. Examples of the postposition as used in Turkish are: *toplantedan sonra* (after) = "after the meeting"; *bir antikaci-dan iciri* (inside) *girdik* = "we went inside an antique dealer's shop."

Direct translation of Moroccan Arabic prepositions into English is tricky because no Moroccan preposition is exactly equivalent to any English preposition.

Chinese employs "localizers," nominal forms used in combination with other elements to indicate position. These words are similar in meaning to English prepositions. Used after a noun, a localizer shows location in regard to the noun itself; used before a verb, the localizer indicates the direction of the action. Chinese also has coverbs that function as English prepositions to signal direction. Modern Chinese prepositions are all verbal in origin; most of them can occur as main verbs as well as prepositions.

Some languages use a principal verb and a supplemental verb. For instance, the Japanese word that is literally translated as "jump-descend" is the equivalent of the English "jump off." Also in Japanese the particle "ni" is regularly used as a place indicator that points to the noun or noun phrase immediately preceding it. The role it plays is similar to the English "at," "in," and "on." A verb's relationship to another word in a sentence (shown either by word order or a preposition in English) is marked by a particle, i.e., "ni" (destination-to) marker; "de" (existence-by) marker; or "kara"- (point of departure-from) marker.

In other Asian languages, such as Korean, particles are to their grammar what word order and prepositions are to English. Substitution of a Korean phrase by an English counterpart is almost impossible. In Tagalog, the Austronesian family language spoken by peoples of the Philippines, "sa" is used as a preposition to indicate the English in, on, at, to, from, by, into, with, etc. It functions as comfortably in the sentence "Sasama ka ba sa Nanay?" (Are you going with Mother?) as it does with "Nagdaan pa kami sa inyong bahay." (We passed by your house).

Native American languages (sometimes called Amerindian languages) differ in their use of prepositions. Some use postpositions and some do not.

The languages of South Africa are English and Afrikaans, the latter of which is derived from the Dutch language and therefore would use prepositions.

Even from such a superficial sampling it becomes clear that more disagreement than agreement exists among the prepositions of the various language families. Although contrastive analysis is not as useful in their study as in the study of other facets of grammar, a general understanding of the great number of variants involved will sensitize the teacher to potential problems.

Using This Book

English prepositions have no neat set of rules to control their use. The rules we do have are often complex; others cannot ensure accuracy. Prepositions are limited in number and can be memorized from a list, but knowing their names does not automatically reveal their true identities or direct them into their proper slots. The exercises offered in this book were devised for the teaching and learning of prepositional usage with minimum rules and maximum repetition.

Example sentences highlighting specific usages, and reading passages focusing on prepositions in context are the basis for the exercises. They build colorful storage places in the mind to hold patterns of prepositions as used in the real world. The intent behind their use is to stir interest, teach culture, elicit questions, increase vocabulary, introduce idioms, and promote a clearer comprehension of the English language in general, not only the targeted preposition.

Because they give us no clues to their meaning through special endings, each preposition must be learned separately. Rather than teaching several prepositions and their various usages at once, each section concentrates on a single preposition. Studying a preposition individually before mixing it in with others allows more complete assimilation and understanding.

The format for each lesson is as follows.

Definition of one of the usages of the targeted preposition.

Example sentences featuring the targeted usage and sometimes including but not stressing other prepositions.

Exercises based on the sentences. These can be selected and adapted by you, and, in cases of individual study, by the students. The example sentences of the more heavily used prepositions are graded from simple to more complex.

Reading passages contextualizing the targeted usages to be read to and by the student. In cases of a less frequently used preposition, or where overuse would result in an awkward-sounding composition, no reading passage is included. The number and length of the passages and exercises also depend on the relative incidence of the individual preposition in everyday speech.

> *Note:* Explain to the students that the passages are not examples of good writing. The artificially frequent use of a single preposition is for saturation purposes only.

Dialogues are included in many of the lessons to introduce the targeted preposition in precise context. These dialogues are designed either for student participation in which two or more students practice and then present them to the class or for small groups to practice among themselves.

Missing Links reading passages, identical to the ones in the lessons but omitting the targeted preposition, are located in the back of the book. In these exercises, the student knows what the correct word is; he/she needs only to find its proper place and insert a "link" (∧) between the words where it belongs. These are integral parts of the units and can be adapted for testing purposes and for individual review.

Combined usage passages featuring two or more of the previously studied prepositions appear at the end of most of the units. Passages with combined usage are presented in cloze form in the Missing Links section.

Review is automatic as the lessons progress. The fewer the occasions of usage of a preposition, the shorter the passage, the less time spent on practice, and the more time spent on review.

An appendix of *Phrasal verbs,* i.e., on, off, in, out, through, over, up, down, which are among the
most widely used, can be used in conjunction with the exercises or for reference and private
study. A definition and example sentence accompanies each one.

Illustrations chosen with an eye toward clarity of meaning accompany representative example
sentences.

The decision to use "Eggies," anthropomorphic versions of the universally known eggplant, was
based on their unethnicity. Their playful naivete and gentle humor help maintain the lightness of spirit
which engenders successful language learning. Certain usages of prepositions cannot be well
illustrated pictorially. In these figurative or abstract cases, involving theory or idioms, several model
sentences are given.

Variations on a Theme

How you implement the material in this book is entirely up to you. Much depends upon your time,
your students, and your imagination. Lessons can be adapted or omitted according to your class's level
and need.

The instructions for each lesson are general guides only. For instance, instead of the class dividing
into teams, you may find it more efficient to be the reader with the class completing the sentences. For
extra practice, you could write missing link or cloze sentences of your own on the board and ask for
volunteers to insert the missing link or the targeted preposition.

Listening practice is important. Just as they do not always see the prepositions, many students do
not hear that a preposition is missing. If the ear is trained to listen for its presence, its absence will be
noted. Missing links can be used as an eye/ear training tool for raising preposition consciousness.
Depending on your particular classroom conditions and student learning levels, you could read the
example sentences and/or the passages minus the prepositions. Alert the students, whose books
should be closed, to listen for the prepositions in the sentences or passages as you read them. Have
them signal missing prepositions in one of several ways, e.g., raising their hands; writing the
preposition on a numbered list; putting a plastic disc in a cup and then counting at the end of reading
to see if all have been heard.

Dictation is an efficient tool for eye/ear training and can be adapted easily. After dictating
sentences from the examples or passages, you might ask the students to underline the prepositions.
Then, after reading the sentences from their papers, have the students try to repeat them from
memory, first in unison, then individually.

Extra exercises based on the reading passages could include dividing the class into teams with one
side making up questions about the passage and the other answering. Questions from you might be
even more effective.

Spatial concepts are the easiest to teach and perhaps the easiest to illustrate. If feasible, plan time
for students to draw simple pictures (stick or geometrical if they prefer) representing prepositions of
location or action. Then display the drawings, or ask the students to exchange them and try to guess
what they symbolize.

Divide the class and provide each side with a list of preposition opposites, e.g., one side has "up"
on its list, the other side has "down." In unison or individually Side A calls out a preposition and Side B
calls out its opposite. At the end of the list Side B calls out first. After a few rounds, the same
prepositions could be called out and responded to in context: go up the stairs/go down the stairs, etc.

Total Physical Response (TPR) lends itself well to spatial prepositions. Distribute strips or slips of
colored construction paper to each student. Give directions quickly: put the blue paper on your desk

under the yellow paper; lift the yellow paper off the blue paper and hold it under your chin; arrange the papers side by side on your desk; take the blue paper in your right hand and hold it over your head; put the red paper between pages five and six of your book; give the orange paper to the student next to you; connect the green and blue papers by folding their top edges together; etc.; etc. The possibilities are countless. After each task is completed, ask: where is the paper?

Games requiring active student participation include hiding objects and either asking or telling the students where to look for them, e.g., behind the books, on the window sill, in the basket. Another, like charades, involves the student in a little acting: each is given a preposition to act out, and the class, divided into teams, must guess which one it is. These games must wait until several prepositions have been mastered.

These extra activities, combined with the exercises included with the lessons, ensure increasing progress in all the ESL objectives: listening and reading comprehension, tense recognition in context, various aspects of grammar, vocabulary, and idiomatic usage.

When the students are as fully involved as they are in these gamelike exercises, both you and they will be having a good, relaxed time in a fertile environment for learning.

Homework can include finding preposition-rich cartoons, magazine and newspaper articles, or pictures, or bringing snapshots to present to the class with the preposition underlined or named and described. Also, you may want to encourage your students to memorize two or more of the example sentences on their own to keep as handy models for their future use of the preposition as used in that particular lesson.

One last suggestion: you do not need to speak your students' first language to be an effective teacher of prepositions, but it will be helpful to both you and them if you research the basic structure of their language. Simple sentence diagrams on the chalkboard contrasting the two language structures make a picture that most students can understand. You might also ask the students of various nationalities to translate sentences with prepositions from English into their own language.

Learning prepositions thoroughly is crucial to the production of spoken-like-a-native English. Teaching prepositions thoroughly ensures a high rate of success toward achieving that goal. Appreciating the importance of prepositions motivates both the learner and the teacher to tackle a difficult job enthusiastically.

Contents

Unit 1
On, Off

Section A: On

Lesson 1. On: touching, supported by, hanging from, connected with, on top of
---

Practice.

S1: I think we're lost. The name on that sign is Main Street and we're supposed to be on Milam Avenue.

S2: But there's no Milam Avenue on this map. Let's ask that guy sitting on the grass for directions.

S1: Wait! Look at the name on the store window. We're in Afton not Alton!

S2: Sorry. I guess I read maps better when my glasses are on my nose instead of on the dashboard!

Example Sentences. With books open, listen to and repeat each sentence as it is read to you.

1. The ivy growing on the brick wall needs trimming.
2. Put the mail on the desk and the groceries on the counter.
3. Goats often graze on the mountainside.
4. Most people wear their watch on their left wrist.
5. The seats on the old bus are very uncomfortable.
6. The tires on his bike are flat.
7. The dog is lying on the rug, snoring.
8. The artist propped her painting on the easel.
9. Uncle Art leans on his cane and waits.
10. The woman carried a basket on her head.
11. His office was on the hundredth floor.
12. Pedro signed on the dotted line.

1

13. She sat on the sofa and read a book.
14. Nori set the large box on the floor.

Now write the *on* phrases.

Exercise 1. With books closed, listen to and repeat each sentence again.

Exercise 2. Use the *on* phrases you have written to answer these questions in turn.

1. What does Uncle Art do?
2. Where do most people wear their watches?
3. Where does the ivy grow?
4. Which tires are flat?
5. Where do goats often graze?
6. Where should we put the mail? The groceries?
7. Where was his office?

Reading Passage 1. Listen, with books closed. Then open your books and take turns reading aloud, sentence by sentence.

     The snow on the ground is white and clean, and the ice on the pond is smooth and thick. The woman on the park bench has a smile on her face. The boots on her feet keep her toes warm. The gloves on her hands keep her fingers warm. The skaters on the pond glide gracefully. The children playing on the slide are laughing. The joggers on the path seem healthy and happy. What a wonderful day to be living on this earth!

Now write the *on* phrases.

Exercise 3. Take turns answering these questions in full sentences. Use your written *on* phrases.

1. Where is the snow?
2. Where is the ice?
3. Where is the woman sitting?
4. Where is the smile?
5. What keeps her toes warm?
6. What keeps her fingers warm?
7. Where is her smile?

8. Where are the skaters gliding?
9. Where are the children playing?
10. Where are the joggers jogging?

Reading Passage 2. Listen, with books closed, as the passage is read to you.

The houses on First Street were painted orange. The houses on Second Street were painted blue. The houses on Third Street were painted yellow. The house on the hill was painted purple. The sign on the courthouse lawn read: Paintbrush, USA, population 147.

Exercise 4. Refer to the book and answer these questions in chorus.

1. Where was the purple house?
2. Where were the orange houses?
3. Where were the yellow houses?
4. Where were the blue houses?
5. Where was the courthouse sign?

Reading Passage 3. Listen, with books closed, as the passage is read to you. Then take turns reading aloud.

The cat on the windowsill washed itself. It didn't see the mouse on the floor. The bell on the cat's collar jingled. The mouse saw the cat on the windowsill and hurried home.

Practice. Write the answers to these questions.

1. Where was the cat?
2. Where was the mouse?
3. Where was the bell?

Practice.

1. Keep both feet on the floor.
2. Put your elbows on your desks.
3. Rest your chin on one hand.
4. Put a book on your head.
5. Sit on your desk.
6. Put your hands on your knees.
7. Put a smile on your face.

Turn to Missing Links, page 239.

Lesson 2a. On: movement in the direction of so as to touch or reach

---

Practice.

S1: Do you remember that New Year's Eve when someone threw a firecracker on our dry wood roof?
S2: Of course I do. Embers fell on our heads and shoulders and Dad sprayed water on the flames. It was terrible.

S1: If the firefighters hadn't climbed up on the roof and squirted foam on it, our house would have burned down.

S2: Dad wrote a letter to the newspaper showering praises on them for what they did.

Example Sentences. With books open, listen to and repeat each sentence as it is read to you.

1. The firefighters sprayed water on the flames.
2. The sun shone on the spring flowers.
3. It rained on the parade but no one cared.
4. Charlie sprinkled sugar on his cereal.
5. Rena threw more wood on the fire.
6. The muddy dog jumped on (onto) the new sofa.
7. The baby spilled milk on the floor.
8. Candle wax dripped on the tablecloth.

Now write the *on* phrases.

Exercise 1. With books closed, listen to and repeat each sentence again.

Exercise 2. Divide the class into two sides. Side A should ask the following questions. Side B, with books closed, should answer, using the *on* phrases you have written. Then switch sides.

1. Where did the baby spill milk?
2. Where did it rain?
3. Where did Charlie sprinkle sugar?
4. Where did the sun shine?
5. Where did the firefighters spray the water?
6. Where did Rena throw more wood?
7. Where did the muddy dog jump?
8. Where did candle wax drip?

Reading Passage 1. Listen, with books closed, to the passage as it is read to you.

One winter morning my mother sprinkled powdered sugar on a warm cake and went calling on our new neighbor. On the way it started to snow on the rooftops, on the trees, on the sidewalk, and on the cake. The snow looked like powdered sugar so no one knew the difference.

Now write the *on* phrases.

Practice. Answer in writing.

1. Where did the mother sprinkle sugar?
2. Name the places where the snow fell.
3. Name some places where rain falls on something.

Reading Passage 2. Listen, with books closed.

   While my mother was gone, my baby brother poured a whole bottle of maple syrup on his cereal. Then he dumped it on the floor and was about to sit down on it when I grabbed him and threw a towel on the mess. My sister said I was a hero.

Exercise 3. Take turns reading the passage, sentence by sentence.

Practice. Answer all together:

1. Where did the baby pour the syrup?
2. Where did he dump it?
3. Where was he about to sit down?
4. Where did the writer throw the towel?

Turn to Missing Links, page 239.

Lesson 2b. On: movement in opposition to or against something

Example Sentences. With books open, listen to and repeat each sentence as it is read to you.

1. The march on the Capitol began early in the morning.
2. That loud music was an assault on our eardrums.
3. Many people were killed during the attack on the village.
4. The children made a raid on the cookie jar.
5. The hailstones pounding on the roof sounded like drumbeats.
6. Alberto bounced the ball on the sidewalk.

Practice. Each student change one of the sentences into a question beginning with *what, when,* or *where.* Start a "chain" of questions and answers with one student asking the next student the question he has composed. That student answers the question and then asks his question of the student on his left.

Lesson 3a. On: at the edge of; alongside; next to

Example Sentences. With books open, listen to and repeat each sentence as it is read to you.

1. Harry waited on the side of the road.
2. The cabin on the river is 100 years old.
3. Goldilocks lived on the edge of the woods.
4. We got seats on the fifty-yard line.
5. The shops on Main Street were open for business.
6. The university is on the busiest street in town.
7. The fans lined up on both sides of the street.
8. Guards were posted on the border between the countries.

Now write the *on* phrases.

Exercise 1. With books closed, listen to and repeat each sentence again.

Practice. Choose any question and ask it of the student next to you, answering his question in turn using your written *on* phrases.

1. Where did Harry wait?
2. Where did we get seats?
3. Where was the cabin?
4. Where did the fans line up?
5. Where did Goldilocks live?
6. What were open for business?
7. Where is the university?
8. Where were guards posted?

Reading Passage 1. Listen, with books closed.

       The house on the beach was empty. The gas station on the highway was closed. The bait house on the river was boarded up. No wonder, it was thirty-five degrees below zero!

Write the passage from dictation.

Practice. Name places that you have seen along the river, the highway, the country road. Use them in sentences with the preposition *on*.

Turn to Missing Links, page 240.

Lesson 3b. On: to indicate direction or proximity

Example Sentences. With books open, listen to and repeat each sentence as it is read to you.

1. My mother sat on my right and my father sat on my left.
2. We watched the full moon rise on the horizon.
3. The bull was on the far side of the arena.
4. The ocean is on the other side of the mountains.
5. On our north is Canada; on our south is Mexico.

Practice. Take turns telling the class who sits on your right and who sits on your left.

Practice. Discuss in groups what is on the north, south, east, and west of the school; of your country.

Lesson 4. On: using, by means of

Practice.

Father: How do kids survive on junk food? They fill up on greasy hamburgers and french fries and then they go on diets to lose weight.

Mother: Yes, and then they spend hours on the telephone instead of going on a walk.

Father: If they would listen to music on their headsets while they were jogging instead of on their stereos while they were sprawling on their beds, they'd be healthier.

Mother: You're absolutely right. How about another slice of pizza, dear?

Father: Sure. And while you're up, would you please turn on the TV?

Example Sentences. With books open, listen to and repeat each sentence as it is read to you.

1. We heard the news on TV.
2. I bought my new car on credit.
3. Most big trucks run on diesel fuel.
4. Some teenagers live on junk food.
5. They spend hours yakking on the telephone.
6. We could save money if we went on a budget.
7. That large family is living on a very small income.
8. The rangers explored the forest on foot because there were no roads.
9. One hundred and fifty-eight scouts arrived on bicycles.
10. Berta found it hard to stay on a thousand-calorie-a-day diet.

Now write the *on* phrases.

Exercise 1. With books closed, listen to and repeat each sentence again.

Exercise 2. Place links where *on* belongs:

1. A good way to save money is to go a budget.
2. It's possible to live a very small income.
3. We heard the news the radio.
4. Most big trucks run diesel fuel.
5. She buys her clothes credit.

Practice. Divide into groups and choose one of these topics for discussion.

1. What does "to go on a budget" mean?
2. What is the fastest way to get news of the world?
3. Would it be safe to explore a wildlife sanctuary on foot?

Reading Passage 1. Listen, with books closed.

      Most college freshmen complain that they gain weight on dorm food so they boycott the dining hall. Of course they soon get hungry and fill up on junk food.

      Our daughter, Marcy, wrote: "It's impossible to stay on a diet here, so a group of us decided to get some exercise. We pedaled to the park on our bicycles and then explored the woods on foot because there are no roads."

      "That night we dined on pizza, fried chicken, and hot fudge sundaes because we were starving after all that exercise. When we weighed ourselves on the restaurant scale we didn't believe what it registered! It must have been out of order."

Now take turns reading the passage, sentence by sentence. Then write the verbs plus the *on* phrases.

Practice. In groups, discuss the meaning of "survive on junk food," "fill up on greasy food."

Practice. Write the answers to these questions.

1. What is a good way to lose weight?   *exescise*
2. What's an easy thing to do for exercise?
3. Where can you hear good music?

Turn to Missing Links, page 240.

Lesson 5. On: telling about (a subject), concerning

Practice.

S1: That scientist is doing research on the intelligence of people who have had their wisdom teeth pulled.

S2: I think someone should do some research on him!

Example Sentences. With books open, listen to and repeat each sentence as it is read to you.

1. The dentist is writing a book on wisdom teeth.
2. The vote on the amendment was close.
3. The graduate student wrote a report on zebras.
4. That article on the royal family is mostly gossip.
5. The new boss attended a seminar on management.
6. The committee finally agreed on a plan.
7. Debates on current politics are not allowed at our dinner table. (But: *we debated current politics,* not *we debated on current politics.*)
8. The ecologist's speech on our environment was quite informative.
9. The paper Jim wrote on astrophysics was well received.
10. What are your thoughts on the economic situation?

Now write the *on* phrases.

Exercise 1. With books closed, listen to and repeat each sentence again.

Exercise 2. Place links where *on* belongs.

1. What are your thoughts the economic situation?
2. The graduate student wrote a report zebras.
3. The vote the new amendment was close.
4. Jim's paper astrophysics was well received.
5. The committee finally agreed a plan.

Reading Passage 1. Listen, with books closed.

Most boys' discussions center on sports; some girls' discussions center on people; the majority of ecologists' discussions center on the environment; a lot of doctors' discussions center on medicine; many artists' discussions center on art; *all* dieters' discussions center on food!

Practice. Take turns reading the passage aloud.

Exercise 3. Choose one or more of the following questions and answer in writing. Share your answers with the class.

When you are with your friends, what do your conversations center on? What do you think your teachers' conversations center on? The president's? Bankers'?

Practice. Divide into groups and discuss.

If you were a scientist, what would you like to do research on? Who are some famous scientists in your native country? What have they done research on?

Practice. What kind of nonfiction books do you enjoy reading? If you wrote a nonfiction book, what kind of book would you write?

Turn to Missing Links, page 240.

Lesson 6. On: used when telling the condition or state of someone or something

---

Example Sentences. With books open, listen to and repeat each sentence as it is read to you.

1. The fire station was on fire!
2. The air conditioner has been on high all summer.
3. Don't talk about work while we're on vacation.
4. They bought their furniture on sale.
5. The captain struggled to keep the ship on course.
6. The operator has put us on hold for twenty minutes.
7. We're on standby for our flight to England.
8. That woman is on trial for murder.
9. The children are on their best behavior before Christmas.
10. The prisoner is out on parole.

Now write the *on* phrases.

Exercise 1. With books closed, listen to and repeat each sentence again.

Exercise 2. Use your written *on* phrases to answer these questions.

1. How did they buy their furniture?
2. Where did the captain struggle to keep the ship?
3. What was wrong with the fire station?
4. How do the children act before Christmas?
5. Where has the operator put us?

Practice. Choose three of the following questions, answer them in complete sentences, and then share your answers with the class.

1. When do you get the best buys on clothes?
2. When you call an office and the person you want to speak to is busy, what does the operator do?
3. When you don't have a reserved seat but are waiting for someone to cancel, you are what?
4. When a person has committed a crime what does she have to do?
5. If a prisoner is let out of prison early but must stay in touch with the prison officials, what is he?

Reading Passage 1. Listen, with books closed.

Your business is on the brink of bankruptcy. Your treasurer is on trial for embezzling company funds; the workers on the payroll have not been paid for three months; the chairman of the board is on extended vacation; your vice president is on sick leave; the bank has put your credit on hold and told you to go on a strict budget. This is no time to go on a spending spree.

Practice. As a class, discuss the meaning of the following phrases.

on the brink, on trial, on vacation, on sick leave, on hold, on a budget, on a spending spree

Reading Passage 2. Listen, with books closed.

The weatherman said it was the worst storm on record. The city workers were all on emergency standby. The doctors on call at the hospital were exhausted. But the mailman delivered the mail on schedule.

Practice. In groups, talk about any or all of these things.

the worst storm on record that you can remember; what "emergency standby" means; a time when you have been on call; about something this school does on schedule.

Turn to Missing Links, page 240.

Lesson 7. On: works for, belongs to, is part of

Example Sentences. With books open, listen to and repeat each sentence as it is read to you.

1. Tay is on the debate team.
2. There are four cheerleaders on the pep squad.
3. Sam has a job on the assembly line.
4. We're all on the side of the underdog.
5. Ann is on the faculty at Great Brains University.
6. The players on our team are motivated by our cheers.
7. Senator Drone is on the Appropriations Committee.
8. Dr. Jones is on the governing board of several institutions.

Note: A few exceptions to using *on* with words about belonging or being a part of are: in the chorus, in the cast of a play, in a dance troupe.

Now write the *on* phrases.

Exercise 1. With books closed, listen to and repeat each sentence again.

Exercise 2. Use your written *on* phrases to complete these sentences.

1. The players _____ are motivated by our cheers.

2. Senator Drone is _____.

3. Tay is _____.

4. Ann is _____ at Great Brains University.

5. There are four cheerleaders _____.

6. Sam has _____.

Reading Passage 1. Listen, with books closed.

      Sara is on the refreshment committee. She has to plan an appreciation dinner for the teachers on the faculty. She's a reporter on the school paper, and she's also on the yearbook staff. She's on the dean's list, too. What a busy person!

Now read aloud, in turn.

Practice. Answer these questions after sharing information.

1. Have you ever been on a committee or known someone who has?
2. Who is on the faculty at this school?

3. What does "being a reporter on the school paper" entail?
4. What must a student do to be on the dean's list (or honor roll)?

Turn to Missing Links, page 241.

Lesson 8. On: directly after and because of

Practice.

S1: I'm teaching my dog to sit on command.

S2: That's nothing. My dog is teaching me to take him for a walk on request.

S1: How does he do that?

S2: After he drops his leash on my lap, licks my face, and puts his paws on my shoulders, I act on instinct. It's called self-preservation.

Example Sentences. With books open, listen to and repeat each sentence as it is read to you.

1. On hearing the news, Pierre left Paris.
2. She will play your favorite songs on request.
3. We hired that young man on your recommendation.
4. He took the medicine on his doctor's orders.
5. The general reacted quickly on reading the report.
6. The soldier said he had been acting on orders.
7. On second thought, I decided my friend was right.
8. We acted on the assumption that they were honest.

Now write the *on* phrases.

Exercise 1. With books closed, listen to and repeat each sentence again.

Reading Passage 1. Listen, with books closed.

The Spanish explorers sailed westward on the premise that India was west of Europe. They charted their course on the calculations of the map makers. Depending on their imperfect knowledge, they became lost.

After several weeks, the sailors continued acting on orders even though they were discouraged. On seeing land, they were relieved and thankful.

Exercise 2. Read the entire passage aloud, sentence by sentence, in turn.

Turn to Missing Links, page 241.

Lesson 9. On: introduces means of conveyance and types of travel

---

Note: Automobiles, trucks, vans, RVs, small boats, canoes, rowboats, motorboats (but *on* a sailboat!) are introduced by *in.*

Practice.

S1: I'd rather go to the Bahamas on a cruise ship than on a raft, wouldn't you?

S2: Of course. And I'd rather go to Alaska on a plane than on a dog sled.

S1: Then why in the world do you want to travel from coast to coast on a motorcycle instead of in a car?

S2: For the same reason you go to work on the subway instead of in a limousine: it's cheaper!

Example Sentences. With books open, listen to and repeat each sentence as it is read to you.

Type of vehicle:

1. They left for Alaska on a cruise ship.
2. They spent several days on the train.
3. The child flew here on a 747.
4. They traveled 2,000 miles on a bus.
5. In New York, most people go to work on the subway.

Kind of travel:

1. We always eat too much on a cruise.
2. The crew on the flight to Atlanta was charming.
3. Mary's on her first trip to California.
4. The geese were on their journey south.
5. Ruth is on a tour of Scotland.

Now write the *on* phrases.

Exercise 1. With books closed, listen to and repeat each sentence again.

Exercise 2. Use the written *on* phrases to answer these questions in writing.

1. Where did they spend several days?
2. How did they leave for Alaska?
3. How do many people go to work in New York?
4. How did they travel 2,000 miles?
5. How did the child fly here?
6. Where do we always eat too much?
7. Where is Mary?
8. What crew was charming?
9. Where were the geese?
10. Where is Ruth?

Practice. In groups, discuss the following.

How would you like to travel to France? To Alaska? To Siberia? To Japan? To any other place you'd like to visit? Or tell about trips you have taken and the means of travel you used.

Lesson 10. On: used with days, dates, and times, i.e., on a day of
the week (Saturday), on a special day (on my birthday), on a
specific date (May 28), on a day or date preceded by an adjective
(a cold day, a sunny afternoon, the second Tuesday) (See unit 12
for prepositions to use for time.)

Note: On is often omitted in conversations when used with days of the week or month, i.e., she
was in class Monday morning and at work Monday afternoon. (An asterisk has been placed after
these sentences.) *On* is always omitted when the day or time of day is preceded by any of these
words: each, every, next, any, this, i.e., the test is next Monday (not *on* next Monday). *On* is not
used with tomorrow or yesterday, i.e., they're arriving tomorrow, (not *on* tomorrow).

Example Sentences. With books open, listen to and repeat each sentence as it is read to you.

1. On weekdays we go to bed early.
2. On December 31, we go to bed late.
3. We arrived at the party exactly on time.
4. Classes begin every hour on the hour.
5. On cold nights we light a fire in the fireplace.
6. Their wedding anniversary is (on) July fifth.*
7. The swallows come back to Capistrano on the same date every year.
8. Labor Day is (on) the first Monday in September.*

Now write the *on* phrases.

Exercise 1. With books closed, listen to and repeat each sentence again.

Practice. Answer in writing using *on* phrases.

1. What day of the week will your birthday fall on this year?
2. Do you go to bed earlier on weekdays than on weekends?
3. When you have a job interview is it better to be late or on time?
4. When is it hardest to get up, on warm summer mornings or on cold winter mornings?
5. When do the swallows come back to Capistrano?
6. Do the buses in your neighborhood run irregularly or on schedule?
7. When is Labor Day?
8. Do you light a fire on warm nights or on cold nights?

Reading Passage 1. Listen, with books closed.

> We have to be at the bus stop on time on school days. Last week on a rainy morning, our alarm
> clock didn't go off and we woke up late.
> The buses run strictly on schedule on weekdays. When our bus didn't come on time, we
> thought we had missed it. Then we remembered: it was July fourth. On holidays we don't have to
> be on schedule for anything. We went back to bed.

Now take turns reading, sentence by sentence.

Practice. Answer these questions in writing, using your books as reference. Then take turns reading your answers to the class.

1. When do we have to be at the bus stop? (Two *on* phrases)
2. When did we wake up late last week?
3. When do the buses run on schedule?
4. Why did we think we had missed our bus?

Practice. In groups, discuss the following. What are some things you must be on time for? What are some things that are done on schedule? Name some of your national holidays and tell what you usually do on them.

Turn to Missing Links, page 241.

Lesson 11. On: combined usages (Includes all of the uses of *on* studied in unit 1.)

Reading Passage 1. With books open, listen to and repeat each sentence as it is read to you.

On a summer day ten years ago, on June 15th to be exact, I contacted my cousins on their fax machine. Since we were all on vacation I asked if they would meet me on Saturday to go fishing on Lake Bluegill. They agreed.

One of my cousins worked on a shrimp boat on weekends and the other cousin worked on a newspaper as fishing editor. They were both up on water sports and fishing. I was relying on their knowledge to help us get a good catch.

On their advice I bought a book on fishing. I read it on the train on the way to the river town. My fishing poles, which I had bought on sale because I'm on a budget, were on the floor on my left. My bait box was on the floor on my right. There was no room for anyone to sit on the seat next to me because my picnic basket was on it. I was surrounded on all sides.

As I got off the train, loaded down with all my gear, I bumped my head on the door frame. I was very dizzy and I couldn't remember why I was standing on a bait shop porch. Then I saw a big houseboat on the water. It had a sign on it: For Sale. On impulse, I found the owner and bought the boat.

Just then my cousins rowed up in a little rowboat and I remembered what I was there for. It was too late to return the houseboat and my budget was ruined, but we've gone on fishing trips on it hundreds of times since then. I'm glad I bumped my head on the train on that summer day ten years ago.

Now write all the *on* phrases.

Exercise 1. Take turns reading the passage, sentence by sentence.

Turn to Missing Links, page 241.

Section B: Off

Lesson 1. Off: to move away from, the opposite of *on*

Practice.

S1: Isn't this photographic safari fun?

S2: Yes, but I keep thinking I've forgotten something. Are you sure you turned off the lights, the television, the oven, the fans, and the air conditioner before we left home?

S1: I'm sure I did. But Harry, I think you've forgotten to take the cover off your camera lens!

Example Sentences. With books open, listen to and repeat each sentence as it is read to you.

1. The boys reluctantly got off the jungle gym.
2. Shiny new cars rolled off the production line.
3. The block of ice slipped off the counter.
4. The Olympic contenders dove off the high board.
5. The speeding car drove off (ran off) the road.
6. The students copied the words off the chalkboard.
7. The hurricane blew the roof off the house.
8. She told her daughter to get off the phone.
9. Please turn off the lights when you leave.
10. He scraped the anchovies off the pizza.

Now write the *off* phrases preceded by the verbs.

Exercise 1. With books closed, listen to and repeat each sentence again.

Exercise 2. Use the written *off* phrases to answer these questions.

1. What happened to the block of ice?
2. What happened to the speeding car?
3. What did the boys do?
4. What did the Olympic contenders do?
5. What did the hurricane do?

Exercise 3. Place links where *off* belongs.

1. Please turn the lights when you leave.
2. The new cars rolled the assembly line.
3. He scraped the anchovies the pizza.
4. She told her daughter to get the phone.
5. The students copied the words the chalkboard.

Lesson 2. Off: turning away from something larger, near, extending or branching off from, no longer having or wanting

---

Example Sentences. With books open, listen to and repeat each sentence as it is read to you.

1. The Appleys lived on a little street off Ocean Drive.
2. We sailed to an island off the coast of Florida.
3. The blockage was in a main artery off the heart.
4. He kept his promise to stay off cigarettes.

Now write the *off* phrases.

Exercise 1. With books closed, listen to and repeat each sentence again.

Practice. In groups, discuss the following.

Is your home on a street off a main one? What island is off the coast of Texas? Name some things it would be wise to stay off?

Lesson 3. Off/Onto: from one place to another

Note: When the subject moves from one place to another the destination is often preceded by the double preposition "onto."

Example Sentences. With books open, listen to and repeat each sentence as it is read to you.

1. The glass fell off the table onto the rug.
2. The squirrel hopped off the branch onto the roof.
3. The block of ice fell off the counter onto the floor.

4. The students copied the cheers off the blackboard onto the posters.
5. The car ran off the road onto the shoulder.

Now write the *off* phrases.

Exercise 1. With books closed, listen to and repeat each sentence again.

Practice. Write two sentences of your own using *off* and *onto* in this way.

Review. On, Off

Reading Passage 1. Listen, with books closed.

> While we were driving on a mountain road several miles off the main highway, our car suddenly slid off the road and landed on its side. Fortunately we had on our seatbelts so we weren't hurt.
> We tried to push off a boulder that had fallen on the door but we couldn't. It was getting dark, so I turned on the emergency lights and turned off the radio so I could make a call for help on the car phone on the dashboard.
> Soon we saw lights on the treetops above us. Someone had turned off the road and was on the incline leading to our car. They had heard our SOS!

Exercise 1. Take turns reading the passage, sentence by sentence.

Turn to Missing Links, page 242.

Exercise 2. On/off usages for extra practice. With books open, listen to and repeat each sentence as it is read to you.

1. Mary got on the bus on the corner of Sixth and Main.
2. She got off the bus on the corner of Tenth and Garland.
3. Please turn on the light when you come home.
4. Please turn off the light when you leave.
5. Put on your hat when you're outside, but take it off when you enter the restaurant.
6. Put on your glasses so you can read the map. Take them off when you drive if you don't need them for distance.

Unit 2
In, Into, Out of, Inside/Outside

Section A: In

Lesson 1. In: surrounded by something, contained by something
---

Practice.

S1: Why isn't Jon in class today?
S2: He's home in bed. He has the flu.
S1: He left his books in my locker. If I put them in a bag could you take them to him?
S2: Well, an article in today's paper said we should stay away from people with the flu.
S1: You could leave it in the hallway outside his apartment, ring the bell, and run.
S2: Okay. I'll put some ice cream in the bag for him, too.
S1: I hope he opens the door right away or his books will be floating in cream!

Example Sentences. With books open, listen to and repeat each sentence as it is read to you.

1. Fish live in the ocean.
2. The children built castles in the sand.
3. Our brains are in our heads.
4. She put the keys in her purse.
5. Drop a coin in the slot before you dial.
6. Joe used to live in Alaska.
7. Cut flowers should be kept in water.
8. Milk should be kept in the refrigerator.
9. We sometimes see monsters in our dreams.
10. I think UFO's exist only in our imaginations.
11. The cartoon in this morning's paper is funny.
12. The piano is in the corner of the room.

Now write the *in* phrases.

 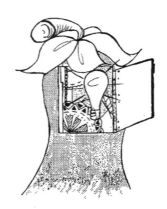 

Exercise 1. With books closed, listen to and repeat each sentence again.

Exercise 2. Use the written *in* phrases to answer these questions.

1. What cartoon was funny?
2. Where should you drop a coin?
3. Where did Joe used to live?
4. Where did she put the keys?
5. Where should milk be kept?
6. Where are our brains?

Practice.

S1: Do you live in this neighborhood?
S2: No, I live in Pine Forest.
S1: Is that in the city?
S2: No, it's out of the city—in the country, really.
S1: Do you enjoy living in the USA?
S2: Yes, and I especially enjoy living here in New Mexico. How about you?
S1: We live in the suburbs. Our house is actually in the next county. Why don't you drive out to see us on Sunday?
S2: I'd like to. What's your address?
S1: We live on Longwood Lane in Breezeville. Here's my card.
S2: Okay, so you live at 1444 Longwood Lane?
S1: Yes, it's right off Highway 30. Here's a little map I had printed. Stay on Highway 30 until you see the Breezeville sign on the right. Turn in there. We're the third street on the left.
S2: It's nice to make friends in the United States. When my plane landed in Los Angeles, I thought, "Here I am in a strange country and I don't know anybody." But now I do.

Practice. Write the answers to as many questions as you can. Then take turns reading them to the class.

1. Where else do fish live besides in the ocean? Where do deer live? Snakes? Monkeys?
2. Where is Los Angeles? Beijing? Chicago? Mexico City? Tokyo? Seoul?
3. Where are our lungs? Our teeth? Where is our blood?

4. Where do you keep your keys? Where do you keep milk? Where do you hang your clothes?
5. What do little children like to play in besides sand?

Practice.

Do all together:

1. Put your pen in your notebook.
2. Put your thumb in your ear.
3. Put your head in your hands.
4. Put your hand in your pocket.

Do individually:

1. Put something in the wastebasket.
2. Set a chair in the corner.
3. Put a book in the teacher's hand.
4. Stand in the doorway.

Reading Passage 1. Listen, with books closed.

When Monica arrived in Houston she rented a small apartment in an old neighborhood and found a job in a doctor's office. She was very happy except for one thing: her piano was back home in Mexico. She was the only one in the family who had learned to play it and it had been very important in her life.

One day a truck with her piano in it pulled up in the driveway. She knew in her heart that her family had pooled their money and sent it. Now she could play it in her new country.

But there was a problem: the piano didn't fit in her little living room. After trying for an hour to get it in, the movers put it down in the middle of the lobby and left. Monica sat on the piano bench with tears in her eyes. Her family should have left the piano in their home!

Her landlady said, "Why don't you leave it here in the lobby? We would all be glad to have some real music in our lives." Monica was very relieved. Now every evening she plays beautiful music for all the other tenants in the building to enjoy.

Exercise 3. Take turns reading the passage, sentence by sentence.

Practice. Answer at least four of these questions in writing and then share your answers with your group or class.

1. Is music important in your life? In what way?
2. What does "in the neighborhood" mean?
3. Have you ever known something "in your heart?"
4. Where did the movers try to put the piano?
5. Where did the landlady suggest that Monica leave her piano?

Turn to Missing Links, page 242.

Lesson 2a. In: used with words that tell how one feels about or reacts to something

Example Sentences. With books open, listen to and repeat each sentence as it is read to you.

1. They watched the air show in amazement.
2. We observed the great whales in awe.
3. The dog, in confusion, ran to the wrong house.
4. He watched in sorrow as his brother was led to prison.
5. She spoke those words in anger.

Now write the *in* phrases.

Exercise 1. With books closed, listen to and repeat each sentence again.

Practice. Use these *in* phrases to write sentences of your own in amusement, in sorrow, in anger.

Lesson 2b. In: used with words that describe the state or condition of someone or something

Example Sentences. With books open, listen to and repeat each sentence as it is read to you.

1. Our team plays in competition with your team.
2. The pirates buried the treasure in secret.
3. The stage hands moved the scenery in full view of the audience.
4. The men were in a hurry to get home for dinner.
5. That magician is in demand for children's parties.
6. Romeo was in love with Juliet.

Now write the *in* phrases.

Exercise 1. With books closed, listen to and repeat each sentence again.

Practice. Discuss the meanings of the sentences and make up sentences of your own using the written *in* phrases.

Practice. Choose two of these questions and answer them in complete sentences. Then take turns reading your answers to the class.

1. Why would pirates bury treasure in secret?
2. Why would people be in a hurry to get on the bus?
3. Who are you in full view of right now?
4. What does "competition" mean?
5. What's the difference between loving someone and being in love with someone?

Reading Passage 1. Listen, with books closed.

      The robber was in full view of the hidden camera when he robbed the bank. The teller screamed in panic. The robber dropped the money in confusion as he ran out the door. No one was in danger because the gun he brandished in desperation was fake.

Practice. Write sentences of your own using the following *in* phrases or any others you choose. In desperation, in fear, in confusion, in full view of, in danger.

Exercise 2. With books closed, listen and write the passage from dictation.

Turn to Missing Links, page 243.

Lesson 3. In: using, with

Example Sentences. With books open, listen to and repeat each sentence as it is read to you.

1. Thanh painted his car in bright colors.
2. Deanna washed the clothes in mild detergent.
3. They spoke only in French.
4. Andrea wrote the music in modern rhythm.
5. Don't write checks in pencil; the bank won't accept them.
6. The scarf was embroidered in silk.
7. Bobby colored all the pictures in orange and blue.
8. The home was decorated in plaid.

Now write the *in* phrases.

Exercise 1. With books closed, listen to and repeat each sentence again.

Exercise 2. Use the *in* phrases to answer these questions.

1. How did they speak?
2. How was the scarf embroidered?
3. How did Thanh paint his car?
4. How did Andrea write the music?
5. How should you write the checks?
6. How did Deanna wash the clothes?
7. How was the home decorated?
8. How did the child color the pictures?

Practice. Write sentences of your own design telling how something was painted, washed, decorated, and written. Then take turns reading them to the class.

Reading Passage 1. Listen, with books closed.

> The woman's portrait had been painted in oils by a famous artist, but she preferred the one her little son had drawn in colored chalk. She had it framed in silver and hung on a wall covered in silk. The other portrait was draped in old rags so no one could compare it to her son's picture. The famous artist never painted in oils again.

Practice. Discuss different media used to paint. Share your feelings about the mother's treatment of the two pictures. How do you think the artist felt?

Reading Passage 2. Listen, with books closed.

> The menu was written in Japanese, the waiter spoke in Spanish, and I could only understand English. So we communicated in sign language.

Exercise 3. With books closed, listen and write the passage from dictation.

Practice. Ask the person sitting next to you what language he/she usually speaks in. Write what he/she told you and share it with the class.

> *Note:* There is a slight difference between saying "He speaks French" (meaning he is able to speak French) and saying "He is speaking in French" (meaning the language being used at the time is French).

Turn to Missing Links, page 243.

Lesson 4. In: as portrayed, described, or depicted

Practice.

S1: That write-up in the paper was misleading.
S2: The coverage in the press is always biased.
S3: I think the stories in the media are excellent.
S1: That's because you agree with them!

Example Sentences. With books open, listen to and repeat each sentence as it is read to you.

1. In the book, the hero dies; in the movie, he lives.
2. The character in the play is not at all likable.
3. I think there is much truth in his statement.
4. The information in your records is outdated.
5. In that account of the accident, Jack was not at fault.
6. The incident as reported in the newspaper isn't true.

Now write the *in* phrases.

Exercise 1. With books closed, listen to and repeat each sentence again.

Exercise 2. Use the written *in* phrases to answer these questions.

1. Where is the information outdated?
2. Where was the untrue incident reported?
3. Where did the hero die? Where did he live?
4. Where is there much truth?
5. Where was Jack not at fault?
6. Where is the character not likable?

Reading Passage 1.

     The actress who plays Annie Warbucks in the musical *Annie* doesn't look like the Annie in the comic strip. In the role of Annie, the young actress gives warmth and life to the character in the cartoon.

Practice. What differences are there in a picture of a friend or relative and in the way he/she looks in real life? Write a sentence or two describing the difference(s).

Turn to Missing Links, page 243.

Lesson 5. In: wearing

Example Sentences. With books open, listen to and repeat each sentence as it is read to you.

1. The man in the tall hat is Uncle Sam.
2. The ballpark ushers are in uniform.
3. It makes me sad to see children in rags.
4. The dancer in the tutu is from the ballet.
5. My friend looks good in glasses.
6. Divers in wet suits and masks look like alien creatures.

Now write the *in* phrases.

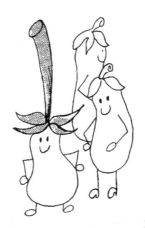

Exercise 1. With books closed, listen to and repeat each sentence again.

Practice. Look around at your classmates and write about one of them using *in* meaning *wearing*. Take turns reading your sentences and see if the others can guess who you're talking about.

Exercise 2. Use the written *in* phrases to complete these sentences.

1. The ball park ushers are _____.

2. Divers _____ and masks look like alien creatures.

3. The man _____ is Uncle Sam.

4. It makes me sad to see children _____.

5. The dancer _____ is from the ballet.

6. My friend looks good _____.

Reading Passage 1. Listen, with books closed.

The woman in white is the bride. The man in the tuxedo is the groom. The other guys in tuxes are groomsmen. They look very uncomfortable. The girls in the pretty dresses are the bridesmaids. The kids in cowboy outfits are in a calf-roping contest.

Practice. Guess why the kids in cowboy outfits are at the wedding.

Practice. Think of another time when people might wear special clothes and write a short paragraph describing the people and their clothes.

Turn to Missing Links, page 243.

Lesson 6. In: shows employment, involvement

Example Sentences. With books open, listen to and repeat each sentence as it is read to you.

1. That family has been in politics for generations.
2. He was in law first; now he's in medicine.
3. A position in publishing can be stressful.
4. She's been in space research since she graduated.
5. People in banking must study all about money.
6. I didn't know your friend was in journalism. I'll give him a great story.
7. Bill's in stocks and bonds. They call him a stockbroker.
8. Ellen's in landscaping. She loves plants and flowers.
9. The women in the bridge club have been friends for years.
10. A career in teaching can be very rewarding.

Now write the *in* phrases.

Exercise 1. With books closed, listen to and repeat each sentence again.

Practice. Discuss what "in politics," "in journalism," and "in landscaping" mean.

Practice. What career are you in now or would you like to be in some day? Do you know anyone in journalism? In nursing? In church ministry? In dentistry? In education? In investing? Write one sentence about him/her or yourself.

Lesson 7. In: so as to be divided or arranged

Example Sentences. With books open, listen to and repeat each sentence as it is read to you.

1. The grapes hung in bunches on the vines.
2. The seats were in tiers around the field.
3. The files were kept in alphabetical order.
4. The magazines were piled in stacks on the shelves.
5. The books were classified in order of their subject.
6. Hungry people waited in long lines for food.
7. The corn and potatoes were planted in straight rows.
8. The chairs were arranged in a circle.

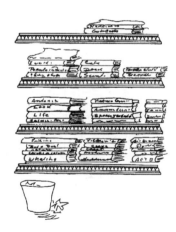

Now write the *in* phrases.

Exercise 1. With books closed, listen to and repeat each sentence again.

Practice. Divide the class into groups and discuss the following. How are the chairs, the desks, and the books arranged in the classroom? Decide how the books in the library and the seats in the stadium are arranged. How is your discussion taking place right now?

Exercise 2. Use the written *in* phrases to answer these questions.

1. How were the files kept?
2. How were the chairs arranged?
3. How were the magazines piled on the shelves?
4. How were the corn and potatoes planted?
5. In what way did the hungry people wait for food?
6. How did the grapes hang on the vines?
7. In what order were the seats around the field?
8. How were the books classified?

Reading Passage 1. Listen, with books closed.

     The teenaged fans went up to the stage in groups of ten. They stood around the singer in a semicircle while he autographed his photographs, which were stacked in piles on the table. Open your books and read silently.

Turn to Missing Links, page 243.

Lesson 8. In: by means of, method of transportation

Example Sentences. With books open, listen to and repeat each sentence as it is read to you.

1. They arrived at the church in a limousine.
2. The Indians crossed the lake in a birchbark canoe.
3. Mark drove to Alaska in his RV (recreational vehicle).
4. The accident victim was brought to the hospital in a helicopter.
5. The pioneers traveled across America in covered wagons.
6. Fresh food is shipped in refrigerated train cars.

Now write the *in* phrases.

Exercise 1. With books closed, listen to and repeat each sentence again.

Practice. In groups, discuss whether you would rather travel across America in a car, a truck, a van, or an RV. Give the reasons why.

Exercise 2. Use the written *in* phrases to answer these questions.

1. How did the pioneers travel across America?
2. How are accident victims sometimes brought to the hospital?
3. How is fresh food shipped?

Reading Passage 1. Listen, with books closed.

      The president arrived in a helicopter and was whisked away in a black limousine. Three hours later he was flying to Antarctica in Air Force One. He would have preferred sitting in his little fishing boat at home, but he had no choice in the matter.

Turn to Missing Links, page 244.

    Note: In/On usages that can't be easily explained:

We say someone is: on a sailboat, but in a canoe; on an ocean liner, but in a rowboat.
We say someone is either in or on an airplane/bus/train, but is always in a car/truck/taxi.
We say someone is in bed (lying or sleeping under the covers), but on (top of) the bed (sitting or lying on top of the covers).
We say someone is sitting in a chair (usually one having arms and cushions), but on a chair/bench/ stool (usually straight-backed and without arms), on a throne, and on a sofa (even though it has arms and cushions!).

Lesson 9. In: used in talking about time, telling when (See unit 12 for prepositions to use for time.)

Note: Use *in* for specific references to the season, year, month, and time of day (morning, afternoon, evening, but not with dawn, noon, night, or midnight—we use *at* with these). Do not use *on* before the words last, next, this, and every. For example: The moon will be full next week; last night it was a crescent. We've had a lot of rain this fall, so we haven't been able to see the moon every night. Exception: if *the* precedes *last, on* may be used. For example: on the last night of the year we celebrate New Year's Eve.

Example Sentences. With books open, listen to and repeat each sentence as it is read to you.

1. When speaking of time, meaning during or when:
   a. Man landed on the moon in 1969.
   b. Paris is lovely in April.
   c. My granddaughter was born in 1982.
   d. In the winter we wear boots; in the summer we wear sandals.
   e. The children take naps in the afternoon.
   f. In September the leaves begin to change color.

2. When speaking of time, meaning not later than:
   a. I'll expect you in an hour.
   b. The plane will land in five minutes.
   c. I'll be back in three weeks.
   d. Dinner will be served in twenty minutes.
   e. You must finish your work in the allotted time.
   f. She finished the race in three minutes.
3. When speaking of an indefinite time in the past or future:
   a. In the past we could walk in the park without fear.
   b. In the future, vacation plans may include a trip to another planet.

Now write the *in* phrases.

Exercise 1. With books closed, listen to and repeat each sentence again.

Practice. In groups, or as a class, take turns answering these questions.

1. In what year did man land on the moon?
2. In what month is your city the loveliest?
3. In what year did you come to this country?
4. During what time of the year do people wear boots in Alaska?
5. When will the bell ring?
6. What is a good time to take a nap?
7. When will it be Sunday?
8. In what month do the leaves begin to change color in Wisconsin?

Reading Passage 1. Listen, with books closed.

    I wonder why Bob is coming to see us in the middle of winter. He usually comes in June when
the weather is nicer. His plane will land in an hour. We'd better leave for the airport in a few
minutes because the traffic is always heavy in the morning.
    If we had a helicopter we could be there in no time, but we'll be lucky to get there in forty-five
minutes by car.

Exercise 2. Take turns reading the passage, sentence by sentence.

Turn to Missing Links, page 244.

Practice. Answer all together with *in* plus a month.

When is Christmas? Valentine's Day? Easter? Fourth of July? Thanksgiving? The last day of school?

Practice. Answer in writing using *in* phrases.

1. When is the most important holiday in your country?
2. When is your birthday?
3. What time of day do we have English lessons?
4. When will the bell ring?
5. How soon will school be over?

Review. In, On

Reading Passage 1. Listen, with books closed.

Her name was on the class chart. It was "Meelia." She looked like a girl on the cover of a book in the school library, but that girl was smiling. I had never seen Meelia with a smile on her face. She sat on the left side of the room in the back corner.

In October we were in the middle of a test when a gust of wind blew in the window and carried my paper up in the air. It landed on Meelia's desk. When she looked at it, her eyes opened wide in disbelief. And then a big smile appeared on her face.

I had drawn kittens in all the margins, because our teacher had just told us about a kitten she had found in her mailbox. On that day Meelia and I became friends. Her smile made her even prettier than the girl on the book cover.

Turn to Missing Links, page 244.

Exercise 1. Take turns reading the passage aloud, sentence by sentence. Then write the *in* and *on* phrases.

Reading Passage 2. Listen with books closed.

It happened in April on a Sunday afternoon. She was sitting on the front porch in her rocking chair. Her baby was on her lap. The sun shone on the grass and on the flowers in the garden.

Suddenly she heard music in the distance. Was it on someone's radio? Then, in amazement she realized the music was in her head. On the night before, she had attended a symphony concert in the Music Bowl in the city. She had read a book on the composer and listened to a tape of one of his concertos when she returned home. In her dreams she had heard the music. And now, in the silence of a sleepy spring afternoon, the music played on in her inner ear.

Exercise 2. Take turns reading the passage, sentence by sentence. Then write the *in* and *on* phrases.

Turn to Missing Links, page 244.

Practice. Answer these questions, in writing, using complete sentences.

1. On what page does chapter ten begin?
2. Where do you eat lunch?
3. Where are you?
4. Are your elbows on the desk?
5. Where is your nose?
6. Where are your ears?
7. Where is your brain?
8. Where are your teeth?
9. Where are your feet?

Practice. After the words *He's sitting* add either *on* or *in* before the following phrases.

a park bench, a sofa, an armchair, a desk chair, a beanbag chair, the driver's seat of a car, a seat on the bus, a church pew, a theater seat, the floor, the grass, a stool, a booth, the sand, the bed.

Section B: Into

Lesson 1. Into: to the inside of

Note: Into implies movement from one place to another.

Example Sentences. With books open, listen to and repeat each sentence as it is read to you.

1. The river runs into the ocean.
2. Carol threw the letter into the fire.
3. The puppy ran into the doghouse.
4. Nick poured the paint into the bucket.
5. Martina broke three eggs into the bowl.
6. When the movie star came into the room we all stared.
7. The rain blew into the house through the open window.
8. The secretary entered the data into the computer.

Now write the *into* phrases.

Exercise 1. With books closed, listen to and repeat each sentence again.

Practice. Complete these sentences using any *into* phrase.

1. Make sure you drop the letter _____.

2. Everyone stood up when the president walked _____.

3. Move the TV set _____.

4. The child reached _____and pulled out her doll.

5. The batter hit the ball _____.

6. Laura dived _____.

Lesson 2. Into: other uses

Example Sentences. With books open, listen to and repeat each sentence as it is read to you.

1. to the action or occupation of:
   a. Three out of the class went into medicine.
   b. Alexa got into gymnastics when she was only five.

2. to the condition, state or form of:
    a. The kids got into trouble for writing on the wall.
    b. Stephen went into debt to buy that car.
    c. The machine tore the paper into shreds.
    d. The magician turned the feather into a duck.
3. so as to be in:
    a. The women got into an argument about politics.
    b. Celia entered into an agreement with the bank.
4. against:
    a. The truck crashed into the guard rail.
    b. The outfielder ran into the fence.
5. toward; in the direction of:
    a. The bus drove into the desert.
    b. Jaime looked into the mirror and combed his hair.
6. as a divisor of:
    a. Three into twelve is four.

Now write the sentences.

Exercise 1. With books closed, listen to and repeat each sentence again.

Section C: Out of

Lesson 1. Out of: from inside to outside, away from, as used with in/into

---

Note: Out used alone is an adverb, not a preposition. *Out of* is used as a preposition.

Example Sentences. With books open, listen to and repeat each sentence as it is read to you.

1. Put the roast in the oven. Take the roast out of the oven.
2. They jumped in/into the water. They jumped out of the water.
3. He put the letter in/into the envelope. He took it out of the envelope.
4. They got in/into the car. They got out of the car.
5. They drove out of the city into the country.
6. When they went into the theatre the sun was shining; when they came out of the theater the moon was shining.
7. Bobby put sixty-five pennies in/into his bank last week. Today he took fifty pennies out of his bank to buy a baseball card.
8. The policeman went into the building alone. Five minutes later he came out of the building with a handcuffed criminal.

Now write the *out of* phrases plus the preceding verbs.

Exercise 1. Complete these sentences, in writing, using any *out of* phrases.

1. The frog jumped _____.

2. The ants crawled _____.

3. The baker took/put the cookies _____.

4. The passengers got _____.

5. We took/put the money _____.

6. She took/put her new dress _____.

7. The birds flew _____.

8. The water ran _____.

Lesson 2. Out of: shows what something is made from

Example Sentences: With books open, listen to and repeat each sentence as it is read to you.

1. Paper is made out of wood.
2. Some furniture is made out of wood.
3. Many containers are made out of plastic.
4. The castle on the beach is made out of sand.
5. These skillets are made out of iron.
6. This coat is very warm because it's made out of wool.
7. This statue was carved out of marble.
8. That statue was shaped out of clay.

Now write the *out of* phrases plus the preceding verbs.

Exercise 1. With books closed, listen to and repeat each sentence again.

Practice: Think of something that was made out of something else, and share it with the class.

Lesson 3. Out of: not having, lacking

Note: To *run out of* something is an idiom meaning having used up or depleted something.

Example Sentences. With books open, listen to and repeat each sentence as it is read to you.

1. We're out of milk. Please go to the store and buy some.
2. If we run out of gas we'll be stuck here all night.
3. We should develop other forms of energy in case we run out of oil.
4. If we don't hurry we're going to run out of time.
5. This pen is out of ink.
6. The restaurant ran out of fish so we ate chicken instead.

7. They're out of coffee so they're drinking tea.
8. We've run out of ideas for a story.

Now write the *out of* phrases.

Exercise 1. With books closed, listen to and repeat each sentence again.

Practice. In groups, discuss what you think is the worst thing that anyone could run out of. Tell each other about times you have run out of something.

Lesson 4. Out of: because of

Example Sentences. With books open, listen to and repeat each sentence as it is read to you.

1. The little boy looked in the box out of curiosity. He couldn't wait until his birthday.
2. We attended the funeral out of sympathy for the widow.
3. When the professor entered the room we stood up out of respect.
4. They gave the poor woman their money out of the kindness of their hearts.
5. He said those nasty things out of meanness.

Now write the *out of* phrases.

Exercise 1. With books closed, listen to and repeat each sentence again.

Practice. Have you ever done something out of curiosity? Out of sympathy? Out of kindness? Out of respect?

Write a sentence telling about this experience. Take turns reading your sentence to the class.

Lesson 5. Out of: other uses

Example Sentences. With books open, listen to and repeat each sentence as it is read to you.

1. from a number of others; a fraction of something
   a. Three out of the ten people at the dinner party were vegetarians.
   b. Only a few kids out of the whole class got an *A* on the test.
2. beyond; farther than
   a. My friend and I have been out of touch for years. (We haven't seen or heard from each other.)
   b. The target was out of his line of vision.
3. absent from
   a. The boss will be out of the office this afternoon.
   b. She'll be out of the country next year.
4. no longer having or being
   a. Her clothes are out of fashion, but they still look great.
   b. It is frightening to be out of work.

5. taking from or losing
   a. The car went out of control and hit a tree.
   b. That salesman talked me out of a thousand dollars.

Now write the *out of* phrases.

Exercise 1. With books closed, listen to and repeat each sentence again.

Practice. In groups, discuss the meaning of the sentences.

Section D: Inside/Outside

Lesson 1. Inside/Outside: in or into or out or out of something or some place

---

Example Sentences. With books open, listen to and repeat each sentence as it is read to you.

1. The children played inside on rainy days but they played outside on sunny days.
2. The outside of her purse is made of leather but the inside is lined with plastic.
3. The world outside her head was drab and dull, but the world inside her head was bright and beautiful.
4. He should be here inside of (within) an hour.
5. She thought it was cool (slang) to wear her shirt inside out.
6. It's cold outside, but inside by the fire it's nice and warm.

Now write the *inside/outside* phrases.

Exercise 1. With books closed, listen to and repeat each sentence again.

Review. On/Off, In/Out, Into/Onto, Inside/Outside

Reading Passage 1. Listen, with books closed.

When we got on the bus in Denver it was cold. When we got off the bus in Houston it was warm. We took our bags off the bus and went into the bus station, where we put a quarter in the telephone slot to call our grandmother.

"Get in a taxi and hurry out here," she said. "I just put a pie in the oven. Be sure to turn off the highway onto Pine Street."

When we got out of the taxi, Grandma was inside the house looking out of the window. Then she came outside and told us to come into the house and take off our coats. We put our bags in the guest room, showered, and put on clean clothes. We brushed the dust off our shoes and shook the wrinkles out of our clothes before we hung them in the closet.

Grandma got out her best crystal glasses, which her mother had bought in England in 1900, and poured iced tea in them. Then she took the apple pie out of the oven and put it on the dining room table. She took off her apron, cut the pie, and said, "Now be sure to clean every crumb off the plate." We were glad to be in Grandma's house again.

Turn to Missing Links, page 245.

Unit 3
At, By

Section A: At

Lesson 1a. At: used to indicate a point in space, the location of someone/something
---

Note: With verbs of motion such as *going,* no preposition is used with *home.* At other times, the preposition is often omitted.

Note: When referring to locations smaller than cities, use *at* with the verb *arrive.*

Practice.

S1: Knock, knock. Is anyone home?
S2: Hi. I'm the only one at home. Can you believe it?
S1: Where is everyone?
S2: Barbara's at the library, Jim's at the golf course, Laura's at her friend's house, and Craig's at school.
S1: When will they be home?
S2: They're going to meet at the cafeteria for dinner and come home from there.
S1: Are you going to stay home alone all afternoon?
S2: Yes, indeed. The peace and quiet are heavenly!

Example Sentences. With books open, listen to and repeat each sentence as it is read to you.

1. Tom arrived at the airport early.
2. I live at 4321 Pinetree Avenue.
3. Sharon stays (at) home on Tuesdays.
4. Let's meet at McDonald's for lunch.
5. Hal bought rolls at the bakery and brought them home.
6. John worked at his computer all night long.
7. The dog is at the vet's getting his rabies shot.
8. Stop at the stop sign, not in the middle of the intersection.

Now write the *at* phrases.

Exercise 1. With books closed, listen to and repeat each sentence again.

Exercise 2. Take turns answering these questions with your written *at* phrases.

1. Where should we meet for lunch?
2. Where is Tom?
3. Where did Hal buy the rolls?
4. Where does Sharon stay on Tuesdays?
5. Where should we stop?
6. Where do I live?
7. Where did John work?
8. Where is the dog?

Practice. In groups, discuss where you enjoy having lunch; whether you like to study at home or at the library; where planes land; where you buy groceries.

Reading Passage 1. Listen, with books closed.

     Professor Think lives at 405 Ogden Street, but he spends most of his time at his desk at the university. One day last week while he was driving to work he forgot to stop at a red light. Now he's spending most of his time in the whirlpool at the rehabilitation hospital and his car is in the shop at the garage.

Exercise 3. Write the *at* phrase that answers these questions.

1. Where does Professor Think live?
2. Where does he spend most of his time?
3. What did he forget to do last week?
4. Where is he spending most of his time now?
5. Where is his car?

Turn to Missing Links, page 245.

Practice. Write four sentences about house and home using *at* where required. Remember:

    We can be home or *at* home
    But we cannot be house or *at* house.
    We can be *at someone's* home or house,
    Or *at the* or at *a* home or house.*

    We cannot go *to* home
    Nor can we go *to* house,
    But we can go *to the* home of someone,
    Or *to* someone's house.†

---

*I.e., Let's go to Dan's house. (Not to the house of Dan) or to our house.
†I.e., We went to the home of a former president. OR Our hosts invited us to their home after the opera.

Lesson 1b. At: used to show the position of something on or within a place or object

Practice.

Reporter 1: The small plane has stopped at the end of the runway.
Reporter 2: We can see the world famous Doctor Kind in the doorway at the back of the plane.
Reporter 1: Hundreds of excited natives have been waiting for hours at the edge of the field.
Reporter 2: Now they're crowding into the area at the front of the terminal, waving and shouting.
Reporter 1: They know that Dr. Kind will soon be at their sides, ready to bring health to their village.

Example Sentences. With books open, listen to and repeat each sentence as it is read to you.

1. Sign your name at the end of the letter.
2. Wild flowers bloom at the side of the road.
3. There's a river at the bottom of the canyon.
4. Karen's blouse has lace at the edge of the collar.
5. At the beginning of the book the hero was a young boy; at the end of the book he was an old man.
6. Bjorn stood at the top of the stairs.
7. A guard was stationed at the front of the bank.
8. Ahmed waited at the corner of 13th and Main.

Now write the *at* phrases.

Exercise 1. With books closed, listen to and repeat each sentence again.

Practice.

1. Write your name at the top of a sheet of paper. What did you do? (Answer all together.)
2. Write *The End* at the bottom of the sheet of paper. What did you do? (Answer all together.)
3. Stand at the side of your desk. What are you doing? (Answer all together.)
4. Put your pencil/pen at the edge of your desk. What did you do? (Answer all together.)
5. Is someone at the door? (Answer all together.)

Practice. Volunteer answers to these questions.

1. Where can coral be found?
2. Where do you write "Dear Sir"?
3. Where in the alphabet is the letter Z?
4. Before you start down the stairs, where are you?
5. Where are the nails on your fingers?
6. Where is the hem of a tablecloth?

Lesson 2. At: used to show attendance or presence in a place, activity, or event

---

Example Sentences. With books open, listen to and repeat each sentence as it is read to you.

1. My father is at work.
2. The president is at a meeting.
3. The office staff is at lunch.
4. Vacation is over. The children are back at school.
5. Rintje is at baseball practice.
6. The sailors are at sea.

Now write the *at* phrases.

Exercise 1. With books closed, listen to and repeat each sentence again.

Practice. Discuss these uses of *at* that sound like locations but are not exactly locations.

Exercise 2. Use your written *at* phrases to answer these questions.

1. Where are the sailors?
2. Where is the office staff?
3. Where are the children now that vacation is over?
4. Where is the president?
5. Where is my father?
6. Where is Rintje?

Practice. Use the *at* phrases to compose two new sentences. Read them to the class.

Reading Passage 1. Listen, with books closed.

> Randy has been at the University of Texas all year but he's home now for the summer. He and his friends are at the beach this afternoon, and tonight they'll be at a party. I'm glad he's having fun today, because tomorrow he'll be at the dentist's having a root canal.

Exercise 3. Take turns answering these questions.

1. Where has Randy been all year?
2. Where will he be for the summer?
3. Where is he this afternoon?
4. Where will he be tonight?
5. Where will he be tomorrow?

Reading Passage 2. Listen, with books closed.

> My brother is at archery practice; my sister is at gymnastics; I'm at the opening of the new water park; my mother is at a garage sale; my father is at his wit's end wondering how he'll pay the bills. He shouldn't worry, because my grandmother's at church praying for us all.

Turn to Missing Links, page 246.

Practice. In groups, take turns telling where each member of the family in the reading passage is. Then think of a place, activity, or event you have been to recently and tell the group about it. Be sure to use *at* in your account.

Lesson 3. At: used to show condition, state, or manner

Example Sentences. With books open, listen to and repeat each sentence as it is read to you.

1. She did the right thing. Her conscience is at peace.
2. Our friends always make us feel at home (comfortable).
3. The boy scouts stood at attention at the flagpole.
4. We are at greater risk of getting the flu in winter.
5. I don't feel at ease with a roomful of strangers.
6. The heart beats more slowly when it's at rest.

Now write the *at* phrases.

Exercise 1. With books closed, listen to and repeat each sentence again.

Practice. Discuss the meaning of the *at* phrases.

Exercise 2. Place a link where *at* belongs.

1. I don't feel ease with a roomful of strangers.
2. Her conscience was peace.
3. The heart beats more slowly when it's rest.
4. The boy scouts stood attention at the flagpole.
5. Our friends make us feel home.
6. We are greater risk of getting the flu in winter.

Practice. In groups, tell each other when you feel most at ease; most ill at ease; how you can make someone feel at home; when your health is at risk.

Lesson 4. At: used to show movement, special attention, or facial expression aimed at a person or object

---

Practice.

S1: Stop staring at me!
S2: I'm not staring at you. I'm staring at Reiko.

S1: Why? It's not polite to stare at people.

S2: Well, Reiko's glaring at Paula. I've never seen Reiko glare at anyone before.

S3: He's glaring at her because she laughed at him.

S1: Why did she laugh at him?

S3: Because of the look on his face when he ate a whole hot pepper, thinking it was pickled okra.

Example Sentences. With books open, listen to and repeat each sentence as it is read to you.

1. Anna shot the ball at the basket.
2. I laughed at my friend's joke.
3. "Look at all the stars!" exclaimed Vera.
4. "Be careful!" Jane yelled at the driver.
5. The mother frowned at her noisy children.
6. The old man glared at the rude boys.
7. The teacher shot questions at the students.
8. I winked at Sara so she'd know I was only teasing.
9. Robert threw a shoe at the raccoon stealing our supper.
10. Don't shout at me! I can hear you.
11. Grant aimed at the target with his bow and arrow.
12. The batter swung at the ball and missed.

Now write the *at* phrases.

Exercise 1. With books closed, listen to and repeat each sentence again.

Practice. Write sentences using the following verbs with *at:* look, aim, scream, toss, frown. Share them with the class.

Reading Passage 1. Listen, with books closed.

The baby stared at the kitten. The kitten stared at the baby. The baby threw a toy at the kitten. The kitten clawed at the baby. The dog growled at the kitten. The kitten scratched at the dog. The mother yelled at the kitten. The kitten ran away.

Exercise 2. Write the passage from dictation.

Practice. Make up sentences using the following verbs with *at:* stare, yell, growl, throw.

Reading Passage 2. Listen, with books closed.

Our family spent Sunday afternoon at the zoo. The elephants sprayed water at us, the monkeys threw bananas at us, the lions roared at us, the snakes hissed at us, and the goats nibbled at our clothes. We decided to go home and watch *Wild Kingdom* on TV.

Exercise 3. Write the passage from dictation.

Practice. Take turns telling what the elephants, the monkeys, the lions, the snakes, and the goats did. Did an animal ever do something like that to you? What was it?

Reading Passage 3. Listen, with books closed.

When Jim was a little boy, his father taught him never to direct insults at anyone, unless he would enjoy having insults directed at him. Years later, that advice kept him from jeering at a young man who would later stand at his side in time of trouble, and who would later still become his best friend.

Turn to Missing Links, page 246.

Lesson 5. At: used to show reaction, how one acts or feels in response (answer) to something

---

Practice.

S1: I was astounded at what we experienced on our trip to Europe.
S2: Were you surprised at the size of the Acropolis?
S1: No, but I was amazed at the taste of Greek baklava.
S2: Were you thrilled at the majesty of the Alps?
S1: No, but I marveled at the rich Swiss chocolate.
S2: Were you speechless at the sight of Michelangelo's sculpture?
S1: No, but I was astonished at the variety of Italian pasta.

Example Sentences. With books open, listen to and repeat each sentence as it is read to you.

1. *at* as used with the expression of feeling or emotion in response to something
   a. We were shocked at hearing the bad news.
   b. Amy was nervous at the prospect of tomorrow's test.
   c. Tansu was indignant at the idea of losing the race.
   d. Neal was upset at hearing the conflicting stories.
   e. Andrei was aghast at the report of the killings.
2. *at* as used with an action in response to something
   a. The workers rebelled at the cut in pay.
   b. Aida trembled at the thought of falling.
   c. The parents rejoiced at their son's success.
   d. The team cheered at learning the name of the winner.
   e. The crowd stood up at the sound of the national anthem.

Now write the *at* phrases.

Exercise 1. With books closed, listen to and repeat each sentence again.

Exercise 2. Use the written *at* phrases to complete these sentences.

1. Neal was upset _____ the conflicting stories.

2. We were shocked _____ .

3. The parents rejoiced _____ .

4. She trembled _____ of falling.

5. Andrei was aghast _____ of the killings.

6. Amy was nervous _____ of the test.

7. The crowd stood up _____ of the national anthem.

8. The team _____ the name of the winner.

9. The workers rebelled _____ the cut in wages.

10. Tansu was indignant _____ losing the race.

Exercise 3. Have you ever been angry at something? Have you ever been annoyed at something? Write a sentence or two about those times and share them with the class.

Practice. Choose one of the example sentences and expand it into a written paragraph.

Exercise 4. Place a link where *at* belongs.

1. Olga began to skate a signal from her coach.
2. Henry stepped on the brakes the sound of the train.
3. Valeri ran the sight of the approaching tornado.
4. The elephants turned a command from the trainer.
5. We all said "Ah!" the smell of freshly baked bread.

Lesson 6. At: used to tell how much skill (or lack of) someone has in doing something

---

Practice.

S1: My father's great at golf.
S2: My mother's wonderful at tennis.
S3: My grandmother's super at aerobics.
S4: My brother's a champion at skiing.
S5: My grandfather's a star at bowling.
S6: The only thing I'm good at is reading the sports page.

Example Sentences. With books open, listen to and repeat each sentence as it is read to you.

 Note: When a verb follows a preposition, it always ends in *-ing.*

 1. My sister is good at swimming.
 2. Jenny is a whiz at math.
 3. The baby is messy at feeding herself.
 4. Craig is accomplished at public speaking.
 5. Most people are slow at learning a new language.
 6. The mechanics are skilled at engine work.
 7. Bill is a natural at gardening.
 8. Sherlock Holmes is an expert at solving mysteries.
 9. I'm not very good at sewing.
10. Andy's great at the piano, but he's not so great at singing.

Now write the *at* phrases.

Exercise 1. With books closed, listen to and repeat each sentence again.

Exercise 2. Divide the class into sides. Side A should read the sentences up to *at.* Side B, with books closed, should use the written *at* phrases to complete the sentences. Then switch sides and repeat the exercise.

Practice. Think of things you—or someone you know—are good at (or maybe not so good at) and write sentences telling what they are. Take turns sharing them with the class.

Reading Passage 1. Listen, with books closed.

 Marta's better at math than she is at history. Jack's better at history than he is at math. They're both good at explaining things, so they help each other with their homework, even though they're brother and sister.

Exercise 3. Answer in complete sentences.

1. What's Jack better at, history or math?
2. What's Marta better at?
3. What are they both good at?

Practice. Use any two school subjects or sports and ask the student next to you whether he/she is better at one or the other. Answer his/her question in turn.

Reading Passage 2. Listen, with books closed.

 My father is lucky at fishing, my mother is great at cooking fish, and my sister and I are expert at eating fish. This is a great way to practice ecology.

Turn to Missing Links, page 246.

Lesson 7. At: a point in time when something happens or when something is done. (See unit 12 for prepositions to use for time.)

Example Sentences. With books open, listen to and repeat each sentence as it is read to you.

1. I'll meet you at 5:30.
2. The new year begins at midnight.
3. The rooster crows at sunrise.
4. At the beginning of the world, man did not exist.
5. The band plays at halftime.
6. We began our long drive at dawn.
7. At the last moment we changed our plans.
8. The children play tag at recess.
9. At the turn of the century, McKinley was president of the United States.
10. At dusk, the bats fly out from under the bridge.
11. At no time will eating be allowed in this class.
12. She always reads a story to her child at bedtime.

Now write the *at* phrases.

Exercise 1. With books closed, listen to and repeat each sentence again.

Practice. Use *at* plus *time* phrases to answer these questions in turn.

1. When does the sun rise?
2. What time of day do you usually watch TV?
3. When do you set your alarm clock?
4. When does this class start?
5. When do the lights go out in the theater, at the beginning or at the end of the movie?
6. When do you eat breakfast?
7. When does the clock strike twelve?
8. When does the news come on TV?

Practice. Ask the person sitting next to you these questions, and write the answers in complete sentences. What time do you get to school? What time do you leave school? What time do you have lunch? Read the answers back to her/him and see if they are correct. Then answer his/her questions in turn.

Practice. Write sentences using these *at* phrases: *at* the same time; *at* different times; *at* one time (once); *at* no time; *at* the present time (now); *at* some time in the future; *at* some point in time.

> *Note:* Some examples are: The bus leaves school *at* the same time every day. My brother and I arrive home *at* different times. *At* one time Bill worked in Sweden. *At* the present time I'm learning English. *At* some time in the future I will speak English well. *At* some point in time (not certain when) she decided to become a nurse. *At* no time (never) has he explained his behavior.

Reading Passage 1. Listen, with books closed.

Blind Spot
At dawn I'm doing sit-ups,
At noon I'm eating fries,
At dusk I'm jogging in the park,
At eight I'm nibbling pies,
At ten my scale informs me
The pounds are on the rise,
I might as well just stay in bed
And skip the exercise!

Exercise 2. With books open, say the poem in unison.

Lesson 8. At: used with measuring degree, level, age, cost, speed, rate

---

Example Sentences. With books open, listen to and repeat each sentence as it is read to you.

1. At his age he should know better.
2. The car was traveling at eighty miles an hour.*
3. The thermometer registered at thirty-two degrees Fahrenheit.*
4. A person can vote at the age of twenty-one in the USA.
5. At that price we could afford to buy several.
6. Arthur always drives at the speed limit.
7. Molly's sailboat is at least thirty feet long.
8. The train was moving at a high rate of speed.
9. At one thousand feet a laser detector's beam is about three feet wide.
10. That car was a good buy at ten thousand dollars.
11. A crash force at sixty-five mph is forty percent greater than at fifty-five mph.
12. At a twenty-five percent discount the stove was affordable.
13. The boxes came off the assembly line ten at a time.
14. The graduates marched across the stage one at a time.

   Note: Omit *at* if *go* or *drive* is used with a number. For example: That car was going seventy miles an hour; we drive thirty-five miles an hour in this neighborhood.

Now write the *at* phrases.

Exercise 1. With books closed, listen to and repeat each sentence again.

---

at may be omitted.

Exercise 2. Use your written *at* phrases to answer these questions.

1. Why should he know better?
2. How fast was the car traveling?
3. What did the thermometer register?
4. When can a person vote in the USA?
5. How long is Molly's sailboat?
6. How fast was the train traveling?
7. How did the boxes come off the assembly line?
8. Under what conditions could we afford to buy several?

Practice. Choose three *at* phrases and use them to write new sentences. Take turns reading your sentences to the class.

Review. At: combined usages

Reading Passage 1. Listen, with books closed.

This story happened last Christmas Eve at seven o'clock at night at my grandparent's house. They live at 128 Cedar Street, at the edge of town.

My sister and I were at the kitchen window looking out at the first snowfall, and the rest of the family was sitting at the kitchen table, talking. Suddenly we heard someone knocking loudly at the front door. At the same time, my little brother, who was standing at the top of the stairs, shouted at us. He was looking down and pointing at the door.

We all crowded into the hall at once. When my father opened the door we were shocked at what we saw. Santa Claus! His sleigh stood at the curb, with his reindeer pawing at the loose gravel. Santa was yelling at someone or something, "Come back, you toy thief!"

My mother's great at tennis and my father's pretty good at running; my grandmother's super at Ping-Pong and my grandfather's a star at badminton. Everything they needed was at hand, so they were prepared.

As they ran down the driveway after the toy thief, my mother aimed a tennis ball at the middle of his back, my father threw a jogging shoe at his legs, my grandmother fired a Ping-Pong ball at his head, and my grandfather pitched his badminton racket at the bag of toys he was dragging away.

The thermometer was at thirty degrees, and ice had formed at the end of the driveway. The thief skidded and dropped the bag of toys. We laughed at him as he ran into the woods at the side of the house. Santa was relieved at the outcome, and so were we. What would a raccoon do with all those toys, anyway?

Now take turns reading the passage, sentence by sentence.

Reading Passage 2. Listen, with books closed.

At six o'clock last evening, my family was at home except for my father, who was still at work. My brother, sister, and I were at the kitchen table doing our homework. Suddenly our mother yelled at us: "Look at the stove! It's on fire!"

At that moment, the fire alarm went off. My brother grabbed a bag of flour that was right at the edge of the counter, and threw the flour at the flames. We were amazed at how quickly he acted.

He was good at knowing what to do at times like this. The fire went out at once, and we all cheered at the same time: "Hurray, John!"

Turn to Missing Links, page 247.

Review. On, In, At: combined usages

Exercise 1. Fill in the blanks. Correct by comparing with each other. Then take turns reading the passage aloud.

The Martians arrived _____ the theater right _____ time _____ spaceships shaped like

taxis. The Martians were very small so twenty of them fit _____ one taxi. Their name was

_____ the marquee (sign) _____ front of the theater: *Musicians* _____ *Miniature.*

Crowds of fans stood _____ the sidewalk _____ the rain. They had arrived _____ seven

P.M. and had waited _____ line for tickets. _____ exactly nine P.M. the show began. _____ least

fifty Martians, dressed _____ every color of the rainbow, stood _____ the stage and danced

_____ circles. They played strange music _____ long blue pipes. _____ the end of the dance

they sat _____ the floor, put their heads _____ their hands, and sang. They were great _____

singing.

The ushers _____ the doors counted seven hundred people _____ the theater. They were

surprised _____ the courtesy of the fans. No one pushed or shoved to get _____ front.

Suddenly they saw a Martian fly up and land _____ the ceiling. He had a motor strapped _____

his back. It had rotors _____ it like a helicopter. Then all the Martians were _____ the air flying

_____ formation. The leader shouted _____ the others:

"Ltmosprz!" he called _____ a loud voice, and _____ an instant they were all gone.

_____ home the next morning, when we were _____ the breakfast table, I told my mother

and father what had happened _____ the theater. They looked _____ me _____ disbelief. I

wonder why.

Section B: By

Lesson 1. By: near, beside, close to

Note: The preposition *beside* can be used interchangeably with *by* when meaning close to or next to.

Practice.

> The dog walked close by his master,
> He sensed what was in store,
> His master was leaving forever,
> His master was going to war.
>
> Maria stood by the window,
> Andrew stood by the door,
> And they waved goodbye to their loved one
> Until they could see him no more.

Example Sentences. With books open, listen to and repeat each sentence as it is read to you.

1. Jozef is standing by the window watching the rain.
2. Grandfather's chair is by the fireplace.
3. The clinic is right by the hospital.
4. The seat by the exit is occupied.
5. Come sit by me so we can look at the pictures together.
6. Helen would love to have a cottage by a lake.
7. The store is right by the freeway.
8. The usher is waiting by the entrance.

Now write the *by* phrases.

Exercise 1. With books closed, listen to and repeat each sentence again.

Exercise 2. Use the written *by* phrases to answer these questions in complete sentences.

1. Where is the store?
2. Where is Jozef standing?
3. Where is the usher waiting?
4. What seat is occupied?
5. Where is Grandfather's chair?
6. Where am I asking you to sit?
7. Where is the hospital?
8. Where would Helen love to have a cottage?

Practice. Using the preposition *by,* write sentences telling where things in the classroom are.

Practice. Look around and take turns telling who is sitting by whom in the classroom. If you are studying alone, write a paragraph about an imaginary dinner table and describe who is sitting by whom.

Lesson 2. By: how something is done using a certain means, through the use of

---

Practice.

S1: Why do you always sit by the door?

S2: Because my next class is way over by the gym. It's only by leaving the minute the bell rings and by running at top speed that I get there in time.

S1: What class is it?

S2: Track. And by doing all that running, I became fast enough to make first team!

Example Sentences. With books open, listen to and repeat each sentence as it is read to you.

1. Maria always pays her bills by check.
2. I plant my garden by the full moon.
3. Philip relaxes by playing golf.
4. The offices communicate by fax.
5. Susan earns money for college by sacking groceries.
6. Al became an Olympic swimmer by practicing every day.
7. The group that traveled by bus arrived first.
8. The group that traveled by plane arrived last.
9. We learn more by listening than by speaking.
10. The sign read: *Leave By This Exit Only.*

Now write the *by* phrases.

Exercise 1. With books closed, listen to and repeat each sentence again.

Exercise 2. Use the written *by* phrases to answer these questions.

1. How did Susan earn money for college?
2. How did the group that arrived first travel?
3. How did the group that arrived last travel?
4. How does Maria always pay her bills?
5. How did Al become an Olympic swimmer?
6. How do the offices communicate?
7. How did the sign tell us to leave?
8. How does Philip relax?
9. How can we learn more?
10. How do I plant my garden?

Exercise 3. Place a link where *by* belongs.

1. I travel plane.
2. We keep in touch exchanging Christmas cards.
3. We left the burning building the fire escape.
4. We got out of the locked room breaking a window.
5. Jane's mother led her to the dentist's office the hand.
6. Have you ever called your own number mistake?

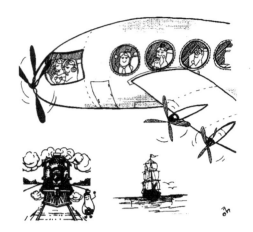

Practice. Answer these questions in writing using *by* phrases.

1. Do you leave a building by the exit or the entrance?
2. How can you learn to play the piano well?
3. Would you rather travel by plane or by car?
4. How can a person earn a living?
5. How can we lower our cholesterol?

Practice. Volunteer answers to these questions using *by* phrases.

1. How do you figure out a difficult problem?
2. How can a person get a diploma?
3. How do you learn what's happening in the world?
4. How can you stay healthy?
5. How can you become an expert at something?

Reading Passage 1. Listen, with books closed.

     I said to my teenage son: "Thomas Edison patented over twelve hundred inventions by using his brains and working hard; Hannibal crossed the Alps by determination and perseverance; Lincoln educated himself by studying by candlelight; your father got his law degree by going to night school. Do you think you're going to raise your grades by playing video games?"

Now take turns reading the passage, sentence by sentence.

Turn to Missing Links, page 247.

Lesson 3. By: introduces a person or thing that creates, produces, causes, or affects

---

Practice.

S1: Our house was designed by the famous architect Frank Lloyd Wright.
S2: Oh, really? Well, our house was redesigned by the most famous architect of all time.

S1: Who is that?

S2: Mother Nature. A tree fell on the roof during a storm.

S1: Did you have it rebuilt by a well-known builder?

S2: Yes, by someone very well-known—to our family, at least—me.

Example Sentences. With books open, listen to and repeat each sentence as it is read to you.

1. Music by Chopin is easy to recognize.
2. That mural was painted by school children.
3. The poor cow was struck by lightning.
4. This garden was planted by a twelve-year-old girl.
5. The prisoner was released by the guard.
6. That dull party was planned by a committee.
7. Reading a play by Shakespeare is very difficult.
8. The jewelry was crafted by the Pueblo Indians.
9. Soil erosion is caused by weather and overuse.
10. The streets were flooded by the heavy rainfall.

Now write the *by* phrases.

Exercise 1. With books closed, listen to and repeat each sentence again.

Practice. Change these sentences into *by* sentences.

1. One thousand people attended the concert.
2. Only one person heard the signal.
3. His brother forgave him.
4. David sang the tenor role.
5. All her friends love Mary.
6. Several people saw the UFO.

Practice. Volunteer answers using *by.*

1. Who wrote your favorite song?
2. Who wrote your favorite book?
3. Who raises potatoes?
4. What controls the tides?
5. What causes thunder?
6. Who/what has influenced your decision to learn English?
7. Who prepares your lunch?

Reading Passage 1. Listen, with books closed.

When Stephen was ten years old, he was urged by his father to take piano lessons. He was advised by all his friends to play baseball instead. He was almost persuaded by them to forget about music. Then he read a story about a great pianist who was inspired by Bach's concertos to study music.

Stephen was impressed by the story and was motivated by them to begin lessons. Sometimes we can be influenced more by what we read than by what we hear.

Now take turns reading the passage, sentence by sentence.

Exercise 2. With your books open, write the answers to these questions using *by* phrases.

1. By whom was Stephen urged to take piano lessons?
2. By whom was Stephen advised to play baseball?
3. What did he read?
4. Which tapes of his father's did Stephen listen to?
5. What can we be influenced by?

Turn to Missing Links, page 248.

Lesson 4. By: not later than, to be completed on or before a certain time (See unit 12 for prepositions to use for time.)

Example Sentences. With books open, listen to and repeat each sentence as it is read to you.

1. The letter should reach Iceland by next week.
2. By this time next year we will be living in Mexico.
3. Be sure to pay your bills by the end of the month.
4. Term papers must be turned in by Friday.
5. The travelers hoped to reach the border by nightfall.
6. Bill will finish his homework by game time.
7. The money must be in the bank by September 7th.
8. It will be dark by nine o'clock.
9. We're usually asleep by eleven.
10. I've got to be at the meeting by two o'clock.

Now write the *by* phrases.

Exercise 1. With books closed, listen to and repeat each sentence again.

Exercise 2. Use the written *by* phrases to answer these questions in complete sentences.

1. When should the letter reach Iceland?
2. When will we be living in Mexico?
3. When must term papers be turned in?
4. When must the money be in the bank?
5. When will it be dark?

Practice. Write sentences telling some things you must do by a certain time, some things you usually do by a certain time, and some things you will do by a certain time.

Lesson 5. By: past, up to and beyond

Practice.

S1: Are you mad at me?

S2: No, why?

S1: When I was waiting for my pie a la mode this noon you walked right by me without saying hello.

S2: I didn't see you. The only way I can pass by the dessert counter without stopping is to close my eyes.

Example Sentences. With books open, listen to and repeat each sentence as it is read to you.

1. A red bird flew by my window.
2. The parade marched by the school.
3. We filed by the dinosaur exhibit.
4. The ship sailed by the Statue of Liberty.
5. The mailman went by our house without stopping.
6. I walk by the toy shop. I don't want to be tempted.
7. We saw the parachute falling right by the plane window.
8. When we drove by the White House the flag was being raised.
9. The ball rolled by the center fielder for a three-base hit.
10. The waitress walked right by our table without taking our order.

Now write the *by* phrases.

Exercise 1. With books closed, listen to and repeat each sentence again.

Exercise 2. Divide the class into sides. Side A should read the sentences up to *by* in mixed order. Side B, with books closed, should take turns completing the sentences with the written *by* phrases. Then switch sides and repeat the exercise.

Note: The preposition *past* may be used in place of *by* in all of these sentences.

Lesson 6. By: special usages

Example Sentences. With books open, listen to and repeat each sentence as it is read to you.

1. as used to point to source, origin, or profession
   a. Mary is cheerful by nature.
   b. Charles is Canadian by birth.
   c. They're conservative by disposition.
   d. They're doctors by profession.
   e. He's a strong man by reputation.

2. without help, *by* oneself (a)
    a. Did you do your homework all by yourself?
    b. Little Polly prepared dinner all by herself.
    c. We planted the entire garden by ourselves.
    d. He learned to read by himself.

3. alone, no one else being there, *by* oneself (b)
    a. I can concentrate best when I'm all by myself.
    b. Young children should never be left by themselves.
    c. When I'm by myself, I enjoy listening to the songs of the birds.
    d. She reads when she's home by herself.

4. as used to show how something is done or is happening by number, size, time, or weight
    a. The painters charge by the size of the room.
    b. It's getting colder by the minute.
    c. They carried flowers to the altar by the armful.
    d. They moved sand by the carload.
    e. I get paid by the week. My friends get paid by the hour.
    f. That movie star gets fan letters by the hundreds.
    g. Fish is sold by the pound.

5. as used informally to introduce a subject not mentioned earlier, or that one just thought of (sometimes interchangeable with "that reminds me")
    a. This fish is delicious. By the way, I saw a new fish cookbook at the bookstore yesterday.
    b. That wall looks blank. By the way, where are those pictures I gave you?
    c. The new cartoon show is coming on TV in a few minutes. By the way, have you done your homework?
    d. I'm glad you enjoyed having dinner here at the Ritz with me. By the way, could you lend me a few dollars?
    e. There sure are a lot of toothpaste ads in this magazine. By the way, I made an appointment at the dentist for you tomorrow.

Now write the *by* phrases.

Practice. Write complete sentences of your own using the written *by* phrases.

Note: The following sentences demonstrate some of the other special usages of *by.*

Always play by the rules. = Never break the rules. = Play according to the rules.

The students walk two by two. = The students follow one another two by two (or three by three, etc.).

I was overcharged/undercharged by one dollar. = I was charged one dollar too much/too little.

The rug is ten by ten. = The rug measures ten feet by ten feet. = Multiply ten by ten (ten × ten) to get the square footage.

Review. By: combined usages (Includes all the uses of *by* studied in Section B.)

Reading Passage 1. Listen, with books closed.

The boy, who was patient by nature, stood by the door all by himself. The door was ten feet by six feet and the boy looked very small by comparison. Suddenly, a big black dog ran by. The boy grabbed it by the collar and held it by force. He called the dog by name: "Toby! Toby! Sit down and stay here by me."

Just then several people, who had arrived by car, walked by the boy, two by two. The child knew they were actors like his mother because they were saying lines from a play by Shakespeare. By that time, his mother had appeared as if by magic.

"I'm afraid you've all come here by mistake," she said. "I know we agreed to meet for rehearsal at four o'clock so we would be through by ten, but we planned to meet by the stage door. Don't you remember? You've overshot the mark by two miles."

Toby, who had become famous by singing *Down by the Old Mill Stream* began to howl it out. The actors quickly moved away. By the time Toby had finished the song, they were standing by the four cars parked by (at) the curb. One had hurried away by another route.

"With the boy and his mother there are twenty of you," said the head driver, just as Toby began tuning up for another song. "Twenty divided by four equals five. That means five in each car. By the way, we charge by the mile, so if we drive you back we've undercharged you by twenty dollars."

"That's better by far than staying here!" cried someone. "Let's leave by the quickest route possible!" And they did.

Now take turns reading the passage, sentence by sentence.

Turn to Missing Links, page 248.

Section C: At, By, On, In, Off, Out of, Inside, Outside

Lesson 1. At, By: combined usage

Reading Passage 1. Listen, with books closed.

When Jennifer and Sarah shopped at the mall, they always walked by the pet shop to look at the animals. At closing time one afternoon, they were horrified by what they saw. Five puppies were crowded together in a cage about four feet by four feet. A spotted puppy was huddled by itself at the far side. A small boy was poking a stick at it. The girls were angered by his behavior and frowned at him as they told him to stop.

The two sisters, who were compassionate by nature, looked at each other and knew what they must do. They asked the girl standing by the desk how much the spotted puppy cost. She pointed at a sign by the cage. It read, "$200.00 each. Payment By Cash Only." Jennifer said, "At that price we may as well forget it." And Sarah replied, "You're right. By the time we earn $200.00 the puppy will be gone."

As they left the shop they saw another sign leaning at an angle by the side of the counter: "Two Helpers Needed." They looked at each other again, and this time they smiled. By noon the next day the girls were being trained by a veterinarian, and by the next morning they were working at the grooming table. They discovered that they were both very good at handling animals.

By working hard, Jennifer and Sarah paid for the puppy all by themselves, and now it lives at their house. They also made a doghouse by following the directions in a book by a famous woodworker. By the end of the summer, they'd been motivated by their work at the pet shop to become veterinarians. Their lives were changed by that day at the mall. And the pet shop was changed by the sisters. At their insistence the cages were enlarged and the customers are now closely watched by the employees.

Now take turns reading the passage, sentence by sentence.

Practice. After writing the prepositional phrases from the reading passage, take turns reading the phrases to the class.

Turn to missing links, page 248.

Review. At, On, In, By

Exercise 1. After filling in the blanks, take turns reading the sentences to the class.

Tim is standing _____ the corner _____ the bus stop _____ the rain. He waves _____ the bus but it drives right _____ him. He presses a button _____ his umbrella. _____ a second he is flying above the bus. _____ the next bus stop Tim lands _____ the bus door. The bus driver looks _____ him _____ amazement. Tim gets _____ the bus. He points _____ his running shoes. "Magic Flyers," he says with a grin _____ his face. The bus driver faints.

Review. On, In, Off, Out of, Inside, Outside, At, By

Exercise 1. After filling in the blanks, take turns reading the sentences to the class.

1. Alan lives _____ 825 Ontario Avenue.

2. The Smith family lives _____ a busy street.

3. They have lived _____ Los Angeles for five years.

4. Margaret enjoys living _____ Australia.

5. Our daughter was born _____ 6:30 A.M.

6. She was born _____ Friday, October 27, 1972.

7. All our children were born early _____ the morning.

8. Three of them were born _____ January.

9. Please try to be here _____ nine o'clock.

10. The mail should be here _____ now.

11. The tornado blew the roof _____ the house.

12. Rain dripped _____ the trees _____ the grass.

13. Stand _____ the window so you can see the parade.

14. We always keep the pot holders _____ the stove.

15. Aunt Em lived _____ fear that another tornado would strike.

16. That man won a million dollars _____ the lottery.

17. Dan became an A student _____ studying hard.

18. Susan is _____ the beauty salon.

19. Young children are quick _____ foreign languages.

20. Would you rather travel _____ car or _____ plane?

21. Foresters are interested _____ trees.

22. We heard the news _____ the radio.

23. Cathy enjoys working _____ the computer.

24. The baby laughed _____ the monkey.

25. Have you ever seen a play _____ Shakespeare?

Reading Passage 1. Listen, with books closed.

On Monday morning, Letty drove by the oriental rug shop on her way to work. She glanced at the rugs in the window in fascination.

Monday evening she parked at the curb by the front of the shop, got out of her car and stood looking at the rugs in the window. She was amazed at their beauty.

Letty was interested in old oriental rugs because she was thinking about starting a business of her own. She was now quite good at appraising their value because she had spent many hours in the library studying books by experts on the subject, as well as examining rugs in galleries. But she was on a small budget and had to be on her guard about spending too much.

It was after five o'clock and no one seemed to be in the shop. On the chance it was still open, she knocked on the door. The owner, with an anxious look on his face, welcomed her into the showroom.

The rugs were heaped in piles on the floor. By 6:00 P.M. he had shown her many of them, one at a time, lifting each one off the floor so she could inspect it more closely. But she had her eye on one in the corner.

It was an antique, woven in the last century in what used to be Persia, by people who were weavers by tradition. They learned to weave at an early age and continued at their craft into old age. This rug had a Tree of Life design in the center, and stylized flowers on either side woven in rich colors.

She decided at once that this rug was quite valuable, but when she looked at the price tag she was shocked. She had estimated it at much less, even though it would rate high on the appraisal list.

The man knew by her expression that she was shocked, and in a weary voice he offered the rug to her at twenty-five percent off. At this point she almost decided to buy it, but first she called her business partner on the phone to ask his opinion. He advised her to think about it.

On hearing her decision to wait, the owner offered her seventy-five percent off.

She answered, "Maybe I'll come by again some other time."

As she stepped outside, she smiled in relief. She had almost put her money into a bad investment. Her guess about the value of the rug had been wrong. She got into her car and drove to the library to take out more books on oriental rugs.

Now take turns reading the passage, sentence by sentence.

Turn to Missing Links, page 249.

Unit 4
To, Toward, From, From/To

Section A: To

Note: To is not a preposition when it is part of the infinitive. The infinitive is: *to* + the simple form of the verb. The simple form of the verb is a verb without *-s, -ed,* or *-ing* endings, e.g., walk, study, want. The infinitives of these words are: to walk, to study, to want.

Lesson 1. To: in the direction of and reaching, as far as

Practice.

S1: How do you get to school?
S2: I walk to my friend's house and then get a ride to school with his brother.
S1: How do you get home?
S2: I take the bus to the library, and after I've done my homework, I walk home.

Note: We say: go home, *not* go to home.

Example Sentences. With books open, listen to and repeat each sentence as it is read to you.

1. Our friends moved to Idaho.
2. Their furniture was trucked to Indiana.
3. Raul returned to America.
4. My parents drove to Arizona.
5. Hank went to bed early last night.
6. The criminal was sent to prison.
7. We read to the end of the chapter.
8. That airline flies to the Orient.
9. The elephants were shipped to a zoo.
10. The silver dollar sank to the bottom of the fountain.

Now write the *to* phrases.

Exercise 1. With books closed, listen to and repeat each sentence again.

61

Exercise 2. Take turns answering these questions with your written *to* phrases.

1. Where did the silver dollar sink?
2. Where did my parents drive?
3. What did he do last night?
4. How far did I read?
5. Where did Raul return?

Exercise 3. Place a link where *to* belongs.

1. Their furniture was shipped Indiana.
2. The criminal was sent prison.
3. That airline flies the Orient.
4. My friends moved Idaho.
5. The elephants were shipped a zoo.

Practice. Tell the person next to you where you have gone in the last year, e.g., to a new restaurant, to a different city or country, to a museum, etc. Make notes of what you tell each other.

Practice. Working with the same person, ask each other the following questions.

1. Would you rather go to the moon or to Montana?
2. Would you rather go to the mall or to the park?
3. Would you rather go to the movies or to the beach?
4. Would you like some free tickets to a football game or to a soccer game?

Reading Passage 1. Listen, with books closed.

> When our father was transferred to Washington, D.C., we kids wanted to stay in Omaha. We didn't want to move to a new city where we couldn't walk to the corner and meet our best friend. We didn't want to go to a school where we wouldn't feel at home. But of course we did move to the new city, and after a few weeks, we were walking to the corner to meet our *new* best friend and attending a new school where we felt very much at home.

Practice. With books open, answer the questions.

1. Where was the father transferred?
2. Why didn't the children want to move?
3. What finally happened?

Practice. With books closed, write about the passage in your own words.

Turn to Missing Links, page 250.

Lesson 2a. To: (as used with nouns) in the direction of, on the way, between starting point and destination

Practice.

S1: Do you study on the way to work?

S2: No, that would be dangerous because I usually drive to work, and I can't read and drive at the same time.

S1: Well, I listen to English tapes when I'm driving to school.

S2: I'm afraid they would distract me from my driving. But I do listen to them when I take the train to Chicago.

Example Sentences. With books open, listen to and repeat each sentence as it is read to you.

1. The road to Dallas is wide and straight.
2. They were on their way to class when the bell rang.
3. Brian slept soundly on the flight to Argentina.
4. The paramedics performed CPR during the trip to the hospital.
5. It was a race to the finish for the tortoise and the hare.
6. The bus ride to school was bumpy.
7. We enjoyed the cruise to the islands.
8. The path to the secret cave was overgrown.

Exercise 1. With books closed, listen to and repeat each sentence again.

Reading Passage 1. Listen, with books closed.

When people from Europe migrated to America one hundred and fifty years ago, the ocean voyage to the shores of the "New World" was long and rough. Now a flight to Europe takes just hours. How long do you think a trip to Europe will take one hundred years from now? How about to the other planets?

Turn to Missing Links, page 251.

Practice. Write sentences containing these phrases: migrate to, travel to, fly to.

Exercise 2. With books closed, listen to the example sentences again, some with *to* and some without *to*. Write the number of each sentence in which *to* is omitted.

Exercise 3. Use the written *to* phrases to answer these questions in complete sentences. Then take turns reading your sentences to the class.

1. On what flight did Brian sleep soundly?
2. What kind of a race was it for the tortoise and the hare?
3. What cruise did we enjoy?
4. On what trip did the paramedics perform CPR?

5. What was bumpy?
6. What path was overgrown?
7. What is wide and straight?
8. What were they doing when the bell rang?

Lesson 2b. To: (as used with verbs) in the direction of, on the way

---

Example Sentences. With books open, listen to and repeat each sentence as it is read to you.

1. The boy scouts were hiking to the campsite.
2. The kite was flying to outer space.
3. The choir traveled to Rome.
4. The Mississippi flows to the Gulf of Mexico.
5. The path led to a waterfall.
6. The ship was sailing to Bermuda.
7. The tour group headed to the museum.
8. Jiro got a flat tire while he was driving to work.

Now write the *to* phrases.

Exercise 1. With books closed, listen to and repeat each sentence again.

Exercise 2. Use your written *to* phrases to answer these questions in complete sentences. Then take turns reading your answers to the class.

1. What was Jiro doing when he got a flat tire?
2. Where does the Mississippi flow?
3. Where does the path lead?
4. Where were the boy scouts hiking?
5. Where was the kite flying?
6. Where did the choir travel?
7. Where did the tour group head?
8. Where was the ship sailing?

Exercise 3. With books closed, listen to the example sentences again, some with *to* and some without *to.* Write the number of each sentence in which *to* is omitted.

Reading Passage 1. Listen, with books closed.

Our class went on a field trip to Space City last week. We were there from early morning to late afternoon. The guide took us to Mission Control.

That night, when I went to sleep, I had a dream. We were in a spaceship on our way to Saturn. The space ship started vibrating, so we radioed to Earth to come to our rescue. To our right and to our left alien ships were attacking us! The trip to Saturn was over; my mother was shaking me awake and saying, "It's time to go to school!"

Turn to Missing Links, page 251.

Lesson 3. To: as used with words about sending, giving, communicating, belonging; being helpful or beneficial

---

Practice.

S1: Do you write to your relatives very often?

S2: Not as often as I should, but I send gifts to them on their birthdays. How about you?

S1: I subscribe to magazines and have them sent to them. That way they think of me at least once a month.

Example Sentences. With books open, listen to and repeat each sentence as it is read to you.

1. The mother sang to her baby.
2. Billy gave his kite to Molly.
3. We write to our parents every week.
4. Carmen sent a package to Alaska.
5. That book belongs to the library.
6. Joan's family belongs to a bicycle club.
7. Philip subscribes to the zoology magazine.
8. The president spoke to the senate.

Now write the *to* phrases.

Exercise 1. With books closed, listen to and repeat each sentence again.

Exercise 2. With books closed, listen to the example sentences again, some with *to* and some without *to.* Write the number of each sentence in which *to* is omitted.

Exercise 3. Place a link where *to* belongs.

1. The king presented a medal the hero.
2. The president spoke the senate.
3. Luke handed the hammer the carpenter.
4. Joan's family belongs a bicycle club.
5. Philip subscribes a zoology magazine.
6. That book belongs the library.

Practice. Fill in the blanks with words of your own to make sentences.

1. _____ sang to _____ .

2. _____ gave _____ to _____ .

3. _____ writes to _____ every day.

4. _____ sent _____ to _____ .

5. _____ spoke to _____ .

6. _____ handed _____ to _____ .

7. _____ showed _____ to _____ .

8. _____ donated _____ to _____ .

Practice. Divide the class into groups. Each group should take turns completing these tasks.

1. Give a piece of paper to each other.
2. Write a short note to the student next to you and hand it to him/her.
3. Talk to each other.

Exercise 4. Write five sentences using *to* after any of these words: send, give, write, show, hand, pass, belong, make a promise, donate, pay attention, listen, lend.

Exercise 5. Write five sentences using any of the following phrases (add the necessary noun or pronoun between the verb and the preposition).

1. apply _____ to the surface

2. confide _____ to the counselor

3. dedicate _____ to her mother

4. describe _____ to her blind friend

5. entrust _____ to the broker

6. introduce _____ to my wife

7. distribute _____ to the crowd

8. furnish _____ to the embassy

9. mention _____ to his wife

10. devote _____ to his work

11. submit _____ to the dean

12. reveal _____ to the secret service

13. recommend _____ to his superiors

14. relate _____ to his grandchildren

15. suggest _____ to the committee

Lesson 4. To: reaching an extreme condition

Example Sentences. With books open, listen to and repeat each sentence as it is read to you.

1. The poem moved Alice to tears.
2. The kitten tore Judy's new hose to shreds.
3. We were almost crushed to a pulp by the crowd.
4. They were starving to death on five hundred calories a day.
5. He was driven to insanity by a nagging wife.
6. The statue was smashed to bits.
7. The stone was ground to powder.
8. The survivors were chilled to the bone.
9. The dinner was cooked to perfection.
10. The decorating was carried to extremes.

Now write the *to* phrases.

Exercise 1. With books closed, listen to and repeat each sentence again.

Exercise 2. Discuss what each phrase means: moved to tears? tear to shreds? crush to death? drive to insanity? smash to bits? grind to powder? cook to perfection? carry to extremes?

Reading Passage 1. Listen, with books closed.

Polar bears, who were starved to a frenzy, attacked the explorers at their camp at the North Pole. The ragged crew drove the bears away, but not before some of the men had been slashed to ribbons. The men who could still move ripped their tents to pieces to make stretchers for the wounded.

They walked for two days and were almost frozen to death. They had gotten to the limit of their endurance and believed they were walking to their doom when they heard a sound. It was a plane. They were saved!

Exercise 3. Take turns reading the passage, sentence by sentence.

Exercise 4. Write the *to* phrases (plus the preceding verb) telling what condition the men were in, what they did or were going to do, and what they believed.

Turn to Missing Links, page 251.

Lesson 5. To: as used after response verbs

Practice.

S1: Are you allergic to tree pollen?
S2: I'm not sure, but I always have a reaction to house dust.
S1: Do you admit to having a dusty house?
S2: My mother would object to that question!

Example Sentences. With books open, listen to and repeat each sentence as it is read to you.

1. The company replied to our inquiry promptly.
2. May responded to the invitation enthusiastically.
3. The crowd reacted to the news calmly.
4. The shop owners agreed to the new closing hours.
5. Her parents consented to her marriage.
6. The criminal confessed to the crime.
7. George did not receive an answer to his letter.
8. You should yield to ambulances on the road.
9. The lawyer objected to the questioning.
10. The judge appealed to the jury's common sense.
11. The suspect adhered to his original story.

Now write the *to* phrases.

Exercise 1. With books open, listen to and repeat each sentence again.

Practice. In groups, tell each other something you object to.

Exercise 2. Divide the class into teams. The team that guesses which of two prepositions, *in* or *on* , the teacher has written, goes first. After the first part of the example sentence is read quickly by the teacher, each team will have five seconds to complete the sentence with one of your written *to* phrases. The team completing the most sentences wins.

Exercise 3. Write a sentence of your own design using the verb + preposition from five of the sentences. Take turns sharing them with the class.

Reading Passage 1. Listen, with books closed.

Most of the animals reverted to their wild states after they were released. They adapted to their natural environments as though they'd never left them. One thing was certain: they all preferred the jungle to the cage.

The experiment demonstrated to the conservationists that they should devote more time to assessing cruelty to animals in captivity.

Turn to Missing Links, page 251.

Exercise 4. Answer these questions in writing using complete sentences.

1. What happened to the animals after they were released?
2. What about their natural environments?
3. How did they feel about the jungle?
4. What did the experiment do?

Lesson 6. To: reaching the condition or state of
(often metaphorical)

Example Sentences. With books open, listen to and repeat each sentence as it is read to you.

1. The way to happiness is contentment.
2. The road to riches was full of potholes.
3. Her rise to power was quick; her fall was quicker.
4. His climb to the top was made on a slippery ladder.
5. Their flight to freedom was made in a rowboat.
6. The path to his destruction was paved with lies.

Now write the *to* phrases.

Exercise 1. With books closed, listen to and repeat each sentence again.

Exercise 2. Discuss what each of the example sentences means.

Lesson 7. To: in contact with, touching or facing

Example Sentences. With books open, listen to and repeat each sentence as it is read to you.

1. The little girl held tightly to her mother's hand.
2. The bubble gum stuck to her shoe.
3. The grocery list was taped to the wall.
4. The paper butterfly was pinned to the curtain.
5. The cards were stapled to the paper.
6. The players stood back-to-back.
7. The teams lined up face-to-face.
8. He applied a tourniquet to the cut.
9. The child stayed close to his father.
10. The windshield wiper froze to the windshield.

Now write the *to* phrases.

Exercise 1. With books closed, listen to the example sentences again, some with *to* and some without *to.* Write the number of each sentence in which *to* is omitted.

Exercise 2. Use your written *to* phrases to complete these sentences.

1. The grocery list was taped _____ .

2. The teams lined up _____ .

3. He applied a tourniquet _____ .

4. The cards were stapled _____ .

5. The child stayed close _____ .

Exercise 3. Place a link where *to* belongs.

1. The windshield wiper froze the windshield.
2. The paper butterfly was pinned the curtain.
3. The little girl clung her mother's hand.
4. The bubble gum stuck her shoe.
5. The players stood back-back.

Practice.

1. Pair off and stand face-to-face and then back-to-back.
2. Tape a paper strip to your sleeve.
3. Apply pressure to your elbow with your hand.
4. Tack a picture to the bulletin board.
5. Hold a piece of paper to the top of your head.

Exercise 4. Write sentences of your own design using these verbs + prepositions: glue to, attach to, nail to, sew to. Take turns reading them to the class.

Lesson 8. To: belonging to something, part of something

Example Sentences. With books open, listen to and repeat each sentence as it is read to you.

1. Diane lost the key to the buffet.
2. Close the door to the closet.
3. Don't tear the cover to that book.
4. Did you flip the switch to the air conditioner?
5. The lid to a pot keeps the steam inside.
6. The table to the dining room set has three leaves.
7. The strap to my purse is broken.
8. The jacket to the suit is too big.
9. The knob to the door won't turn.
10. What would I do without the eraser to my pencil?

Now write the *to* phrases.

Exercise 1. With books closed, listen to and repeat each sentence again.

Exercise 2. Take turns answering these questions.

1. What shouldn't you tear?
2. What keeps steam inside a pot?
3. What did Diane lose?
4. What is broken?
5. What won't turn?

Exercise 3. Use your written *to* phrases to complete these sentences.

1. Don't tear the cover _____ .

2. The jacket _____ is too big.

3. Diane lost the key _____ .

4. What would I do without the eraser _____ .

5. The knob _____ won't turn.

Exercise 4. Divide the class into teams. With books closed, listen to the example sentences again, some with *to* and some without *to*. As soon as you hear a sentence missing a *to,* write the number of that sentence. Whichever team has the most correct numbers wins.

Exercise 5. Replace the *to* phrases with double words (e.g., key to the typewriter = typewriter key). Take turns reading the new sentences to the class.

Lesson 9. To: indicating an accompaniment or background for doing something

---

Example Sentences. With books open, listen to and repeat each sentence as it is read to you.

1. Jan likes to sleep to the sound of the rain.
2. The drill team marches to the beat of the band.
3. They danced to the rhythm of the calypso music.
4. It's fun to sing to the tapes of famous bands.
5. Sally plays the piano to the tick of the metronome.
6. Sean studies to the buzz of his computer.
7. Baby claps her hands to the cadence of the poem.
8. Mother hums to the radio broadcast of the opera.

Now write the *to* phrases.

Exercise 1. With books closed, listen to and repeat each sentence again.

Exercise 2. With books closed, listen to the example sentences again, all without *to*. Raise your hand when you notice *to* is missing. Then, with books open, place a link where *to* belongs in the following sentences.

1. Sean studies the buzz of his computer.
2. The drill team marches the beat of the band.
3. It's fun to sing the tapes of famous bands.
4. Jan likes to sleep the sound of the rain.
5. Baby claps her hands the cadence of the poem.
6. They danced the rhythm of the calypso music.
7. Mother hums the radio broadcast of the opera.
8. Sally plays the piano the tick of the metronome.

Practice. Discuss which is harder, studying to the sound of a symphony orchestra or the sound of a marching band; the sound of people talking or birds singing; a TV comedy show or complete silence.

Practice. In groups ask one another what kind of music you like to study to.

Lesson 10. To: used to show how one thing is affected by another (used with nouns plus *to*)

Example Sentences. With books open, listen to and repeat each sentence as it is read to you.

1. The old bridge was a threat to safe travel.
2. Work is an antidote to boredom.
3. Energy is the secret to her success.
4. The solution to the puzzle was in the code.
5. A good job was the answer to his problem.
6. Fingerprints are often first clues to mysteries.

7. Disrespect is an obstacle to love.
8. Dishonesty is a barrier to honor.
9. Applause is a boost to ego.
10. Education is a bridge to a better life.

Now write the *to* phrases.

Exercise 1. With books closed, listen to and repeat each sentence again.

Exercise 2. Divide the class into sides. Side A should take turns reading the sentences up to the *to* phrases. (Be sure to mix up the order in which you read them.) Side B, with books closed, should use your written *to* phrases to complete the sentences in turn. Then switch sides and repeat the exercise.

Practice. Divide the class into groups. Each group should choose one of the following questions to discuss.

1. What besides applause is a boost to the ego?
2. What besides old bridges could be threats to safe travel?
3. How could a good job be an answer to someone's problems?

Then share your conclusions with the class.

Lesson 11. To: used to connect an adjective to its prepositional object

---

Example Sentences. With books open, listen to and repeat each sentence as it is read to you.

1. The nurse is attentive to her patients' needs.
2. We are all indebted to our parents.
3. Rude behavior is unacceptable to the coach.
4. Crying is natural to a baby.
5. The auditorium is adjacent to the gym.
6. People should remain faithful to their promises.
7. Too much sun can be detrimental to your skin.
8. Your handwriting is similar to my daughter's.
9. Children should be obedient to their parents.
10. The rebels were hostile to the government.

Now write the *to* phrases plus the preceding adjective.

Exercise 1. With books closed, listen to and repeat each sentence again.

Exercise 2. Place a link where *to* belongs.

1. The rebels are hostile the government.
2. Crying is natural a baby.
3. We are all indebted our parents.
4. The nurse is attentive her patients' needs.
5. Rude behavior is unacceptable the coach.

Exercise 3. Complete each sentence with any *to* phrase.

1. The theater is adjacent _____ .

2. Lack of exercise is harmful _____ .

3. Children should be attentive _____ .

4. Smoking can be dangerous _____ .

5. Your name is similar _____ .

6. We should be grateful _____ .

7. The old man remained faithful _____ .

8. The rebels were hostile _____ .

Practice. Choose three of these adjectives, plus *to,* and use them to write sentences of your own. acceptable, helpful, natural, distasteful, pleasing

Reading Passage 1. Listen, with books closed.

Ellen knew her job was important to her family's independence. The food, clothing, and shelter that it paid for were essential to their well-being. But she was shy, and shyness was a barrier to communication. Would it be an obstacle to her chance to succeed?

Turn to Missing Links, page 251.

Lesson 12. To: other usages

Example Sentences. With books open, listen to and repeat each sentence as it is read to you.

1. in addition
   a. Add some pepper to the soup.
   b. Add two to three and get five.
2. in expressions of time meaning before
   a. It's ten to one.
   b. It's an hour to game time.
3. in comparing
   a. The score is seven to six.
   b. She has two plums to his three oranges.
4. in honor of someone
   a. A toast to his success!
   b. A salute to her memory!
5. making up or consisting of
   a. There are four cups to a quart.
   b. There are three feet to a yard.
6. relationship in space of one thing to another
   a. The streets run parallel to each other.

b. The building is perpendicular to the wall.
c. He placed the screen at an angle to the bookcase.

Exercise 1. With books open, listen to and repeat each sentence again. Then write the complete sentences from dictation.

Exercise 2. Write parallel sentences to as many of the example sentences as you can. Take turns sharing them with the class.

Section B: Toward

Lesson 1. Toward: moving or looking in the general direction of

Practice.

S1: The funniest thing happened this morning when I was walking my dog, Tiny.
S2: What happened?
S1: He saw another dog and they were running toward each other, ready to fight. As the other dog got closer, it was easy to see that he was huge!
S2: What did Tiny do?
S1: He growled and the big dog turned and ran toward the park.

Example Sentences. With books open, listen to and repeat each sentence as it is read to you.

1. The dog is running toward the cats.
2. The wind is blowing toward shore.
3. This plane is flying toward the horizon.
4. The ship is sailing toward an iceberg!
5. Point the robot toward the computer.
6. The soldiers were marching toward freedom.
7. We're headed toward the north. (Or: We're headed north.)
8. You'll see the sun rising if you look toward the east.
   (Or: Look east and see the sun rise.)
9. He was walking toward the book store when he saw her.
10. Look out! That car is speeding right toward us!

Now write the *toward* phrases.

Exercise 1. With books closed, listen to and repeat each sentence again.

Exercise 2. Use the written *toward* phrases to answer these questions.

1. Where are we headed?
2. Where is the wind blowing?
3. Where were the soldiers marching?
4. Where is the plane flying?
5. Where is the dog running?

Exercise 3. Discuss the following questions.

1. If you look out the classroom window, what are you looking toward; the north, the south, the east, or the west?
2. When rain leaves the clouds, where is it going?
3. When a spaceship blasts off, where is it headed?

Lesson 2. Toward: not long before

Example Sentences. With books open, listen to and repeat each sentence as it is read to you.

1. Toward dawn the sky began to lighten.
2. Toward evening it cooled off a bit.
3. Toward the end of life things become a little clearer.
4. Toward the middle of the second act, the villain appears.
5. Toward noon he began to think of lunch.

Now write the *toward* phrases.

Exercise 1. With books closed, listen to and repeat each sentence again.

Exercise 2. Answer these questions with your written *toward* phrases.

1. When did the villain appear?
2. When did he begin to think of lunch?
3. When did the sky begin to lighten?
4. When did it cool off a bit?
5. When do things become a little clearer?

Reading Passage 1. Listen, with books closed.

Soon after the early settlers migrated to America, they continued their trek to the West in covered wagons. They were often crowded several to a wagon.

As they moved toward the interior of the country, the rough trails to each new campsite ground the horses' shoes down to their hooves and the wagon wheels to filings.

Progress toward their destination was slow, but everyone contributed their labor, expertise, and emotional support to the rest of the settlers. Children adapted to the hard life and shouted to each other from dawn to dusk. Babies slept to the rhythm of the turning wheels and the clopping hooves.

Toward evening, families passed travel information to each other as they rested to the eerie howls of the coyotes. The covers to the wagons provided a bit of shelter and privacy as the weary families slept.

Severe winters were threats to their lives but not an obstacle to their determination. Some almost starved to death, and others succumbed to illness, but they were never abandoned to the elements by their companions.

These people were committed to a dream, and they remained faithful to that commitment.

Turn to Missing Links, page 252.

Section C: From

Lesson 1. From: the source, the starting point

Practice.

S1: I got a letter from my friend, Lee, this morning.
S2: Is he the one from Indonesia?
S1: Yes, but this letter came from California.
S2: Were you glad to hear from him?
S1: Yes, and I'll soon see him. His plane from Los Angeles arrives here in two hours. I have to hurry to get some groceries from the supermarket, a folding bed from the furniture store, and some towels and linens from the department store.
S2: Would you like a little help from me?
S1: Thanks, I sure would. Could you get me some aspirin from the pharmacy?

Example Sentences. With books open, listen to and repeat each sentence as it is read to you.

1. The plane from Ohio arrives at gate ten.
2. Where do whooping cranes come from?
3. NASA received a signal from the satellite.
4. Fruit comes from orchards.
5. Fish come from lakes, streams, and oceans.
6. The cowboy comes from Texas.
7. Bobby received a gift from Santa Claus.
8. We got the information from a book.
9. Silk comes from silkworms.
10. Snow comes from snow clouds.

Now write the *from* phrases.

Exercise 1. With books closed, listen to and repeat each sentence again.

Exercise 2. Write five sentences telling where people or things come from. Take turns reading them to the class.

Practice. In groups, take turns asking what country each person comes from, who you enjoy getting mail from, where the freshest fish comes from, or any other questions using *from.*

Reading Passage 1.

In the USA
Willa's folks hail from Wales,
Jose's kin came from Spain,
Marya's grandma comes from Russia,
Ali's father from Bahrain.

Cheryl's dad comes from China,
Tomo's mom from Japan,
But their children rightly say,
"I am American."

Lesson 2. From: using, made of, or as a result of something

Example Sentences. With books closed, listen to and repeat each sentence as it is read to you.

1. Bread is made from flour, yeast, and a liquid.
2. She recited the poem from memory.
3. Those bowls are made from clay.
4. The furniture is made from oak.
5. This clean house comes from hard work.
6. Her good grades come from long hours of study.
7. His bright teeth come from frequent brushings.
8. Paper is made from wood pulp.
9. Their drinking water comes from melted snow.
10. This jewelry is fashioned from silver.

Now write the *from* phrases.

Exercise 1. With books closed, listen to and repeat each sentence again.

Practice. In groups, discuss what different things come from or are made from (e.g., pickles, shoes, coffee, tea, towels, glass, cheese, etc.).

Exercise 2. Listen to the example sentences again, some with *from* and some without *from*. Write the number of each sentence in which *from* is omitted.

Lesson 3. From: shows separation, taking away, or difference of some kind

---

Example Sentences. With books closed, listen to and repeat each sentence as it is read to you.

1. The ship is five miles from shore.
2. Sunscreen shields us from ultraviolet rays.
3. Umbrellas protect us from the rain.
4. The drums are separated from the violins.
5. The teacher collected the homework from the students.
6. Five from ten equals five.
7. It's hard to tell one twin from the other.
8. The children ran from the big waves.

Now write the *from* sentences.

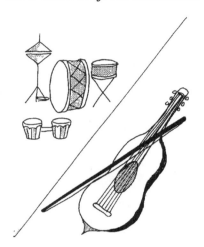

Exercise 1. With books closed, listen to and repeat each sentence again.

Exercise 2. Use the written *from* phrases to complete these sentences.

1. Five _____ equals five.

2. The children ran _____ .

3. Umbrellas protect us _____ .

4. The ship is five miles _____ .

5. It's hard to tell one twin _____ .

6. Sunscreen shields us _____ .

7. The teacher collected the homework _____ .

8. The drums are separated _____ .

Exercise 3. Write three sentences, using *from,* meaning separation, taking away, or difference. Take turns sharing them with the class.

Lesson 4. From: because of

Example Sentences. With books open, listen to and repeat each sentence as it is read to you.

1. Gina was bored from waiting so long.
2. The children are tired from playing.
3. Jeff is exhausted from lack of sleep.
4. The kittens have gotten fat from overeating.
5. The desert caravan almost died from thirst.
6. Their feet are sore from walking twelve miles.
7. Every fall, Paul suffers from allergies.
8. From the way he dresses you'd think he was rich.

Now write the *from* phrases.

Exercise 1. With books closed, listen to and repeat each sentence again.

Exercise 2. Use the written *from* phrases to complete these sentences.

1. Jeff is exhausted _____ .

2. The desert caravan almost died _____ .

3. The kittens have gotten fat _____ .

4. _____ the way he dresses, you'd think he was rich.

5. Gina was bored _____ .

6. Every fall, Paul suffers _____ .

7. The children are tired _____ .

8. Their feet are sore _____ .

Reading Passage 1. Listen, with books closed.

When Charles arrived at the University from his home town, he had to borrow money from his new roommate to buy a soft drink from the machine in the cafeteria. His brains may have come from his genes, but his money came from summer jobs that hadn't paid very much.

Even with the extra income he had earned from selling fishing poles he made from willow trees, he was several hundred dollars away from the total of his book bill. He was exhausted from all the nights spent worrying over finances.

The next day he took some good advice from his roommate and applied for a job at the student union, which was only one block from his dormitory. He got the job. He works from 4:00 to 8:00 P.M. from Monday to Friday, and from 10:00 A.M. to 4:00 P.M. on Saturday.

At last he's free from financial worries. Now his headaches come from his studies instead.

Turn to Missing Links, page 252.

Section D: From/To

Lesson 1. From/To: starting at a certain time or place and ending at a certain time or place

---

Example Sentences. With books closed, listen to and repeat each sentence as it is read to you.

1. I read that book from beginning to end.
2. Do you read books from front to back or from back to front?
3. The children will be in school from September to May.
4. The Civil War raged from 1861 to 1865.
5. The parade stretched from one side of town to the other.
6. How far is it from your house to the supermarket?
7. Arteries carry blood from the heart to the lungs.
8. She brought him from sickness to health.
9. His love brought her from despair to hope.
10. Aunt Minnie cleaned the house from top to bottom.

Now write the *from/to* phrases.

Exercise 1. With books closed, listen to and repeat each sentence again.

Exercise 2. Divide the class into two teams. Have your written phrases ready. The team that guesses which preposition (one out of three) your teacher has written goes first. With books closed, listen as the first part of the sentence is read to you. Each team has five seconds to complete the sentence with the correct phrase. The team that completes the most sentences correctly wins.

Practice.
1. Walk from your desk to the window.
2. Change your watch from your left hand to your right hand.
3. Drop a piece of paper from your hand to the floor.
4. Slide a pencil from one side of the desk to the other.
5. Take a book from the student next to you and then give it back to him/her.

Exercise 3. Write your own sentences using these phrases.

1. from top to bottom
2. from the river to the sea
3. from the city to the country
4. from A to Z
5. from here to there

Take turns sharing them with the class.

Reading Passage 1. Listen, with books closed.

From July 1st to July 14th every summer, I take the train from Chicago to a little town in Colorado to visit my cousin Jerry. Last summer he received two free tickets to the county fair. They came from a friend who had some connection to the rodeo.

We went to bed early the night before the fair, and toward dawn the next morning we started out toward town. We rode from the ranch to the fairgrounds on horseback and when we got there, Jerry tied the horses to a post not far from the main tent. A sign to the side of the gate said the show was from 2:00 to 3:00, so we went in and stood close to the stage. It was crowded—about two people to every seat—but we intended to stay from the beginning to the end, even though everyone was standing shoulder to shoulder.

The tent was at least a block from one end to the other. A big band was playing, and the crowd swayed from side to side with the music. Many rodeo riders from all over the Southwest were in the crowd, waiting for their special events. Coming from a big city, I wasn't accustomed to this kind of entertainment and I was thrilled to the core.

Suddenly a back door to the stage opened and a masked man walked from the back to the front of the stage. He grabbed a handful of souvenirs from a table and threw them to the audience. Then he began to juggle glass balls from one hand to the other. From his appearance you would have thought he was pretty old, but from his agility he seemed young. He was the introduction to the main act.

Just then a voice came from the loud speaker. To our astonishment we heard: "Two horses are pulling down the tent! They're trying to break away from a tent post close to the entrance. They're a danger to the crowd. Whoever owns them, hurry and stop them. They're too wild even for the cowboys!"

Our reaction to this announcement was to run from the tent with great speed. When we got outside, the horses were heading toward the ranch. Some men were retying the ropes to the post to keep the tent from caving in. We shamefacedly followed the horses down the road toward home. We'll never know what the main act was.

Turn to Missing Links, page 253.

Unit 5
For, Against

Section A: For

Lesson 1. For: directed or sent to; given to, usually to help or benefit; intended to be used by or in
---

Practice.

S1: The telephone's for you.

S2: Tell them I'm busy.

S1: It's the lottery company. They have a million-dollar prize for you.

S2: For me? Really?

S1: No, not really. I just wanted to get you to the phone. It's Pieter. He wants you to buy tickets for the school raffle.

Example Sentences. With books open, listen to and repeat each sentence as it is read to you.

1. Grandma made cookies for her grandchildren.
2. The father built a house for his family.
3. A big package came for you.
4. Jerry made a swing for the children.
5. Cam wrote a story for the magazine.
6. Pat brought cold drinks for the athletes.
7. The band gives free concerts for the students.
8. The owner bought a desk for the office.
9. The Indians wove colorful blankets for their tribes.
10. The clinic offers good health care for everyone.

Now write the *for* phrases.

Exercise 1. With books closed, listen to and repeat each sentence again.

Practice. Write your own beginnings to the *for* phrases you have written.

Exercise 2. Place a link where *for* belongs and answer each question in turn.

1. The dog dug a hole its bone. Why did the dog dig a hole?
2. Alma bought a new dress the party. Why did Alma buy a new dress?

3. That department store has something everyone. What does the department store have?
4. The mother got books her children at the library. What did the mother do at the library?
5. Casey bought groceries dinner. Why did Casey buy groceries?
6. We collect cans the recycling drive. Why do we collect cans?
7. Aunt Vi knit socks Luis. Why did Aunt Vi knit socks?
8. The kids washed cars money. Why did the kids wash cars?

Practice. Answer in complete sentences using *for* phrases.

1. You answer the phone and it's Scott's friend. What do you say to Scott?
2. A package comes in the mail. It's addressed to Ingrid. What do you say to Ingrid?
3. You make a big bowl of popcorn and put it on the table. One of your guests asks if she could have some. What will you reply? (Use "everyone" in your answer.)
4. At the furniture store, you buy a small wooden chair. Your friend asks you what room you are going to put it in. What do you reply?

Practice.

S1: Did you remember to buy a present for Naoko?
S2: No, I forgot. What did you get for her?
S1: Well, since she writes articles for the newspaper, I planned to buy her some floppy disks for her computer, but I forgot to stop at the store.
S2: I think I'll buy her something for her garden. She gave me some of her flowers for my birthday. I can't remember what kind.
S1: Who's bringing the candles for the cake?
S2: You are. Did you forget? I left a message for Juanita to bring the cake. I hope she remembers.
S1: This is going to be a surprise for Naoko and fun for us all—provided we don't forget the date of the party!

Reading Passage 1. Listen, with books closed.

Grandma cooked dinner for my brother and me last night. We brought our guitars to play for her while she was cooking. She had left a message for our cousin on his mother's answering machine inviting him, too. He was busy writing an article for the school newspaper so he didn't come. That was okay—we shared the food meant for him.

Grandma keeps a cheerful home for Grandpa and herself—and for us to visit. She always picks flowers for the table, and she makes sure there are plenty of games for us to play and books for us to read. We supply music and company for her, and she provides food and attention for us. A good trade for us all.

Turn to Missing Links, page 254.

Practice. In groups, talk about something nice someone has done for you, and/or something that someone has made for you.

Practice. Volunteer to sing a song from your native country, singly or in groups, for the class.

Lesson 2. For: used when showing special use or purpose

Example Sentences. With books open, listen to and repeat each sentence as it is read to you.

1. with nouns or pronouns
   a. The turkey is for Thanksgiving dinner.
   b. Those lemons are for lemonade.
   c. Anita bought a coat for cold weather.
   d. The new class is for adults.
   e. The arena is used for sports events.
   f. The author adapted his book for the movies.
   g. A dance for teenagers will be held next week.
   h. She's a computer consultant for small businesses.
2. with *-ing* verbs
   a. We bought shoes for walking.
   b. The small broom is for sweeping the kitchen floor.
   c. The big broom is for sweeping the sidewalk.
   d. They used the fireplace for heating the house.
   e. Maki used a screwdriver for opening the paint can.
   f. Eva has special glasses for sewing.
   g. A long-handled brush is good for painting ceilings.
   h. A spatula is for lifting, mixing, and spreading.

Now write the *for* phrases.

Exercise 1. With books closed, listen to and repeat each sentence again.

Exercise 2. Divide the class into teams. As the first part of the example sentence is read to you by the teacher, the teams should take turns supplying the rest of the sentence. Use your written *for* phrases. The team that supplies the most correct endings, wins.

Practice. Starting with one student, follow this routine.

S1: I use a pencil for writing. What do you use an eraser for?
S2: I use an eraser for erasing mistakes. (And turning to *S3*.) What do you use water for?

Then continue around the class with questions about these objects: shoes, the telephone, the library, a refrigerator, paper, an umbrella, a knife, a fork, a spoon, a microwave oven, scissors, a cup, ice cubes, rice, beans, eggplants, a bicycle, money, a chair, TV, a radio, a water hose, electric lights, a candle.

Practice. Take turns answering these questions in complete sentences using one of these *for* phrases: for cars; for transportation; for cooking; for communicating; for light and power; for protection; for cold winters; for processing information.

1. We need heavy clothing _____ .

2. Garages are _____ .

3. We use electricity _____ .

4. We use telephones _____ .

5. Some people have burglar alarms _____ .

6. We use a stove _____ .

7. Computers are _____ .

8. Cars are _____ .

Reading Passage 1. Listen, with books closed.

In my suitcase I packed a skating outfit for skating, a swimming suit for the pool, nice clothes for dining and dancing, ski clothes for skiing, boots for hiking, and plenty of casual clothes.

At the lodge, the restaurant was closed for remodeling, so meals for guests were served in the kitchen. The power for the ski lift was cut off, so there was no skiing. It was forty degrees so there was no ice for skating. The guide for our hikes and tours quit, and the pump for the indoor pool was broken. It poured every day.

Thank goodness I had gone to the library for a good book the day I left home. It had fourteen hundred pages, just enough for a week's read. By the way, do you know anyone who needs some very nice secondhand resort clothes?

Turn to Missing Links, page 254.

Lesson 3a. For: as being, as a substitute for something

Example Sentences. With books open, listen to and repeat each sentence as it is read to you.

1. Uncle Will used a stick for a cane.
2. I use a table for a desk.
3. The child used a blade of grass for a whistle.
4. The gardener used a piece of plastic for a raincoat.
5. My friends use sheets for curtains.
6. I mistook a shopper for a sales clerk.
7. We ate our lunch for dinner.
8. Mindy ate a peach for dessert.
9. The dieters use mustard for a dip for vegetables.
10. The children used cardboard for sleds.

Now write the *for* phrases.

Exercise 1. With books closed, listen to and repeat each sentence again.

Practice. Turn one of the example sentences into a question. Ask this question of the student next to you. Make any changes to the sentence that you wish, and start the question with: "Have you ever___ " (i.e., "Have you ever mistaken a stranger for a friend?") The second student should answer your question and ask you one of his/her own.

Exercise 2. Use your written *for* phrases to complete these sentences.

1. Uncle Will used a stick _____ .

2. We ate our lunch _____ .

3. The dieters used mustard as a dip _____ .

4. The child used a blade of grass _____ .

5. Mindy ate a peach _____ .

6. My friends use sheets _____ .

7. I use a table-top _____ .

8. The gardener used a piece of plastic _____ .

9. The children used cardboard _____ .

10. We mistook a shopper _____ .

Practice. Do these tasks all together.

1. Use your fingers for a comb.
2. Use a book for a paperweight.
3. At the chalkboard, use a tissue for an eraser.
4. Use a rolled up paper for a flyswatter.
5. Put your arms on your desks and use them for a pillow.
6. Use a finger for a bookmark.

Exercise 3. Place a link where *for* belongs.

1. We used the tank a swimming pool.
2. The lost campers ate berries breakfast.
3. The little kids used a blanket a tent.
4. They ate melons dessert.
5. She wore a palm leaf a rain hat.

Practice. In pairs, ask each other what you usually eat for breakfast, lunch, and dinner in your native countries (even if you are both from the same country). Write whatever you hear, and then check with each other to make sure you have the correct information.

Practice. Have you ever used something in place of (or *for*) something else? Take turns sharing your answers with the class.

Reading Passage 1. Listen, with books closed.

      The shipwrecked people on the island used bamboo mats for roofs and floors, seashells for cups and spoons, and coconut shells for bowls. They used fish bones for needles, seaweed for thread, and vines for rope. They ate fish for breakfast, for lunch, and for dinner. They even ate it for snacks.

Turn to Missing Links, page 255.

Lesson 3b. For: to help by doing something in place of someone/ something else
---

Practice.

S1: Would you please hold the baby for me while I get my keys?

S2: Surely. Let me hold your grocery bags for you, too.

S1: Thanks. I did my mother's shopping for her; that's why there are so many bags.

S2: Is she ill?

S1: No, she's substituting for a friend in a cross-country skiing competition.

Example Sentences. With books open, listen to and repeat each sentence as it is read to you.

1. The boy carried our luggage for us.
2. The bus company does the driving for you.
3. Our teacher was sick, so Miss Blue taught for her.
4. The dog does the blind man's seeing for him.
5. You won't learn much if someone does your homework for you.
6. Andy asked Ross to move his motorcycle for him.
7. Could you please walk the dog for us while we're away?
8. Nadia filled in for the absent secretary.
9. Mother sprained her ankle, so we did the ironing for her.
10. Abdul's arm was broken, so I wrote the application for him.

 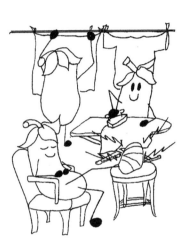

Exercise 1. With books closed, listen to and repeat each sentence again.

Exercise 2. With books open, take turns answering these questions.

1. What did Andy ask Ross to do?
2. What did I do when Abdul broke his arm?
3. What did the boy do?
4. What does the dog do?
5. What did Nadia do?
6. When won't you learn much?
7. What does the bus company do?
8. What did we do for Mother when she sprained her ankle?
9. What did Miss Blue do when our teacher was sick?
10. What did we ask you to do while we were away?

Practice. Think of things others have done for you and write sentences about them using *for.* Then think of things you have done for others and write sentences about them using *for.*

Reading Passage 1. Listen, with books closed.

On Monday my wife was sick so I did the dishes for her.
On Tuesday she was busy so I did our laundry for her.
On Wednesday she was out of town so I paid our bills for her.
On Thursday she got home late so I cooked our dinner for her.
On Friday she was at a meeting so I cleaned our house for her.
On Saturday she was grocery shopping so I mowed our grass for her.
On Sunday, when I told her all I'd done for her, she said, "For me?! You did it for both of us!"

Exercise 3. Take turns reading the sentences.

Lesson 4. For: in favor, support, or defense of; to save or keep

---

Example Sentences. With books open, listen to and repeat each sentence as it is read to you.

1. Vote for the honest man.
2. Show support for your candidate.
3. Send help for the injured victims.
4. We must work for justice.
5. The soldiers fought for their lives.
6. The citizen stood up for his rights.
7. Tony is campaigning for Ross for class president.
8. We cheered for our team when they lost.
9. The students showed respect for authority.
10. Bren spoke up for the absent employees.

Now write the *for* phrases.

Exercise 1. With books closed, listen to and repeat each sentence again.

Practice. Write two sentences of your own design using any of these *for* phrases: vote for, play for, cheer for, send help for, fight for, stand up for, work for, show support for, show respect for. Then take turns reading them to the class.

Reading Passage 1. Listen, with books closed.

The Parents
"We had a family meeting to get support for our plan for dividing the housework. We put up a good defense for equal work for each member of the family. We spoke strongly for the idea of *work in exchange for privilege!*"

The Children
Fran: "Since I play soccer for the school team, I should be excused from chores."
Nan: "Since I'm working hard for the debate team, I don't have time for chores."

Van: "Since I'm busy campaigning for student council president, I'm not home enough for chores."

Dan: "We stand together: no chores for children."

The Parents

"Since there's no enthusiasm for our ideas, we made a new rule: only those over the age of twenty-one may vote. We vote for equality in household chores. Mothers and fathers must stand up for their rights, too."

Now take turns reading the parts.

Turn to Missing Links, page 255.

Lesson 5. For: so as to reach, in order to go to

Example Sentences. With books open, listen to and repeat each sentence as it is read to you.

1. The kids leave for school at 7:45 A.M.
2. The plane took off for California.
3. Elena swam for shore.
4. The ship is sailing for the island.
5. We left for the airport early.
6. This train departs for Baltimore at noon.
7. Our friends started off for Montana this morning.
8. The balloon is headed for France.
9. The ballcarrier ran for the goal line.
10. The prisoner made a break for freedom.

Now write the *for* phrases.

Exercise 1. With books closed, listen to and repeat each sentence again.

Practice. The teacher will put the trash basket in an open spot on the floor. Everyone should wad up a piece of used paper and shoot for the basket. Then answer all together: What did you do?

Exercise 2. Use the *for* phrases you have written to complete these sentences.

1. Elena swam _____ .

2. This train departs _____ at noon.

3. The ballcarrier ran _____ .

4. The prisoner made a break _____ .

5. The kids leave _____ at 7:45 A.M.

6. We left _____ early.

7. The plane took off _____ .

8. Our friends started off _____ this morning.

9. The ship is sailing _____ .

10. The balloon is headed _____ .

Practice. Write the answers to these questions in full sentences using *for.*

1. If it starts to rain and you don't have an umbrella, where do you head?
2. What do Olympic runners race for?
3. If you were in a boat on a lake and a storm came up, what would you do?

Reading Passage 1. Listen, with books closed.

Every morning at 6:15, my wife leaves for the hospital where she's a nurse. At 7:30, the children get on the bus for school. At 8:00, I take off for the university where I teach.

At 3:00 P.M., my wife leaves the hospital for the parking lot where she parks her car. At 3:30, the children leave school for home. At 2:50, I leave my last class for the bus station, where I catch a bus for our street. We all arrive at home together and head for the refrigerator for a cold drink.

Practice. With books open, take turns answering these questions.

1. What does his wife do at 6:15 A.M.?
2. What do his children do at 7:30 A.M.?
3. What does he do at 8 A.M.?
4. What does his wife do at 3 P.M.?
5. What do his children do at 3:30 P.M.?
6. What does he do at 2:50 P.M.?
7. Where do they all head when they get home?

Turn to Missing Links, page 255.

Lesson 6a. For: in order to have or get something

Example Sentences. With books open, listen to and repeat each sentence as it is read to you.

1. Ben whistled for the dog.
2. Alice went for a walk.
3. Alex studied for his degree.
4. The player ran for the pass.
5. The woman shopped for food.
6. John looked for a good book at the library.
7. The line for pizza is the longest.
8. The pilot asked for landing instructions.
9. Astroworld is accepting applications for summer jobs.
10. Eighty Boy Scouts registered for camp.

Now write the *for* phrases.

Exercise 1. With books closed, listen to and repeat each sentence again.

Exercise 2. Use the *for* phrases you have written to complete these sentences.

1. The woman shopped _____ .

2. Astroworld is accepting applications _____ .

3. The pilot asked _____ .

4. Eighty Boy Scouts registered _____ .

5. Alex studied _____ .

Exercise 3. Place a link where *for* belongs.

1. The line pizza is longest.
2. John looked a good book at the library.
3. Ben whistled the dog.
4. The player ran the pass.
5. Alice went a walk.

Practice. Start with a volunteer who will be *S1*. *S1* should turn to another student, who will be *S2*, and ask the following question: I go to the supermarket for groceries, why do you go to the office supply store? *S2* should answer the question and then turn to another student, *S3*, and ask: Why do you go to the bakery? Continue around the class with these questions: Why do you go to the beach? to school? to a yogurt parlor? to a shoe store? to a flower shop? to an information booth? to the library? to a travel agent? to a bank? to the post office? to a card shop? to the fish market?

Exercise 4. With books open, write the answers to these questions in complete sentences.

1. What did Ben do?
2. What line is longest?
3. Where did Alice go?
4. What did John do at the library?
5. What did Alex study?
6. What did the player do?
7. What kind of applications is Astroworld accepting?
8. What did the pilot do?
9. What did the woman do?
10. What did eighty Boy Scouts do?

Lesson 6b. For: with an aim to having something intangible

Practice.

S1: Why are you raking leaves on a beautiful Saturday afternoon?
S2: Oh, I work in the yard for relaxation.
S1: Why don't you come surfing with us for relaxation?

S2: That wouldn't be for relaxation, that would be for excitement and danger.

S1: Why? The waves aren't very high where we surf.

S2: But I can't swim.

Example Sentences. With books open, listen to and repeat each sentence as it is read to you.

1. We read for relaxation.
2. Elise cooks for pleasure.
3. Children watch cartoons for amusement.
4. The boys in-line skate for fun.
5. Sam bungee-jumps for excitement.
6. Olivia plays the piano for enjoyment.
7. Kids ride the roller coaster for a thrill.
8. Hannah meditates for tranquillity.
9. Some people rent videos for entertainment.
10. The poet went to the mountains for inspiration.

Now write the *for* phrases.

Exercise 1. With books closed, listen to and repeat each sentence again.

Exercise 2. Divide the class into sides. Side A should take turns reading the sentences up to *for.* Mix up the order of the sentences. Side B should take turns completing the sentences using your written *for* phrases. Choose any of the phrases that seem appropriate. Then switch sides and repeat the exercise.

Practice. Write sentences using these *for* phrases: for experience; for peace of mind; for comfort; for control.

Exercise 3. Place a link where *for* belongs.

1. He gave up money happiness.
2. He diets his health.
3. The Smiths go to the beach fun.
4. The teacher showed a film diversion.
5. The poet reads poetry inspiration.
6. My sister goes to concerts recreation.
7. I always go to my friend encouragement.
8. The clinic plays tapes of old comedy shows easing stress.

Practice. In groups, discuss what you enjoy doing for relaxation, for exercise, and for entertainment.

Lesson 7. For: with a desire or longing for

Example Sentences. With books open, listen to and repeat each sentence as it is read to you.

1. The baby cried for her mother.
2. Amanda pleaded for forgiveness.
3. The lions were starved for meat.

 4. I often get a yen for chocolate.
 5. That man is greedy for money.
 6. Patrick is eager for fame.
 7. The criminal begged for mercy.
 8. The crowd is anxious for news of the earthquake.
 9. Jana longs for her homeland.
10. The desert traveler thirsted for water.

Now write the *for* phrases.

Exercise 1. With books closed, listen to and repeat each sentence again.

Exercise 2. Use the *for* phrases you have written to complete these sentences.

1. The desert traveler thirsted _____ .

2. The criminal begged _____ .

3. The lions were starved _____ .

4. Amanda pleaded _____ .

5. Patrick is eager _____ .

Practice. Write five sentences of your own design using any of the following *for* phrases: cry for, long for, beg for, hunger for, yearn for, be anxious for, be greedy for, be ambitious for, be starved for.

Lesson 8. For: used to show something representing something, to mark a symbol or sign of

---

Example Sentences. With books open, listen to and repeat each sentence as it is read to you (the symbols in sentences 7 and 8 must be written on the board).

 1. Green is for go; red is for stop.
 2. H_2O is the symbol for water.
 3. The Spanish word for cat is *gato.*
 4. On the weather map, zigzag lines stand for lightning.
 5. The plus sign is for adding.
 6. The minus sign is for subtracting.
 7. ♀ is the symbol for female.
 8. ♂ is the symbol for male.
 9. *Fax* is short for *facsimile transmission.*
10. The letters *e.g.* stand for the Latin *exempli gratis* which means *for example.*

Exercise 1. Read the sentences again quietly and then write them.

Practice. Think of some road signs and symbols that you've seen. Take turns putting them on the board without identifying them. The rest of the class should try to tell what they are.

Practice. The word *abbreviate* means *to make shorter. MPH* is the abbreviation for *miles per hour.* Think of some names or phrases that are often used in abbreviated form. Write sentences about the abbreviations, using this as a model: *USA* is the abbreviation for *United States of America.* Take turns reading the sentences to the class.

Lesson 9. For: shows payment, price, or amount

Practice.

S1: Have you found a place to live yet?

S2: No, I haven't. They're asking too much for the junky apartments around here.

S1: I know. You'd think you could get a nice one for that much rent. What are you going to do?

S2: If I can't find a decent one for the amount I can afford, I'll look for one farther away from school, where I can get something better for my money.

S3: I'm lucky. I live in a nice place near school for almost nothing.

S2: Where's that?

S3: At my parents' house.

Example Sentences. With books open, listen to and repeat each sentence as it is read to you.

1. Bananas were two pounds for a dollar.
2. Two of us had dinner for thirty dollars.
3. Greg bought the old boat for almost nothing.
4. At that store you can buy more for less.
5. Chris traded his bike for in-line skates.
6. You can't buy peace of mind for a million dollars.
7. Senior citizens can travel for lower fares.
8. That's a nice house for the money.
9. Tal is lucky to find a good car for that price.
10. That book store sells books for fifty percent off the regular price.

Now write the *for* phrases.

Exercise 1. With books closed, listen to and repeat each sentence again.

Exercise 2. Divide the class into sides. Side A should read the sentences up to *for.* Mix up the order of the sentences. Side B should take turns completing the sentence using your written *for* phrases. Then switch sides and repeat the exercise.

Practice. Using the example sentences as models, write five new sentences substituting your own names, nouns, and prices.

Lesson 10. For: because of, as a result of

Example Sentences. With books open, listen to and repeat each sentence as it is read to you.

1. Nancy apologized for being late.
2. The boys were scolded for fighting.
3. The child was praised for her honesty.
4. The reunited family was crying for joy.
5. Pete was honored for his volunteer work.
6. The criminals were punished for their crime.
7. Monica got an *A* for her excellent work.
8. Henry was cited for bravery.
9. We congratulated Chung for winning the scholarship.
10. Paul rewarded the boy for returning the lost wallet.
11. Zoe criticized the employee for his carelessness.
12. The company failed for lack of funds.

Now write the *for* phrases.

Exercise 1. With books closed, listen to and repeat each sentence again.

Exercise 2. Take turns answering these questions with one of the *for* phrases you have written.

1. Why were the criminals punished?
2. Why was the child praised?
3. Why did the company fail?
4. Why was Pete honored?
5. Why did Zoe criticize the employee?
6. Why was Chung congratulated?
7. Why did Monica get an *A*?
8. Why did Nancy apologize?
9. Why did Paul reward the boy?
10. Why was the reunited family crying?
11. Why was Henry cited?
12. Why were the boys scolded?

Practice. Use the example sentences as models and write other sentences of your own design telling what happened as a result of something else (e.g., Jonas was congratulated for winning the race).

Practice. What do you say in these situations? Take turns responding to each situation. Begin each response with "Thank you for . . ."

> to the host/hostess when leaving a party
> to the crew after a pleasant flight
> to the waiter/waitress after receiving good service

when answering someone's letter
to someone who has given you helpful information
to your supporters in an election
when someone tells you that you look very nice
at the end of a telephone call from someone

Practice. In groups, discuss when you would ask forgiveness or pardon for something, and how you would use these phrases: excuse me for _____ ; forgive me for _____ ; pardon me for _____ ; I'm sorry for _____ . Some of the endings might be: interrupting; the inconvenience; asking; making you wait.

Lesson 11. For: in connection with or in regard to someone or something, in its effect on

---

Example Sentences. With books open, listen to and repeat each sentence as it is read to you.

1. Vegetables and fruits are good for you.
2. Wisconsin is known for its lakes.
3. Milwaukee is famous for its beer.
4. The coach has plans for the new season.
5. Sunshine is a great cure for depression.
6. Aunt Kate has a good recipe for fruitcake.
7. Enough rain is necessary for a good crop.
8. The criminal has no respect for authority.
9. Find three sentences using *for,* for homework.
10. Good accounting is important for a business.

Now write the *for* phrases.

Exercise 1. With books closed, listen to and repeat each sentence again.

Exercise 2. Divide the class into two sides. Side A should take turns reading the example sentences up to *for.* Side B should take turns adding the correct *for* phrase. Then switch sides and repeat the exercise.

Practice. Make six headings on the board: Good for Health; Bad for Health; Good for Crops; Bad for Crops; Good for Business; Bad for Business. Volunteer as many items as you can think of to enter under the proper heading.

Practice. Write a sentence about a place that is known for: its scenery, its restaurants, its art, its traffic, or its weather. Then take turns reading your sentences to the class.

Lesson 12. For: length of time or distance, to the extent of

Example Sentences. With books open, listen to and repeat each sentence as it is read.

1. We waited for* two hours in the rain.
2. The band practiced for a week in the sun.
3. The pool was closed for the winter.
4. The ship sailed for* ten thousand miles last month.
5. Barbara hasn't had a vacation for years.
6. Boil the eggs for* five minutes.
7. He didn't stop laughing for at least two minutes.
8. The road is closed for three hundred yards.
9. Stay on this street for* six blocks.
10. He paid interest on his loan for twenty years.
11. He hadn't seen a movie for months.
12. The ski slopes were closed for the summer.

    *preposition may be omitted

Now write the *for* phrases.

Exercise 1. With books closed, listen to and repeat each sentence again.

Exercise 2. Use the written *for* phrases to answer these questions in complete sentences.

1. How many miles did the ship sail last month?
2. How far should we stay on this street?
3. How long did we wait in the rain?
4. How far is the road closed?
5. How long should we boil the eggs?

Practice. Volunteer the answers using *for.*

1. How long do you study for this class?
2. How long does a tape usually play?
3. How far do you walk every day?
4. How long does this class last?
5. When are outdoor skating rinks closed?

Exercise 3. Write five sentences of your own design using *for* with these phrases: for a little while; for a short time; for a long time; for the rest of my life; forever.

Lesson 13. For: at the time of, at an appointed time

Practice.

S1: The children came home for Thanksgiving, and we planned our turkey dinner for 1 P.M.

S2: But the football game was scheduled for 1:30. Didn't you watch it?

S1: Oh, yes. You have never seen a dinner disappear so fast. It took us hours to prepare and twenty minutes to eat.

S2: You should have sheduled dinner for noon.

S1: Next year we're going to plan it for ten in the morning!

Example Sentences. With books open, listen to and repeat each sentence as it is read to you.

1. Bob arranged the meeting for Thursday.
2. We're going to Michigan for Christmas.
3. The shuttle liftoff was scheduled for tomorrow.
4. We're scheduled for yearly dental checkups.
5. Rain is forecast for tonight.
6. More hurricanes are predicted for this summer.

Now write the *for* phrases.

Exercise 1. With books closed, listen to and repeat each sentence again.

Practice. Choose two of the following questions and answer in complete sentences using *for.* Take turns reading one of your sentences to the class.

1. When does your family usually get together?
2. When is your next class scheduled for?
3. What is the weather forecast for tomorrow?
4. What time would you invite guests for dinner?

Exercise 2. Use your written *for* phrases to complete these sentences.

1. We're scheduled _____ .

2. More hurricanes are predicted _____ .

3. The shuttle liftoff was scheduled _____ .

4. Rain is forecast _____ .

5. Bob arranged the meeting _____ .

6. We're going to Michigan _____ .

Practice. Write sentences using *for,* telling about times when you have, or have had, something planned. Take turns reading one of your sentences to the class.

Lesson 14. For: special phrases using *for* to get what you need

---

Practice. Take turns reading and then answering the question.

Dial 911 for emergency help: "My house is on fire! Come quickly!" (What did you do?)

Scream for help: "I've been robbed. He took my purse! Help!" (What did you do?)

Ask for assistance in a store: "Could you please help me? I can't read the label on this coat." (What did you do?)

Call for assistance at home by phone: "My electricity went out during the storm. Will you please come out and check it?" (What did you do?)

Ask for information: "What time does the store close?" (What did you do?)

Signal for service: Raise your cup and say, "Miss (or Waiter)! More coffee, please?" (What did you do?)

Practice. Answer these questions in turn using *for.*

1. Why would you dial 911?
2. Why would you call information?
3. Why would you call "Waiter!" at a restaurant?
4. Why would you call the service department at the electric company?

Practice. As a class, take turns reading the following sentences aloud.

1. in honor of
   a. We had a party for her birthday.
   b. A reception will be held for the president.
2. considering or comparing
   a. He's strong for his age.
   b. It's warm for this time of year.
3. in spite of, even with
   a. For all her experience she is still inefficient.
   b. For all his wealth he is still poor in spirit.
4. that someone should act in a certain way
   a. It's ridiculous for him to pay so much for clothes.
   b. It's dangerous for children to be left alone.
5. without justification
   a. There's no excuse for you to be late.
   b. There's no reason for them to be frightened.
6. without the help of
   a. If it weren't for you I wouldn't be here.
   b. If it weren't for you I couldn't stay here.
7. specializing in
   a. Sue has a talent for drawing faces.
   b. Henri has a knack for solving mysteries.
   c. Margo has a gift for public speaking.
   d. Klaus has a nose for news.
8. in order to serve or succeed in something
   a. Drew studied for the priesthood.
   b. Bonnie trained for the Olympics.
   c. We crammed for our finals.
   d. Kay tried out for a part in a movie.

Practice. Write your own sentences using the example sentences as models. Choose one from each *for* usage group. Then take turns reading them to the class.

Review. For: combined usage

Exercise 1. Place a link where *for* belongs.

1. The postman brought a letter you.
2. This knife is used cutting cheese.
3. Ken received a medal bravery.
4. We're waiting the phone to ring.
5. I'm writing a poem you.
6. These books are students only.
7. We eat cereal breakfast.
8. The kids have been camping two weeks.
9. Pam is reading the book homework.
10. Let us push that car you.
11. New Orleans is known its jazz music.
12. Sue draws well her age.
13. The meeting has been scheduled 10 A.M.
14. We all come home holidays.
15. Tim got a star good behavior.
16. We have to stand in line lunch.
17. Isn't he rather old a sky diver?
18. If it hadn't been that shrimp boat, we might still be in the life raft.
19. There's no excuse rudeness.
20. We paid too much this car.
21. This sign — $ — stands dollar.
22. They used a piece of tin a roof.

Reading Passage 1. Listen, with books closed.

1. Grandma baked cookies for us every Saturday.
2. She had a red tin for the cookies.
3. She was tired last Saturday, so we washed dishes for her.
4. She worked for a living five days a week.
5. She had fought for independence and won.
6. This Saturday she headed for the mountains.
7. We waited for her to answer her door.
8. We had the key for her house, so we went in.
9. Inside she had left a note for us. "Aloha!" it said.
10. *Aloha* is Hawaiian for *Until later.*
11. Our tin of cookies was there, so we ate them for breakfast.
12. Then we went out and walked for about an hour.
13. We bought four bananas for twenty-five cents.
14. Lunch was planned for noon, so we only ate one each.
15. When we got home we were scolded for being late.
16. When we didn't eat our vegetables, our father said, "Broccoli is good for you!"
17. It was warm for March, so after lunch we invited all our friends over to play.

18. My mother said, "Where can I go for some peace and quiet?"
19. Then she left, and she may be at the North Pole for all we know.
20. If it weren't for our father making us cut the grass, we would have left for the movies.

Now take turns reading the passage, sentence by sentence.

Turn to Missing Links, page 255.

Section B: Against

Lesson 1a. Against: in an opposite direction to, the other way
---

Practice.

S1: I'm exhausted by the time I get to work.

S2: Do you have to drive far?

S1: Only five miles, but most people are going toward town at that time. Driving with the traffic is slow.

S2: I work ten miles out of town, but because I'm driving against the traffic coming into town, it's a pleasant drive.

S1: Maybe I'll change jobs.

Example Sentences. With books open, listen to and repeat each sentence as it is read to you.

1. The bird flew against the storm.
2. Lissa walked home against the crowd.
3. The doctors raced against time.
4. Ed drove against the five o'clock traffic.
5. The plane slowed against the headwind.
6. The salmon swam against the current.
7. Dora pushed against the heavy gate.
8. The rider galloped on against the driving rain.

Now write the *against* phrases.

Exercise 1. With books closed, listen to and repeat each sentence again.

Practice. Volunteer for the following tasks.

1. Two students stand on opposite sides of the door. With hands flat against the door, each pushes hard. (Answer in unison: What are they doing?)
2. Several students walk together across the room. One student walks alone in their direction. (Answer in unison: What is the one student doing?)
3. One student faces the windows and pretends they are wide open. A forty mile an hour wind is blowing through them. The student demonstrates how he/she would walk in order to shut them. (Answer in unison: What is the student doing?)

Exercise 2. Use the written *against* phrases to complete these sentences.

1. The plane slowed _____ .

2. Ed drove _____ .

3. The bird flew _____ .

4. Dora pushed _____ .

5. Lissa walked home _____ .

6. The rider galloped on _____ .

7. The doctors raced _____ .

8. The salmon swam _____ .

Lesson 1b. Against: in forcible contact with, in the direction of and meeting

---

Example Sentences. With books open, listen to and repeat each sentence as it is read to you.

1. Hailstones beat against the roof.
2. Someone was pounding against the window.
3. Waves crashed against the shore.
4. He dashed his foot against a rock.
5. The snarling dog threw himself against the burglar.
6. The policeman hurled himself against the door.
7. The elephant butted his head against the tree.
8. The boxer's blows fell against his opponent's back.

Now write the *against* phrases.

Exercise 1. With books closed, listen to and repeat each sentence again.

Exercise 2. Use your written *against* phrases to answer these questions.

1. Someone was pounding _____ .

2. Waves crashed _____ .

3. The dog threw himself _____ .

4. Hailstones beat _____ .

5. He hurled himself _____ .

6. The elephant butted his head _____ .

7. He dashed his foot _____ .

8. The boxer's blows fell _____ .

Practice. Write sentences of your design, similar to the ones in Exercise 2, using *against* along with the following verbs: beat, pound, crash, throw, and fall.

Practice. Volunteer for the following tasks.

1. Throw an eraser against the board. (Answer in unison: What did he/she do?)
2. Slap one hand against the other several times. (Answer in unison: What did he/she do?)
3. Pound your fist against the door. (Answer in unison: What did he/she do?)

Lesson 2a. Against: in hostile opposition to, resisting

Example Sentences. With books open, listen to and repeat each sentence as it is read to you.

1. The lawyer defended his client against the accusers.
2. The angry lion strained against the tether.
3. The townspeople guarded the town against the enemy.
4. The citizens voted against the unjust law.
5. Their spiritual leader spoke against violence.
6. The rebels shouted threats against the mayor.
7. They battled against the invaders.
8. They struggled against temptation.

Now write the *against* phrases plus the verbs from each sentence.

Exercise 1. With books closed, listen to and repeat each sentence again.

Exercise 2. Copy the complete sentences from dictation.

Practice. Write a complete sentence answering one of these questions.

1. What would you fight against?
2. What would you guard against?
3. What would you vote against?

Lesson 2b. Against: contrary to

Example Sentences. With books open, listen to and repeat each sentence as it is read to you.

1. Stealing is against the law.
2. The girl left against her mother's wishes.
3. They bet against the odds.
4. That book went against his beliefs.
5. The plan went against his conscience.

6. Jean acted against her better judgment.
7. The gaudy jewelry went against her taste.
8. His statement goes against what the records show.

Now write the *against* phrases.

Exercise 1. With books closed, listen to and repeat each sentence again.

Practice. Discuss the meaning of each example sentence.

Practice. Write sentences of your own design about some things that are: against the law; against your beliefs; against the odds; against your conscience.

Exercise 2. Place a link where *against* belongs.

1. The plan went his conscience.
2. Stealing is the law.
3. Jean acted her better judgment.
4. The girl left her mother's wishes.
5. The book went his beliefs.
6. They bet the odds.

Lesson 3. Against: as a defense or protection from, in preparation for

---

Example Sentences. With books open, listen to and repeat each sentence as it is read to you.

1. The children were vaccinated against smallpox.
2. We take vitamin C as a protection against colds.
3. Sunscreen is a good shield against the sun's rays.
4. The right diet is good insurance against health problems.
5. The farmers put in supplies against the approaching hurricane.
6. The settlers put in firewood against the long winter.
7. Ivan warned Jacob against leaving the shelter.
8. The villagers built a dam against the rising river.

Now write the *against* phrases.

Exercise 1. With books closed, listen to and repeat each sentence again.

Exercise 2. Divide the class into sides. Side A should take turns reading the sentences up to *against*. Mix up the order. Side B should take turns using the written *against* phrases to complete the sentences. Then switch sides and repeat the exercise.

Lesson 4. Against: as contrast, in comparison with

Example Sentences. With books open, listen to and repeat each sentence as it is read to you.

1. That red tie looks good against that blue shirt.
2. His sales record stands up well against hers.
3. Put the shoes against the dress to see if they match.
4. She didn't see the black car against the dark wall.
5. We weighed the advantages against the disadvantages.

Now write the *against* phrases.

Exercise 1. With books closed, listen to and repeat each sentence again.

Practice. Write two sentences of your own using the example sentences as models. Then take turns reading them to the class.

Lesson 5. Against: touching, leaning on for support

Example Sentences. With books open, listen to and repeat each sentence as it is read to you.

1. The tired child leaned against her mother.
2. Eleanor propped the poster against the chalkboard.
3. The workmen sat with their backs against the tree.
4. Grandpa leaned against the wall.
5. Martin rested the rake against the barn.
6. The boat was moored against the pier.
7. The little boy pressed his nose against the bakery window.
8. Ellen placed her hand against her forehead.

Now write the *against* phrases.

Exercise 1. With books closed, listen to and repeat each sentence again.

Exercise 2. With your books closed, after the first part of a sentence is read to you, take turns using your written *against* phrases to complete it.

Reading Passage 1. Listen, with books closed.

    Joe could hear the crash of the falls against the rocks just behind him. He had acted against the guide's advice, and against his own better judgment, when he had taken the kayak out on the river alone. He had worn a life jacket as a safety measure against overturning, and he was glad he had.

He put his shoulder against the boat and pushed against it with all his might. His feet slipped against the slick stones. It was almost impossible to make headway against the current. He inched slowly against the spray of the rapids. The reflection of the sun against the water was blinding, but the wind against his face was freezing. He was struggling against the elements.

Now take turns reading the passage, sentence by sentence.

Turn to Missing Links, page 256.

Review. For, Against: combined usage

Practice. On a sheet of paper make two headings for two separate columns: *for* and *against.* Enter each of the following words in either one of the columns, as if you were voting for or against it: sunshine, crime, noise, freedom, cruelty, goodness, smiles, gloom, truth, beauty, frowns, dirt, music, hunger, laughs, hate, fun, lies, happiness, food, war, kindness, children. Add words of your own to the lists.

Unit 6
Of, About

Section A: Of

Lesson 1a. Of: belonging to or connected to something

Practice.

S1: The keys of this old piano are yellow.

S2: So are the pages of these old music books.

S1: What's the name of the nearest antique shop? Maybe we could sell them.

S2: Never. Too many memories of the happiest times of our lives would be sold with them.

S1: You can't sell memories of happy times. They live in our hearts and minds. And they don't turn yellow.

Example Sentences. With books open, listen to and repeat each sentence as it is read to you.

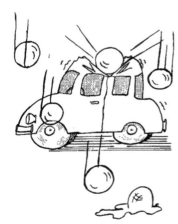

1. The bark of an oak tree is rough.
2. The heels of my black shoes need to be replaced.
3. The fingers of the old man's gloves were holey.
4. Donna read the title of the book.
5. The colors of the flag were red, white, and blue.
6. The roof of the car was dented by hail.
7. The hands of his watch stopped at 2:30.
8. The sailors mopped the deck of the ship.
9. The wheels of the train went clickety-clack.
10. She has never had a house of her own.
11. We had a picnic on the banks of the river.
12. The white of the eye is called the *sclera.*

Now write the *of* phrases plus the two words preceding each one (i.e., the bark of an oak tree).

Exercise 1. With books closed, listen to and repeat each sentence again.

Note: Of is not usually used in this way when talking about something alive (especially a person). The possessive form is used instead. For example:

Nan's hand	*not*	the hand of Nan
the cat's whiskers	*not*	the whiskers of the cat
Joan's car	*not*	the car of Joan
Mother's cooking	*not*	the cooking of Mother
the boy's hair	*not*	the hair of the boy

Note: Many of these *belonging* phrases can be used without the apostrophes and without *of* (e.g., book title, United States flag, ship deck, her own house, river bank, chair back, car roof, train wheels, coat pocket, etc.). These variations can be learned by careful listening and reading.

Practice. Pass along the following questions from one student to the next. Each student should answer one question using the written *of* phrases, then ask the next question of the next student. After all eight questions have been asked and answered, the next student should start over with question 1. Continue until each student has asked and answered at least one question.

1. What did Donna read?
2. What stopped at 2:30?
3. What went clickety-clack?
4. What is red, white, and blue?
5. What did the sailors mop?
6. What were holey?
7. What was dented by hail?
8. What is called the *sclera*?

Practice. Write *of* sentences of your own that include these words: clock hands, book pages, table legs, coat sleeves. Then take turns reading them to the class.

Exercise 2. Place a link where *of* belongs.

1. The handle the spoon is bent.
2. The handkerchief was in the pocket his coat.
3. We had a picnic on the banks the river.
4. The bark a birch tree is smooth.
5. The soles my shoes need to be replaced.
6. Marya wanted a room her own.
7. The walls the building were very thick.
8. The keys the typewriter need cleaning.

Lesson 1b. Of: as used with words such as smell, taste, size, texture, and shape, to connect them with the things they describe

---

Practice.

S1: Mmmm. The smell of popcorn always makes me hungry.

S2: Me, too. They have three sizes of bags. Which should we get: large, giant, or humongous?

S1: Let's each get a large. I don't like the taste of the chili flavored kind, do you?

S2: No, it's too strong. And the texture of the caramel corn is weird. Let's get regular. Do you have any money?

S1: No, don't you?

S2: So why were we so interested in the size of it, the taste of it, and the texture of it? We're going to have to be satisfied with the smell of it.

Example Sentences. With books open, listen to and repeat each sentence as it is read to you.

1. The smell of fish was strong.
2. The taste of lemon is refreshing.
3. The texture of the cloth was coarse.
4. The shoe store had every size of shoes.
5. The flowers were the colors of the rainbow.
6. The potter carefully molded the shape of the bowl.
7. We studied many styles of architecture.
8. Iron does not have the strength of steel.
9. An angel took the form of a human being.
10. The curvature of the earth can be seen from space.

Now write the *of* phrases with the preceding nouns.

Exercise 1. With books closed, listen to and repeat each sentence again.

Practice. Make up sentences using these beginnings plus the preposition *of* : the color
_____ ; the taste _____ ; the shape _____ ; the strength _____ ;
the style _____ ; the smell _____ ; the texture _____ .

Practice.

S1: The design of that dress is quite stylish.
S2: But the pattern of the print makes me dizzy.
S1: The length of the skirt is definitely *mini.*
S2: But the price of it is definitely *maxi.*

Practice. Write answers to these questions in complete sentences. Use the example sentences as models.

1. Is the cost of living in your native country high?
2. What is refreshing?
3. What does a clothing salesperson ask?
4. What fills the air during a band concert?
5. In a candy factory, what is strong?
6. What makes a garden beautiful?

Exercise 2. Use your written *of* phrases to complete these sentences. Then take turns reading the sentences to the class.

1. The shoe store had every _____ shoes.

2. The potter carefully molded the _____ the bowl.

3. The _____ the earth can be seen from space.

4. The _____ fish was strong.

5. The _____ lemon is refreshing.

6. Iron does not have the _____ steel.

7. The flowers were the _____ the rainbow.

8. An angel took the _____ a human being.

9. We studied many _____ architecture.

10. The _____ the cloth was coarse.

Lesson 1c. Of: used to connect a position word to a certain place or object

---

Example Sentences. With books open, listen to and repeat each sentence as it is read to you.

1. The side of the building is painted blue.
2. The captain saw the tip of an iceberg.
3. The garage is in front of the house.
4. The boys ran to the end of the block.
5. The cow stood in the middle of the road.
6. Water lilies floated on the surface of the pond.
7. The climbers reached the top of the mountain.
8. Molten rock fills the center of the earth.
9. The best apples were at the bottom of the barrel.
10. A signal came from the edge of the solar system.

Now write the *of* phrases plus the two words preceding each phrase.

Exercise 1. With books closed, listen to and repeat each sentence again.

Practice. Volunteer to perform one of the tasks from the following list. The teacher should give each volunteer a slip of paper assigning him/her a task. (Be sure to mix up the order.) After each volunteer has performed his/her task, the other members of the class should try to determine which task was performed.

1. Stand at the side of your desk.
2. Look at the bottom of your shoe.
3. Touch the back of your head.
4. Balance a book on the edge of a desk.
5. Write a short question on top of the board.
6. Stand in the middle of the room.
7. Stand in the front of the room.
8. Stand in the back of the room.
9. On the board, put a question mark at the end of a question.
10. On the board, put quotation marks at the beginning and at the end of a short sentence.

Practice. Write sentences using these position words plus an *of* phrase: the side, the top, the bottom, the beginning, the end, the inside, the outside, the surface, the head, the foot.

Note: When speaking of a bed, table, or stairs, head and foot are often used instead of top and bottom. When speaking of lines, i.e., standing in line, *head* is often used with *end.*

Exercise 2. Using your written *of* phrases, plus any other words necessary, take turns answering these questions.

1. Where did water lilies float?
2. What did the captain see?
3. Where did a signal come from?
4. What does molten rock fill?
5. Where did the boys run?
6. Where is the garage?
7. What did the climbers reach?
8. What is painted blue?
9. Where were the best apples?
10. Where did the cow stand?

Review

Exercise 1. Place a link where *of* belongs.

1. The wings a butterfly are beautiful.
2. What are the colors the rainbow?
3. The branch the tree broke off during the storm.
4. Sara has a room her own.
5. The sleeves the coat were too long.
6. Do you like the smell garlic?
7. We saw snow on top the mountain.
8. Meet me on the north side the building.
9. Most people like the taste sushi.
10. They coasted to the bottom the hill.

Reading Passage 1. Listen, with books closed.

The flashlights of the searchers dotted the side of the hill. Someone cried out: "I've found a button of a coat! Maybe it's Gary's! It was lying at the bottom of a fork of this tree. A strip of a handkerchief was tied to the top of a twig and stuck in the crevice. Some petals of a red flower were scattered on top of it, but I used the sleeve of my sweater to brush them off. The button was lying on the bottom of the crevice!"

The mother of the missing boy was elated. "I recognize the shape and color of the button. It's Gary's! Now I understand the value of his scouting lessons. He left a kind of clue for us."

The mood of the searchers lifted. As the light of the moon grew brighter, it reflected on the surface of the pond. Now they could see more clearly into the dark places of the forest.

Suddenly they heard a rustling of leaves. The little boy stood at the edge of the pond, with the collar of his coat pulled up around his ears, and the brim of his hat pulled down over his eyes. "Here I am!" he cried. The long search of the weary townspeople was over.

Exercise 2. With books open, take turns answering these questions.

1. What did someone find?
2. Where was it?
3. What did he use to brush off the petals?
4. Where was the button lying?
5. Who was elated?
6. What grew brighter?
7. Where did it reflect?
8. Where could they see more clearly?
9. What did they hear?
10. Where did the boy stand?
11. What was pulled up around his ears?
12. What was pulled down over his eyes?
13. What was over?

Turn to Missing Links, page 256.

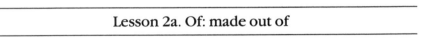

Lesson 2a. Of: made out of

Practice.

S1: My pots and pans are all made of stainless steel.
S2: My favorite skillet is made of iron.
S3: Since I got a microwave the only cooking utensils I use are made of plastic or glass.
S4: I buy my food at the deli in cartons made of recyclable cardboard, and I eat off plates made of recyclable paper. I save time, fuel, detergent, and water.
S1: Sure, everything but money.

Example Sentences. With books open, listen to and repeat each sentence as it is read to you.

1. She wore a jacket made of wool.
2. The piñatas are made of papier-mâché.
3. Boots (made) of fine leather were on sale at the market.
4. Lincoln lived in a cabin made of logs.
5. The crown (made) of gold was heavy.

Exercise 1. With books closed, listen to and repeat each sentence again.

Exercise 2. Write the complete sentences from dictation.

>   *Note: Out of* is often used when naming the material something is made from.

Lesson 2b. Of: that has, containing or consisting of

Example Sentences. With books open, listen to and repeat each sentence as it is read to you.

1. Joyce wrote a book of poetry.
2. They had a salad of avocados and oranges.
3. Louis directed a play of three acts.
4. Paloma owned a collection of geodes.
5. Eloise read an anthology of short stories.

Exercise 1. With books closed, listen to and repeat each sentence again.

Exercise 2. Write the complete sentences from dictation.

>   *Note:* We often say: wool jacket; papier-mâché piñatas; fine leather boots; log cabin; gold crown;
>   three-act play; short story anthology; geode collection; avocado and orange salad. However, using
>   the object of the preposition *of* as an adjective preceding the noun is not always acceptable. Here
>   are a few examples of when it is not: an onion bunch, a yarn ball, a thread spool. Since there are no
>   definite rules to guide us in this, correct usage must be learned by listening and reading.

Practice. Exchange objects of some kind with the person sitting next to you. Ask each other what you
think the objects are made of.

Review

Practice. Write your answers to the following questions.

1. Which is warmer, a coat of wool or a coat of silk?
2. Which is colder, a cube of ice or an ice cube?
3. Which smells better, a bunch of roses or a bunch of onions?
4. Which is longer, a ball of yarn or a spool of thread?

Practice. Think of some things that are made of: wood, steel, Styrofoam, plastic, concrete, clay, or cotton. Write phrases about them using *of.*

Practice. Volunteer answers to these questions.
1. What is paper made of?
2. What are pencils made of?
3. What are microchips made of?
4. What are bricks made of?
5. What is your desk made of?

Practice. Name the things that consist of: lettuce, tomatoes, and cucumbers; loose-leaf paper; several stories; strings, woodwinds, brass, and percussion instruments; teachers and students.

Lesson 3. Of: containing, holding, or carrying

Example Sentences. With books open, listen to and repeat each sentence as it is read to you.

1. The cat tried to reach the bowl of goldfish.
2. Teddy had a pocketful of pennies.
3. A cup of tea soothes the spirit.
4. The basket of fresh bread smelled delicious.
5. A sinkful of dirty dishes is unsightly.
6. One can of paint didn't cover the four walls.
7. A bag of popcorn makes the movies more fun.
8. A planeload of passengers walked down the ramp.
9. When I have a cold, I keep a box of tissues nearby.
10. We started the trip with a tankful of gas.
11. A carful of teenagers passed us on the road.
12. Philip brought an armload of books from the library.

Now write the *of* phrases plus the two words preceding each phrase.

Exercise 1. With books closed, listen to and repeat each sentence again.

Exercise 2. Divide the class into two sides. Side A, with books open, should make questions out of the sentences (e.g., What did the cat try to reach? What did Teddy have? What do you keep nearby when you have a cold?). Ask them in any order. Side B, using the written *of* phrases, should answer the questions. Then switch sides and repeat the exercise.

Practice. Take turns answering these questions.

1. Which weighs more, a bag of potatoes or a bag of potato chips?
2. Is a two-pound bag of rocks heavier than a two-pound bag of feathers?
3. Which tastes better, a cup of water or a cup of vinegar?
4. On a cold day, would you rather have a bowl of soup or a bowl of ice cream?
5. On a hot day, would you rather have a glass of lemonade or a cup of coffee?
6. Which is more useful, a box of light bulbs or a box of tulip bulbs?
7. Which has more calories, a bag of doughnuts or a package of gum?
8. Which has more nourishment, a carton of milk or a bottle of soda?

Practice. Write complete sentences using *of* after these words: a crate, a bucket, a truckload, a trunkful, a drawerful, a vase, a tub, a pool, a pile, a stack. Use your dictionaries if necessary. Some nouns that you might use as objects of *of* are: flowers, groceries, mail, syrup, jewelry, oranges, books, furniture.

> *Note:* A bowl of goldfish is not the same as a goldfish bowl. A goldfish bowl may or may not have fish in it. The same is true of a tea cup, a gas tank, a paint can, a bread basket, and a tissue box.

Practice. Volunteer answers to the following questions. If twenty people were in a small room, how would you describe it? If a quart bottle had a quart of juice in it, what would you say it was? If a basket was filled with apples up to the top, how would you describe it?

Lesson 4 Of: from a total or group, a fraction or amount

Example Sentences. With books open, listen to and repeat each sentence as it is read to you.

1. Three of his brothers are dentists.
2. Monday is the second day of the week.
3. A piece of pie was left on the plate.
4. Some of the students stayed after class.
5. Abbie is the youngest child of their family.
6. Doris gave Dennis a bite of her ice cream cone.
7. Half of the garden is planted with rosebushes.
8. The last of the crowd left NASA at noon.
9. A pound of sugar lasts for years at our house.
10. Several of the teenagers brought food.
11. One flake of snow was the beginning of the blizzard.
12. One slice of bread was all she ate.

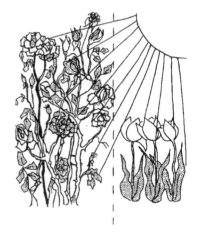  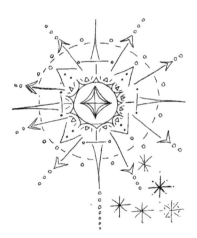

Now write the *of* phrases plus the word that precedes them.

Exercise 1. With books closed, listen to and repeat the sentences again.

Practice. Take turns answering in complete sentences.

1. Would you rather have a slice of bread or a slice of cake?
2. How many hours of the day should we sleep?
3. Have you ever had a wedge of apple pie with ice cream?
4. Have you ever had a sip of very hot soup?
5. Do all of us have the same name?
6. Do you put a teaspoon of sugar on your cereal?
7. Have you ever gotten a grain of sand in your eye?
8. Is a drop of oil or a drop of rain easier to get out of a shirt?

Note: Of must be used after such words (determiners) as _enough, some, many, all, each, every, most, and least_ if determiners such as _the, her, our, your, his, this,_ or _that_ precede the object. For example, we would say _some of the students,_ not _some the students._ If there is no other determiner, _of_ is not used. For example, we would say _most students,_ not _most of students. Of_ may be omitted after _all, both,_ or _half_ before another determiner, for example, _all the students, both the students,_ or _half the students._

Practice. Repeat the following phrases aloud together: all of us, all of you, all of them, some of us, some of you, some of them, either of us, either of you, either of them, neither of you, neither of us, neither of them, none of us, none of you, none of them, each of us, each of you, each of them, both of us, both of you, both of them, most of us, most of you, most of them, half of us, half of you, half of them.

Practice. Raise your hands in response to these questions. Count the number of hands raised, and record the number. How many in this class are male? female? speak another language? have studied English before? have lived here for more than a year? Then use all of us, most of us, or some of us, and complete these sentences in writing.

1. In this class, _____ are male, and _____ are female.

2. In this class, _____ speak another language.

3. In this class, _____ have studied English before.

4. In this class, _____ have lived here for more than a year.

Practice. All together, perform each task. After each task, answer the question in unison using _of:_

1. Raise your hands. Who raised their hands? (All _____ .)

2. Put half of your books on one side of your desk and the other half on the other side. What did you do? (We put _____ .)

3. Two students from each row stand up. How many from each row are standing up? (Two _____ .)

4. Your teacher will hold up objects of different shapes and/or colors. How many of them are red/ green/blue, or round/square/rectangular, etc.?

Exercise 2. Answer these questions using the written _of_ phrases from the example sentences at the beginning of this lesson.

1. Who left NASA at noon?
2. Who is Abbie?
3. Who are dentists?
4. What was the beginning of the blizzard?
5. What is planted with roses?
6. Who stayed after class?
7. What lasts for years?
8. What was left on the plate?
9. Who brought food?

10. What did Doris give Dennis?
11. What was all she ate?
12. What is Monday?

Exercise 3. Place a link where *of* belongs.

1. A gust wind blew down the tree.
2. She didn't eat any the vegetables.
3. A few the students study in the library.
4. Zack always chews a stick gum on the plane.
5. A series lectures will be held in October.
6. Ernest got a lot the data from the old records.
7. Most the bananas were ripe; just one them was green.
8. Some the lessons are easy, but a few them are difficult.
9. Timmy has learned all the letters the alphabet.
10. Six the ten answers were correct.

Reading Passage 1. Listen, with books closed.

A Lover's Lament
Goblets of silver, platters of gold,
Bracelets of diamonds too bright to behold,
Earrings of rubies, emeralds and jade,
The finest of jewelry that's ever been made,
I'd offer you all of that mentioned above,
But the best I can give is a lifetime of love.

Lesson 5a. Of: used to name what someone/something is or does; how someone/something is associated with a place, occupation, or activity; to connect a title or name with a place or thing

---

Practice.

S1: Tomoei's father is a doctor. I wonder what kind of doctor he is.
S2: I think he's a doctor of cardiology. What's your father?
S1: He's the head of an important political house.
S2: What house is he the head of, the House of Representatives?
S1: No, he's the head of our house. He runs it like a dictator.

Example Sentences. With books open, listen to and repeat each sentence as it is read to you.

1. David is the leader of the band.
2. Therese is president of her class.
3. The Sea of Galilee is in Israel.
4. The children love the Museum of Natural History.
5. Mr. Bontello is the manager of that store.
6. The Chamber of Commerce promotes our town.

7. The state of Minnesota has more than a thousand lakes.
8. The town of Minocqua is in the north woods.
9. Charles wants to be a teacher of languages.
10. The mayor of Houston is a very busy person.

Now write the *of* phrases plus the preceding word.

Exercise 1. With books closed, listen to and repeat each sentence again.

Practice. Take turns answering these questions, using *of* in complete sentences.

1. What colors are in the flag of your native country?
2. What colors are in the flag of the United States?
3. What state are we in?
4. What kind of teacher is your teacher?
5. What does your doctor specialize in?
6. What do you call a museum that houses modern art?
7. What is the full title of the person who presides over your native country?
8. What is the full title of the person who presides over this city's government?
9. Are you a student of French?
10. Are you a native of America?

Exercise 2. Answer these questions using your list of *of* phrases.

1. What is Mr. Bontello?
2. What is David?
3. What kind of chamber promotes our town?
4. What has more than a thousand lakes?
5. What is in Israel?
6. What do the children love?
7. Who is very busy?
8. What is in the north woods?
9. What does Charles want to be?
10. What is Therese?

Lesson 5b. Of: used when telling where someone/something comes from or is derived from

---

Example Sentences. With books open, listen to and repeat each sentence as it is read to you.

1. The Indians of the Southwest make beautiful pots.
2. Some animals of the jungle are in danger of extinction.
3. Some natives of the Arctic live in igloos.
4. Graduates of that trade school all get jobs easily.

5. Dogs of that breed make good pets for children.
6. The women of her family are tall and strong.
7. That wealthy man was born of poor parents.
8. My friends of Irish descent all have a good sense of humor.
9. People of all races should live in peace with each other.
10. Birds of the tropics are the most colorful.

Now write the *of* phrases plus the preceding words.

Exercise 1. With books closed, listen to and repeat each sentence again.

Exercise 2. Use the *of* phrases you have written to complete the following sentences.

1. People _____ should live in peace with each other.

2. The Indians _____ made beautiful baskets.

3. Some animals _____ are in danger of extinction.

4. My friends _____ all have a good sense of humor.

5. Birds _____ are the most colorful.

Lesson 5c. Of: used to connect people to the special groups they belong to

---

Example Sentences. With books open, listen to and repeat each sentence as it is read to you.

1. Members of the Republican Party are republicans.
2. Members of the Democratic Party are democrats.
3. Members of the plumbing trade are plumbers.

4. Members of the building trade are builders.
5. Members of the Jewish religion are Jews.
6. Members of the Catholic religion are Catholics.
7. Members of the Protestant religions are Protestants.
8. Members of the medical profession are doctors.
9. Members of the legal profession are lawyers.
10. Members of the Senate are senators.
11. Members of the House of Representatives are representatives.
12. Members of the jury are jurors.

Exercise 1. Divide the class into two sides. Side A, with books open, should take turns changing the example sentences into questions (in random order), asking: "What are _____ ?" Side B should use the written *of* phrases to answer with complete sentences. Then switch sides and repeat the exercise.

Practice. Working together, think of examples of other groups, religions, or forms of government. Write these examples on the board. What are their members called?

Reading Passage 1. Listen, with books closed.

Margaret is a teacher of English at the school of adult education at the University of the North. In her class is the pastor of a Lutheran church who is from Germany, a professor of Russian from Moscow, a doctor of orthopedics of Korean descent, and two members of the Japanese-American Society. The rest of the class is made up of college students of many different language backgrounds, including Thai, Chinese, and French, plus seven natives of Mexico, and three of Central America.

Before the beginning of class, Margaret asks each student to greet the class and to announce the date and time in the language of his/her native country. Margaret sometimes feels as if she's been sent to the Tower of Babel of biblical times, to get everyone speaking in one language again.

Take turns reading the passage, sentence by sentence.

Turn to Missing Links, page 257.

Lesson 6a. Of: produced by or coming from when referring to works of music, art, and literature

---

Example Sentences. With books open, listen to and repeat each sentence as it is read to you.

1. Dennis enjoys the films of the forties.
2. They studied the works of Leonardo da Vinci.
3. The music of J. S. Bach is magnificent.
4. The poetry of T. S. Eliot is famous.
5. Felix has read all the plays of Shakespeare.
6. The paintings of Salvador Dali are surrealistic.
7. The musicals of Andrew Lloyd Webber are popular.
8. The mysteries of Agatha Christie are fun to read.

Exercise 1. With books closed, listen to and repeat each sentence again.

Practice. Write complete sentences of your own about other books, paintings, or music. Use *of* to tell who produced them. Take turns sharing them with the class.

Lesson 6b. Of: used to connect things that have been recorded to the form in which they were recorded

---

Example Sentences. With books open, listen to and repeat each sentence as it is read to you.

1. Audubon made many paintings of birds.
2. Carol takes beautiful photographs of flowers.
3. The new graduate sent out a resume of his education.
4. Bill kept an account of their expenses.
5. Always keep a record of your oil changes.
6. We get a statement of our purchases every month.
7. George is writing a history book of the American West.

Now write the *of* phrases plus the preceding word.

Exercise 1. With books closed, listen to and repeat each sentence again.

Practice. Using the example sentences as models, write sentences of your own about these subjects: keeping records, taking photographs, writing books, painting pictures.

Practice. Volunteer answers to these questions.

1. What do you write before going to the supermarket?
2. What is required for a job application?
3. If you have a savings account, what do you get in the mail every month?
4. If you have a car, how do you know when to change the oil?
5. What tells you what is in a book?

Exercise 2. Complete these sentences using *of* phrases.

1. Always keep _____ your oil changes.
2. Carol takes beautiful _____ .
3. A resume _____ is required.
4. Audubon made many _____ .
5. Bill kept an _____ their expenses.
6. The _____ is famous.
7. We get a _____ every month.
8. The _____ is full of adventure.

Exercise 3. Take turns reading the completed sentences to the class.

Lesson 6c. Of: produced by or coming from in reference to sounds

S1: The screech of tires was frightening.
S2: Did someone try to stop suddenly?
S1: Yes, me. I almost ran into the car in front of me.

Example Sentences. With books open, listen to and repeat each sentence as it is read to you.

1. The hiss of a snake made the boy stand still.
2. The cry of the loon is a lonely sound.
3. The crash of thunder startled them.
4. The laughter of the children brightened the day.
5. Every morning we were awakened by a chorus of birds.
6. Ann could hear the howl of the coyotes in the distance.
7. The growl of the watchdog frightened the burglar.
8. The neighbors listened to the buzzing of saws.
9. The humming of machinery filled the factory.
10. The stamping of the dancers' feet disturbed the sleepers.

Now write the *of* phrases plus the preceding word.

Exercise 1. With books closed, listen to and repeat each sentence again.

Practice. Volunteer to answer these questions.

1. What sounds like a jet plane flying by?
2. What wakes people up on a farm?
3. What do you hear when you are on a sea coast?
4. What do you hear when you are near a waterfall?
5. What do you hear when you play a teenager's tapes?
6. What do you hear when your roof is being replaced?

Exercise 2. Use the written *of* phrases to answer these questions.

1. What did the neighbors listen to?
2. What could Ann hear?
3. What made the boy stand still?
4. What startled them?
5. What were they awakened by?
6. What brightened the day?
7. What is a lonely sound?
8. What disturbed the sleepers?
9. What frightened the burglar?
10. What filled the factory?

Reading Passage 1. Listen, with books closed.

The drama department of the University of Oldhall invited the graduates of our school to attend a play. We were told that we would see one of the historical plays of Shakespeare, but we didn't. The title of the play was "Puzzles," and it was the creation of the president of the university's son.

In an account of the play in the program, the background of the playwright seemed hazy. The list of characters was exceedingly long, and the members of the cast numbered one hundred and thirty.

The designer of the sets was a genius; the lighting of the stage was brilliant; the star of the evening was talented; the director of the production had done his best; but the meaning of the play was unclear, and the words of the actors made no sense. Worst of all, the number of scenes was eighteen. We had to sit through six acts of three scenes each! Our sighs of boredom and loud yawns of weariness were noisier than the voices of the cast.

The ending of the play was abrupt, because the members of the audience were suddenly awakened by the bright lights of the theater, which came on after the curtain closed. There was no sound of clapping.

We were sure of one thing: this was not a play of Shakespeare's!

Now take turns reading the passage, sentence by sentence.

Practice. With books open, answer these questions in turn.

1. Who were invited to the play?
2. Who invited them?
3. What was the play?
4. What was in the program?
5. What seemed hazy?
6. What was long?
7. What numbered one hundred and thirty?
8. Who was a genius?
9. What was brilliant?
10. Who was talented?
11. Who had done his best?
12. What was unclear?
13. What made no sense?
14. How many acts did they sit through?
15. What kind of sighs and yawns were noisy?
16. What was abrupt?
17. What were they sure of?

Turn to Missing Links, page 257.

Lesson 7a. Of: filled with, showing, used with words of emotion causing or resulting in a reaction

---

Example Sentences. With books open, listen to and repeat each sentence as it is read to you.

1. Words of anger spoiled the evening.
2. Tears of sadness rolled down her cheeks.
3. Jenni gave a gasp of surprise when she saw the puppy.
4. Cries of delight greeted the clown's antics.

5. Screams of terror came from the theater where the horror movie was playing.
6. A frown of annoyance crossed Alan's face when the audience began to boo him.
7. Margaret breathed a sigh of relief when she knew the children were safe.
8. A shout of excitement rose from the crowd when their team scored a touchdown.

Now write the *of* phrases.

Exercise 1. With books closed, listen to and repeat each sentence again.

Exercise 2. As the words preceding the *of* phrases are called out (in random order), take turns trying to match them with the *of* phrases you have written.

Exercise 3. With books open, write the answers to these questions in full sentences.

1. What came from the theater?
2. What did Jenni give when she saw the puppy?
3. What greeted the clown's antics?
4. What crossed Alan's face?
5. What rose from the crowd?
6. What spoiled the evening?
7. What did Margaret breathe?
8. What rolled down her cheeks?

Exercise 4. Take turns reading your sentences to the class.

Lesson 7b. Of: caused by, that comes from, used to connect an event or occurrence with its result

---

Example Sentences. With books open, listen to and repeat each sentence as it is read to you.

1. The stress of worry affects one's work.
2. The enjoyment of reading adds zest to life.
3. The fear of flying grounds many people.
4. The harm of gossip cannot be calculated.
5. The destruction of hurricanes can be terrible.
6. The benefits of a good night's sleep are many.
7. The anxiety of having to give a speech is universal.
8. The satisfaction of work well done was enough reward.
9. The effect of his fishing trip was better than medicine.
10. The pleasure of travel is only equaled by the pleasure of returning home.

Now write the *of* phrases plus the word preceding each phrase.

Exercise 1. With books closed, listen to and repeat each sentence again.

Exercise 2. Use the written *of* phrases to complete these sentences.

1. The _____ adds zest to life.

2. The _____ is only equaled by the _____ home.

3. The _____ affects one's work.

4. The _____ grounds many people.

5. The _____ can be terrible.

Reading Passage 1. Listen, with books closed.

Dr. Jean Taline's face wore a smile of contentment. She had just written a report of her team's research work and had asked her assistant, Barbara, to make a copy of it. Now she was enjoying the feeling of satisfaction of a year of accomplishment.

Suddenly a cry of alarm came from the area of the animal cages. A squeal of protest soon followed. Dr. Taline hurried to check on the source of the noise. She soon found it.

Primo, the chimp of Africa, and Barbara, the research assistant of Ohio, were having a tug-of-war, with Dr. Taline's report as the prize! With grunts of effort, Primo tugged at one end of the report, and Barbara tugged at the other.

One word of command and a frown of disapproval from the boss stopped the contest. Dr. Taline retrieved the pages of the tattered report and said a prayer of thanks. It was still readable and, though full of rips and tears, could be copied.

Primo uttered a squeak of embarrassment, and Barbara gave a speech of apology. She had stopped to feed the chimp a snack, holding the report in one hand and the cracker in the other. Of the two, Primo had preferred the report and grabbed it.

The stress of the moment was replaced by a laugh of amusement as Primo, full of shame, draped a piece of newspaper over his head. All was forgiven.

Exercise 3. With books open, take turns answering these questions.

1. What did Dr. Taline's face wear?
2. What had she just written?
3. What did she ask Barbara to do?
4. What was she enjoying?
5. What came from the animal cages?
6. What soon followed?
7. What did Dr. Taline hurry to check?
8. Who was Primo?
9. Who was Barbara?
10. What did they tug at?
11. What did Dr. Taline retrieve?
12. What did she say?
13. How did the report look?
14. What did Primo do?
15. What did Barbara do?
16. What replaced what?

17. How did Primo feel?
18. What did Primo drape over his head?

Turn to Missing Links, page 257.

Lesson 8. Of: with, having, possessing

Example Sentences. With books open, listen to and repeat each sentence as it is read to you.

1. America is a land of many people.
2. George is a man of integrity.
3. Mother's garden was a place of beauty.
4. That story has the ring of truth.
5. Adelia is a woman of silence.
6. L. Frank Baum was a writer of wonderful imagination.
7. The Smythes are people of wealth.
8. Spring is a season of flowers and rain.
9. A centipede is a creature of many legs.
10. Isaac Stern is a violinist of genius.

Now write the *of* phrases.

Exercise 1. With books closed, listen to and repeat each sentence again.

Exercise 2. Take turns matching the written *of* phrases to the sentences as they are read to you in random order.

Exercise 3. Place a link where *of* belongs.

1. The Smythes are people wealth.
2. A centipede is a creature many legs.
3. L. Frank Baum was a writer wonderful imagination.

4. Spring is a season flowers and rain.
5. America is a land many people.
6. Isaac Stern is a violinist genius.
7. Adelia is a woman silence.
8. That story has the ring truth.
9. Their home is a place warmth and contentment.
10. George is a man integrity.

Lesson 9. Of: set aside for, especially for, taken up by

Example Sentences. With books open, listen to and repeat each sentence as it is read to you.

1. A church is a house of prayer.
2. Sunday is a day of rest.
3. A library is a treasury of books.
4. Lent is a period of fasting.
5. An hour of reading calmed her nerves.
6. A school is an institution of learning.
7. A moment of silence preceded the meeting.
8. Thanksgiving is a time of giving thanks.
9. A resort is a place of relaxation and enjoyment.
10. The sun shone on their day of celebration.
11. They wrote a book about the year of famine.
12. That family is observing a period of mourning.

Now write the *of* phrases plus the word preceding each phrase.

Exercise 1. With books closed, listen to and repeat each sentence again.

Exercise 2. As the first part of each sentence is read to you in random order, use your written *of* phrases to complete the sentences.

Practice. Write the answers to these questions in complete sentences.

1. What is a temple?
2. What is Monday?
3. What is a holiday?
4. What is a family reunion?
5. What is a factory?

Practice. What special occasions does your family observe? How would you describe them using the preposition *of*?

Reading Passage 1. Listen, with books closed.

As the moment of her marriage drew near, Jane was not sure she could live through the next twelve hours of pageantry. She was a woman of composure and gentleness, while her husband-to-be, Ken, was a man of restless energy and charm. Jane would have preferred a quiet ceremony attended by family and close friends, but Ken had insisted on a wedding of great size and expense.

Jane's mother was a person of sensitivity; she had seen the aura of unhappiness surrounding her daughter. On the evening of the rehearsal, she drew Jane aside. In the stillness of the Chapel of Prayer, she said, "Jane, now is the moment of truth. Do you want a life of glamour and excitement, or a life of peace and serenity? This is your time of decision."

Jane finally realized that Ken's need of excitement and her need of tranquillity would result in a marriage of misery. She told Ken of her concerns, and he, being a man of understanding, agreed to a plan.

The morning of the expected nuptials, the guests were asked to stay for a reception without a wedding. They toasted two wise people, who had spared themselves a lifetime of unhappiness.

Now take turns reading the passage, sentence by sentence.

Exercise 3. With books open, answer these question.

1. What drew near?
2. What kind of woman was she?
3. What kind of man was Ken?
4. What kind of wedding did Ken insist on?
5. What kind of person was Jane's mother?
6. When did she draw Jane aside?
7. What did Jane's mother ask her?
8. What did Ken have?
9. What did Jane have?
10. What would their differing needs result in?
11. What did she tell Ken?
12. What had they saved themselves from?

Turn to Missing Links, page 258.

Lesson 10. Of: used with words meaning to be separated or freed from

---

Example Sentences. With books open, listen to and repeat each sentence as it is read to you.

1. She was cured of pneumonia in three days.
2. Rob pulled the kite free of the branches.
3. They were glad to be rid of the rats.
4. The old lady was robbed of all her money.
5. The dismissal of school is at three P.M.
6. The children ran clear of the smoke.
7. The loss of jobs affected the economy.
8. The loss of his wallet affected Al's budget.
9. It is heartbreaking to see babies deprived of love.
10. The injured man was relieved of some of his duties.
11. The students worked independently of the teacher.
12. The release of the prisoner was ordered by the judge.

Now write the *of* phrases.

Exercise 1. With books closed, listen to and repeat each sentence again.

Practice. Write answers in complete sentences using *of.*

1. What have you, or someone you know, been cured of?
2. Have you, or someone you know, ever been robbed of something?
3. When there is a pile of trash in your house, what do you do with it?
4. How would the loss of your watch affect you?

Exercise 2. Use the written *of* phrases to complete these sentences.

1. It is heartbreaking to see babies deprived ＿＿＿＿＿＿＿ .

2. The injured man was relieved ＿＿＿＿＿＿ .

3. The students worked independently ＿＿＿＿＿＿ .

4. The release ＿＿＿＿＿＿ was ordered by the judge.

5. The loss ＿＿＿＿＿ affected Al's budget.

6. The loss ＿＿＿＿＿ affected the economy.

Now take turns reading the completed sentences.

Lesson 11a. Of: used in time and dates (See unit 12 for prepositions to use for time.)

Example Sentences. With books open, listen to and repeat each sentence as it is read to you.

1. On the 15th of April, Americans pay taxes.
2. The first day of April is April Fool's Day.
3. Christmas always falls on the 25th of December.
4. The beginning of October is a beautiful time of year.
5. We usually have exams in the middle of May.
6. The meetings are held at a quarter of twelve.
7. Tanya always calls at five minutes of seven.
8. At one minute of midnight the lights went out.
9. We pay our rent at the end of the month.
10. The last day of February is not always the 28th.

Exercise 1. With books closed, listen to and repeat each sentence again.

Lesson 11b. Of: at a distance from

Example Sentences. With books open, listen to and repeat each sentence as it is read to you.

1. School is within a block of our house.
2. The lake is within three miles of here.
3. Houston is two hundred and forty miles south of Dallas.

Now write the sentences.

Practice. Write the directions to the city you are in, using north of, south of, east of, or west of another city. Tell how close the nearest lake, river, or ocean is, using the phrase within _____ of here.

Reading Passage 1. Listen, with books closed.

It was five minutes of four, on the afternoon of the sixth of July, when Timmy let go of his kite. It had been a day of strange happenings, but what happened next was the strangest of them all.

A blue heron, a bird of placid disposition, flapped its wings and followed the flight of the kite. As we watched, the heron caught the kite in the grip of its long bill. Little Timmy cried for his lost kite.

All of us who were gathered on the beach watched in amazement. This bird of the seashore circled overhead and then swooped within feet of the spot where Timmy stood sobbing. The heron's release of the kite was a miracle of accuracy, and the glow of joy on Timmy's face was as bright as the sunlight on the bird's wings.

We'll always remember that day of our family reunion as a symbol of the wonders and mysteries of the world of nature.

Exercise 1. With books open, answer these questions using complete sentences.

1. When did Timmy let go of his kite?
2. What kind of day had it been?
3. What is a blue heron?
4. What did the blue heron follow?
5. How did the blue heron catch the kite?
6. Who gathered on the beach?
7. How close did the bird swoop?
8. What was a miracle of accuracy?
9. What was on Timmy's face?
10. How will they remember their family reunion?

Turn to Missing Links, page 258.

Lesson 12a. Of: regarding, used in prepositional phrases that act as adjectives that answer the question: *about what?*

Practice.

S1: What is your opinion of our team?
S2: I think the stress of their tight schedule is hard on them.
S1: The challenge of winning this game should motivate them.
S2: Yes, a lot depends on the outcome of today's game.
S1: Right. The championship of the fourth grade series is at stake.

Example Sentences. With books open, listen to and repeat each sentence as it is read to you.

1. Their judgment of the case was biased.
2. Jimmy's view of life was optimistic.
3. The outcome of the meeting was kept secret.
4. The stress of owning a business made Bud ill.
5. Mike's knowledge of poisons saved his life.
6. Their anticipation of the trip was great.
7. The critics' opinion of the play was unfavorable.
8. My impression of the new magazine is favorable.
9. The prospect of a better economy was encouraging.
10. Einstein's theory of relativity changed physics.
11. Her version of the story is different from his.
12. The coach's schedule of games is exciting.

Now write the *of* phrases plus the preceding word in each sentence.

Exercise 1. With books closed, listen to and repeat each sentence again.

Practice. Discuss what these sentences mean.

1. His impression of the country was based on what he had seen as a tourist.
2. The bad review of the movie kept many people away.
3. The criticism of the new courthouse led to changes.
4. His report on the library was based on hearsay.
5. The girl's version of the incident was different from her sister's.
6. The punishment of the dog was unfair.

Practice. Write five complete sentences of your own using the example sentences as models. Then take turns reading your sentences to the class.

Exercise 2. With books open, answer these questions.

1. What saved Mike's life?
2. What is exciting?
3. What was biased?
4. What made Bud ill?
5. What was great?
6. What did the critics have?

Lesson 12b. Of: more *of* phrases used as adjectives answering
the question: *what?* or *which?*

Example Sentences. With books open, listen to and repeat each sentence as it is read to you.

1. The winners of the lottery bought a new house.
2. The losers of the lottery bought more tickets.
3. The patients of that doctor are all poor.

4. The survivors of the fire were very thankful.
5. The results of the research were encouraging.
6. Their method of farming is more modern than ours.
7. The star of the show is a lion.
8. Her description of the Alps was vivid.

Now write the *of* phrases plus the preceding word in each sentence.

Exercise 1. With books closed, listen to and repeat each sentence again.

Practice. Answer these questions in complete sentences using *of.*

1. What would you call people who lived through an earthquake? (survivors)
2. If scientists had been doing research on a disease and found a cure, what would you call the cure? (result)
3. If you read a story about skiing that was so real that you felt as though you were actually on the mountain, what would you say about it? (description)

Exercise 2. Divide the class into sides. Side A should take turns reading the sentences without the *of* phrases. Mix up the order. Side B should take turns completing the sentences using the written *of* phrases. Then switch sides and repeat the exercise.

Lesson 13. Of: used to connect adjectives denoting feelings or conditions to the objects of those feelings and conditions

---

Practice.

S1: I'm fond of double fudge ice cream, aren't you?
S2: Yes, but I'm afraid of its calories.
S1: Are you capable of saying no to it?
S2: Only if I'm aware of everyone else at the table ordering low-calorie yogurt.

Example Sentences. With books open, listen to and repeat each sentence as it is read to you.

1. Mimi is fond of her niece and nephew.
2. Those parents are proud of their children.
3. Angela is afraid of rats but not of mice.
4. Alvin was aware of a change in temperature.
5. People who cheat should be ashamed of themselves.
6. We got tired of waiting for the bus, so we walked.
7. The detective was suspicious of that young man.
8. A computer is not capable of thinking.
9. It is silly to be envious of anyone.
10. I was not conscious of the passage of time.

Now write *of* plus the preceding word in each sentence.

Exercise 1. With books closed, listen to and repeat each sentence again.

Exercise 2. Use your written *of* combinations to complete these sentences.

1. Angela is _____ rats but not of mice.

2. A computer is not _____ thinking.

3. We got _____ waiting for the bus, so we walked.

4. It is silly to be _____ anyone.

5. Those parents are _____ their children.

6. I was not _____ the passage of time.

7. Mimi is _____ her niece and nephew.

8. Alvin was _____ a change in temperature.

9. The detective was _____ that young man.

10. People who cheat should be _____ themselves.

Lesson 14a. Of: used to connect verbs with their objects

Example Sentences. With books open, listen to and repeat each sentence as it is read to you.

1. William approved of the new office schedule.
2. The kitchen smelled of onions and garlic.
3. The campers never despaired of being rescued.
4. The sign says, "Beware of the dog!"
5. The criminal repented of his crime.

Now write the verb plus *of* in each sentence.

Exercise 1. With books closed, listen to and repeat each sentence again.

Practice. Volunteer answers to these questions.

1. What does a bakery smell of?
2. What do you approve of in this school?
3. What do you disapprove of in this school?
4. What should we all be aware of?
5. What should we all beware of?

Exercise 2. Use the written combinations to complete these sentences.

1. The kitchen _____ onions and garlic.

2. The criminal _____ his crime.

3. The sign says, " _____ the dog!"

4. William _____ the new office schedule.

5. The campers never _____ being rescued.

Lesson 14b. Of: verbs after *of* end in *-ing*

Example Sentences. With books open, listen to and repeat each sentence as it is read to you.

1. Have you ever thought of learning French?
2. Hisako dreamed of playing the violin.
3. Tracy's mother approved of studying long hours.
4. Denny's father disapproved of smoking.
5. She was afraid of going into the cave alone.

Now write the verb, plus *of*, plus the *-ing* word.

Exercise 1. With books closed, listen to and repeat each sentence again.

Practice. Volunteer answers to this question: What are you most afraid of doing?

Exercise 2. Complete the sentences with the verb, plus *of*, plus the correct *-ing* verb.

1. Tracy's mother _____ long hours.

2. She was _____ into the cave alone.

3. Denny's father _____ .

4. Have you ever _____ French?

5. Hisako _____ the violin.

Lesson 15. Of: used to connect persons to the way they act

Example Sentences. With books open, listen to and repeat each sentence as it is read to you.

1. It was nice of them to call.
2. It was silly of me to be afraid.
3. It was selfish of her not to share her food.
4. It was kind of him to help her find her luggage.
5. It was cruel of the boys to shoot at the birds.
6. It was rude of him to interrupt the speaker.
7. It was inconsiderate of her to be so late.
8. It was generous of them to contribute to the fund.

Now write the adjective plus *of* in each sentence.

Exercise 1. With books closed, listen to and repeat each sentence again.

Practice. Write complete sentences of your own using nice of, inconsiderate of, clever of, thoughtful of, or careless of. Then take turns reading your sentences to the class.

Practice. Answer these questions with complete sentences using *of.*

1. Do you think it's wise of anyone to walk alone at night?
2. Do you think it's considerate of a person to make another person wait for an hour?
3. Is it kind of a person to care for an injured animal?
4. Would it be rude of you to interrupt me while I'm speaking?
5. Is it silly of anyone to be afraid of mice?

Exercise 2. Complete these sentences with the written adjectives plus *of.*

1. It was _____ them to contribute to the fund.

2. It was _____ her not to share her food.

3. It was _____ them to call.

4. It was _____ her to be so late.

5. It was _____ him to interrupt the speaker.

6. It was _____ me to be afraid.

7. It was _____ the boys to shoot at the birds.

8. It was _____ him to help her find her luggage.

Lesson 16. Of: more *of* usages

Example Sentences. With books open, listen to and repeat each sentence as it is read to you.

1. in case of, in the event of, if something happens
   a. The sign on the fire extinguisher read: "In Case of Fire Break Glass."
   b. In the event of a hurricane, you should keep your radios tuned to a weather station.
2. regardless of, in spite of, without concern about, taking no notice of
   a. He is going to buy the car regardless of the high price.
   b. In spite of the bad weather, they left for the beach.
3. right-of-way, an avenue of passage open to one
   a. At an intersection, the car to your right has the right-of-way.
4. because of, by reason of
   a. He used a cane because of his broken leg.
   b. The flight was canceled on account of bad weather.
5. type of, kind of, sort of, classifies by characteristics
   a. She is the type of person you can always depend on.
   b. What kind of sandwich would you like, tuna or cheese?
   c. That sort of behavior is unacceptable.

Exercise 1. With books closed, listen to and repeat each sentence again.

Section B: About

Lesson 1. Of/About: specializing in, representing or concerning a certain subject

---

Note: The words *book, story, tale, report, saga, news,* and *discussion,* are some of the nouns that can be followed by either *of* or *about.*

Example Sentences. With books open, listen to and repeat each sentence as it is read to you.

1. Books about astronomy filled his shelves.
2. Stories about the old west are his favorites.
3. Ruth read an article about Alaskan pioneer days.
4. Timmy loved tales about dinosaurs.
5. The reports about the meeting are in the notebook.
6. A saga is a long narrative about Icelandic legends and history.
7. The news about the moon landing was exciting.
8. The lawyers had a discussion about the case.

Now write the *about* phrases plus the preceding noun (i.e., discussion about the case).

Exercise 1. With books closed, listen to and repeat each sentence again.

Practice. Using *about* in complete written sentences, tell what kind of books you like best, or what type of newspaper article interests you the most. Then take turns reading your sentences to the class.

Practice. In groups, discuss the meaning of rumors. Think of some examples of rumors (e.g., rumors about a government official) and discuss the effect they could have.

Practice. Starting anywhere in the classroom, each student should pass along to the next student this question: "Have you heard the news about the new baby elephant at the zoo?" The last student should announce the final version of the question.

Practice. Starting anywhere in the classroom, one student should ask the next student this question, adding his/her own ending: "Have you heard the news about_____ ?" The question should then be passed around the classroom from student to student. The last student should announce the final version of the question.

Exercise 2. Take turns answering these questions with the noun plus *about* phrases.

1. What kind of books filled his shelves?
2. What did Timmy love?
3. What did Ruth read?
4. What stories are his favorites.
5. What were in the notebook?
6. What is exciting?
7. What did the lawyers have?
8. What is a saga?

Lesson 2. Of/About: after verbs

Note: Either *of* or *about* may be used after certain verbs. These are some of them: *talk, speak, tell, dream, complain, hear, write.*

Example Sentences. With books open, listen to and repeat each sentence as it is read to you.

1. Bart thought about his brother when he saw the picture.
2. Judy often spoke about her adventures in India.
3. Margo dreamed about a house of her own.
4. The students talked about nothing but the exam.
5. The restaurant patrons complained about the poor service.
6. We just heard about the plans for the new highway.
7. The poet wrote about love and sadness.
8. The students worried about the exam.
9. Ari forgot about the meeting.
10. We argued about the spelling of *judgment.*

Now write the verbs plus *about.*

Exercise 1. With books closed, listen to and repeat each sentence again.

Practice. Write the answers in complete sentences using *about.*

1. What do you write about in your letters home?
2. Have you ever forgotten about a party you were invited to?
3. What do you dislike arguing about?
4. Do you know about the new class in astronomy?
5. Have you ever dreamed about being lost?
6. Do you worry about world problems?
7. Do you enjoy talking about sports?
8. What do you think about when you're hungry?
9. What do you complain about when it's ninety-five degrees in the shade?

Now take turns reading your sentences to the class.

Exercise 2. Use your written *about* phrases in complete sentences to answer these questions.

1. What did the restaurant patrons do?
2. What did Bart do when he saw the picture?
3. What did Margo do?
4. What did the students do?
5. What did the poet write?
6. What did Judy often do?
7. Why did we argue?
8. What did Ari forget?

9. Why did the students worry?
10. What did we just hear?

Lesson 3. About: not exactly, but somewhere near the amount, distance, or time

Example Sentences. With books open, listen to and repeat each sentence as it is read to you.

1. The dog eats about a pound of meat a day.
2. Tory studies about three hours every night.
3. The lake is about five miles from the house.
4. They will return to this country about the middle of May.
5. I've done about half of my homework.

Now write the *about* phrases.

Exercise 1. With books closed, listen to and repeat each sentence again.

Exercise 2. Write three sentences of your own using *about* meaning *not exactly, but near to.*

Practice. Complete these sentences with the written *about* phrases.

1. They will return to this country _____ .

2. The dog eats _____ a day.

3. Tory studies _____ every night.

4. The lake is _____ from the house.

5. I've done _____ of my homework.

Lesson 4. About: other usages

Example Sentences. With books open, listen to and repeat each sentence as it is read to you.

1. to be ready or prepared to do something
   a. The race is about to start.
   b. He looks as if he's about to lose his temper.
2. here and there, throughout
   a. Guards were stationed about the palace grounds.
   b. Newspapers were scattered about the room.
3. surrounding, as part of
   a. She has an aura of self-assurance about her.
   b. The house has a mysterious atmosphere about it.

Now write the complete sentences.

Review

Reading Passage 1. Listen, with books closed.

On the first of October of my twenty-third year, my trip to the Orient turned from dreams into reality. From the time I was a child, I had loved stories about travel and especially about the countries of Asia. Every night when I went to bed I would look forward to my dreams. They were about far-off places.

For years I saved my pennies for a trip. I worked for my father for about a dollar an hour, removing brush from our land and dragging fallen trees to the clearing for firewood against the winter. A farm is never short of jobs. When I got to college, I worked part of the time as a waiter, and for about a year in the library of the school of engineering.

After years of planning, the day of departure finally arrived. I worried about being late for my flight and got to the airport about two hours early. My carry-on bag was full of maps of Asian cities and, of course, my camera and film. I planned on taking many pictures of these lands of mystery, and thought about writing a book about them. The plane took off from San Francisco and headed west toward the East!

The first stop of the trip was Japan. The memory of that day is one of the clearest of my life. I sat in the front of the plane and pressed my forehead against the window as we came in sight of the Tokyo airport. It was the end of a long flight and the beginning of a wonderful adventure.

Practice. With books open, take turns answering these questions using complete sentences.

1. When did his dreams turn to reality?
2. What kind of stories did he like?
3. What were his dreams about?
4. How long had he saved his pennies?
5. What did he do for a dollar an hour?
6. What is a farm never short of?
7. How long during college did he work as a waiter?
8. How long did he work in the library?
9. What finally arrived?
10. What did he worry about?
11. Where did he get to two hours early?
12. Describe his carry-on bag.
13. What kind of pictures did he plan on taking?
14. What did he think about writing?
15. When the plane took off, where did it head?
16. Describe his memory of that day.
17. Where did he sit?
18. Where did he press his forehead?
19. What did they come in sight of?
20. What was it the end of, and what was it the beginning of?

Turn to Missing Links, page 259.

Unit 7
With, Without, Through, Throughout

Section A: With

Lesson 1a. With: in the company of, as a companion or partner of, in the presence of
---

Example Sentences. With books open, listen to and repeat each sentence as it is read to you.

1. He eats lunch with his wife every noon.
2. Joanne often takes walks with her children.
3. The students study with each other.
4. Elise plays with her friends every day.
5. Robert plays softball with the college team.
6. The president travels with body guards.
7. Jackie went to the movies with Mike.
8. The man playing chess with Philip is his uncle, Gary.

Exercise 1. With books closed, listen to and repeat each sentence again.

Practice. Write five complete sentences of your own using *with*. Use the example sentences as models. Then take turns reading them to the class.

Practice. Take turns walking somewhere in the room with the student sitting next to you. Then each of you should tell the class what you have done.

Practice. Ask the student next to you who he/she usually has lunch with, studies with, goes shopping with, and then answer the same question(s) in turn. Write down the answers, and then turn these answers into complete sentences using *with*.

Practice. Answer these questions in writing, using *with* phrases.

1. If you could play tennis (or golf, baseball, basketball, bingo, etc.) with anybody in the world, who would you choose?
2. If you were taking a two-day bus trip, would you rather be traveling alone or with a talkative friend?
3. Who do children like to play with?
4. What animal does a sightless person often walk with?

To Remember:
I walked a mile with Sorrow
And not a word said she;
But, oh, the things I learned from her
When Sorrow walked with me.

—Robert Browning Hamilton, *Along the Road*

Lesson 1b. With: including, added to

Practice.

S1: I know I put my tickets with my passport.
S2: Where is your passport?
S1: With my boarding pass.
S2: Where's your boarding pass?
S1: It was right here with the newspaper I was reading, but now it's gone.
S2: Oh, oh. I saw the custodian throw the newspaper in the shredder with the rest of the trash.
S1: Well, I guess I won't be going to Spain with you after all. Here's my camera. Take it with you and bring back some pictures so I can see what I missed.

Example Sentences. With books open, listen to and repeat each sentence as it is read to you.

1. Betsy likes crackers with peanut butter.
2. Ice cream with strawberries is delicious.
3. He always takes sugar with his coffee.
4. She put the daisies in a vase with the marigolds.
5. The taxi drove away with three passengers.
6. The space shuttle blasted off with a crew of ten.
7. The family, with the grandparents included, numbered ten.
8. Red paint mixed with yellow paint results in orange paint.

Exercise 1. With books closed, listen to and repeat each sentence again.

Practice. Volunteer answers to these questions using *with* phrases.

1. How can you make paste? (mix)
2. How do some people like coffee?
3. How can you make green paint? (mix)
4. If you have a bowl of oranges and you add an apple, what have you done? (put)
5. If an elevator full of clowns stops and you get on, what have you done?

Practice. First, each student should draw a circle, a square, and a triangle on a piece of paper. Then, inside each of these shapes, write, print, or draw one thing (i.e., your initials, a geometrical form, a face). Then, exchange papers with the student next to you. Finally, tell each other what you see on the papers using *with* phrases.

Exercise 2. Write three sentences of your own using any of the *with* phrases you have written. Then take turns reading them to the class.

> *To Remember:*
> To carry care to bed is to sleep with a pack on your back.
>
> —T. C. Haliburton

Lesson 1c. With: at the home of, in the charge or keeping of

Note: When used in this way, *with* usually answers the question *where,* rather than *with whom.*

Note: At may be used in this way when referring to a place. In those cases, the possessive must be used, i.e., Timmy spent the night at his grandparent's (house); Nilsa left her broken bracelet at the jeweler's (shop).

Example Sentences. With books open, listen to and repeat each sentence as it is read to you.

1. Mary stayed with her cousin in Seattle last week.
2. Timmy spent the night with his grandparents.
3. Randy often visits with his parents at the lake.
4. Shari's daughter lives with her family in India.
5. Clara left her baby with her mother.
6. Nilsa left her broken bracelet with the jeweler.
7. Tucker left the keys to the office with the custodian.
8. We leave copies of important papers with our attorney.

Exercise 1. With books closed, listen to and repeat each sentence again.

Exercise 2. Write questions from the example sentences using *where did* or *where does* or *where do.*

Practice. Take turns answering these questions.

1. Do you leave your homework assignment with the bus driver?
2. Do you stay in a hotel when you go back to your own country?
3. Where do people leave their pets when they go out of town?
4. Do people leave their important papers with the grocer?
5. Do hotel guests leave their keys with the maid when they go out for the evening?

Reading Passage 1. Listen, with books closed.

The Johnsons like to listen to music with their dessert. Joanne sits at one end of the table with Robert, with their tape recorder playing classical music. Philip sits at the other end of the table with Elise, with the CD playing opera arias. Combined with that is the sound of the VCR in the next room playing reggae music.

When I spent the week with them last summer, I always took a walk with my dog at dessert time, even when they served my favorite — ice cream with chocolate sauce — because my dog liked to howl along with the music.

The next time I visit with the Johnsons, I'm going to bring some earplugs with me and leave my dog with a friend.

Turn to Missing Links, page 260.

Lesson 2a. With: having, showing an attribute or possession, answers the questions *what kind?* or *which?*

Practice.

S1: Look at that white dog with the black spots.
S2: That's not a white dog with black spots, that's a black dog with white spots.
S1: I suppose you think a zebra is black with white stripes, too.
S2: Well, it is, isn't it?

Example Sentences. With books open, listen to and repeat each sentence as it is read to you.

1. Pat has a dog with blue eyes.
2. Carmen likes the shoes with the silver buckles.
3. The car with the broken window is Bob's.
4. The man with the beard is a professor.
5. The girl with the red hair is my friend.
6. Alice wore a hat with a green feather on it.
7. Marta is blessed with a happy nature.

Now write the *with* phrases.

Exercise 1. With books closed, listen to and repeat each sentence again.

Practice. Each of you look around the room and choose one person to be your *mystery person.* Then, ask the student next to you to guess who you have in mind by asking, for example, "Who is the girl with the green sweater?" After your mystery person has been identified, you in turn must guess who the other student has in mind.

Practice. Write one sentence describing anyone in the world, using a *with* phrase.

Exercise 2. Answer these questions using your written *with* phrases.

1. Which girl is my friend?
2. What kind of hat did Alice wear?
3. What kind of shoes does Carmen like?
4. Which car is Bob's?
5. Which man is a professor?
6. What kind of dog does Pat have?

To Remember:

Men are born with two eyes, but with one tongue, in order that they should see twice as much as they say.

—Charles Caleb Colton

Lesson 2b. With: answers the question *in what manner?*

Example Sentences. With books open, listen to and repeat each sentence as it is read to you.

1. The children danced with grace.
2. The doctor performs surgery with skill.
3. Paola accepted the award with humility.
4. Lissa does her work with enthusiasm.
5. Jim acted with courage when he saved the child.
6. The children greeted Mickey Mouse with delight.
7. The driver of the other car reacted with anger.
8. The sisters spoke to the patients with compassion.

Now write the *with* phrases.

Exercise 1. With books closed, listen to and repeat each sentence again.

Practice. Write the answers to these questions using *with* phrases. (Some words that could be used are: grace, skill, strength, shyness, anger, excitement, tact, courage, and daring.)

1. How do children sometimes act when another child takes their toys? When they're invited to go to Disneyland? When they meet someone for the first time?
2. How do watchmakers repair watches? How do figure skaters skate? How do wrestlers wrestle?
3. How do firefighters act when fighting a fire? How do parachutists act when they jump out of planes?
4. How do you tell someone that they are blocking your view?

Exercise 2. Close your books and answer these questions with the written *with* phrases.

1. How did Paola accept the award?
2. How did the driver of the other car react?
3. How does Lissa do her work?
4. How did the children greet Mickey Mouse?
5. How did the sisters speak to the patients?
6. How did Jim act when he saved the child?

Reading Passage 1. Listen, with books closed.

My sister and I went to meet our aunt at the train station. Aunt Ella said she'd be the one with the flower in her lapel. At least thirty people with carnations on their coats got off the train. It was Memorial Day, which we celebrate with parades—and by wearing red or white carnations!

We finally found Aunt Ella in spite of all the people with flowers. She was the only one with a yellow rose in her lapel. We yelled at her with excitement and we hugged each other with relief.

As she rode home with us in the taxi, she said she would have found us, even though we hadn't seen each other in years. We were the only twins with bright red hair in the station!

Now take turns reading the *with* phrases.

Turn to Missing Links, page 260.

Lesson 3. With: by means of, using

Example Sentences. With books open, listen to and repeat each sentence as it is read to you.

1. Julia washed her car with the hose.
2. The butcher cut the meat with a cleaver.
3. Teresa served the soup with a ladle.
4. Scott drew the picture with a pen.
5. They lit up the garden with lanterns.
6. The plumber dug a hole with a shovel.
7. Malynda seasoned the sauce with herbs.
8. Hallie cleaned the sink with a sponge.
9. The farmer plowed the field with a tractor.
10. The forester cut down the tree with an axe.

Now write the *with* phrases.

Exercise 1. With books closed, listen to and repeat each sentence again.

Practice. Take turns answering these questions. How (with what) do you eat? write? sew? cut bread? mow the lawn? drive a nail into the wall? write a letter? pay for groceries? protect yourself from rain? measure a room? stir something cooking? apply paint? type a report? draw a picture? rake leaves? light a fire? chop down a tree? iron a shirt? find your way on a long trip? clean pots and pans? water the grass? open a locked door?

Practice. Volunteer to do one or all of these tasks.

1. Write your name on the board with chalk.
2. Clean the board with an eraser.
3. Wipe your forehead with the back of your hand.
4. Pretend to sweep the floor with a broom.

Exercise 2. Divide the class into two sides. Side A should take turns reading the first part of the example sentences in random order. Side B, with books closed, should take turns completing the sentences with the *with* phrases. Then switch sides and repeat the exercise.

To Remember:
It is easier to catch flies with honey than with vinegar.

—English Proverb

Lesson 4. With: used with verbs meaning to cover, fill, or contain

---

Practice.

S1: Look through the window! The house is packed with people.

S2: And the tables are covered with white linen and brimming with food.

S1: Listen! The air is alive with music and laughter.

S2: They're having a party, and we weren't invited.

S1: The sky is filled with stars, and I have a bag filled with doughnuts. Let's sit out here and have our own party.

S2: Good idea. But watch where you sit! The ground is covered with red ants!

Example Sentences. With books open, listen to and repeat each sentence as it is read to you.

1. We packed the boxes with books.
2. Yuri spread the toast with jelly.
3. Sheila filled the vases with flowers.
4. My wife covered the sleeping children with a blanket.
5. Sherrita filled the kettle with boiling water.
6. The train was loaded with new cars.
7. Shun planted the garden with roses.
8. The table was heaped with presents.
9. The olives were stuffed with pimientos.
10. The cake was iced with chocolate frosting.

Now write the *with* phrases.

Exercise 1. With books closed, listen to and repeat each sentence again.

Practice. Using *with,* describe in writing: a library, how you pack a suitcase, a lawn after all the leaves have fallen, a balloon, a pillow, how you prepare jelly toast, and a jar full of candy. (Some words you could use are: filled, covered, stuffed, and spread.)

Exercise 2. Answer these sentences using the written *with* phrases.

1. What happened to the olives?
2. What did Sherrita do to the kettle?
3. What did Yuri do to the toast?
4. What happened to the cake?
5. What happened to the train?

Reading Passage 1. Listen, with books closed.

The campers made a fire with kindling and lit it with matches. Their supper was a can of beans, flavored with tomato sauce, and some hot dogs, covered with mustard and onions.

After supper they filled a pot with creek water, heated it over the fire, and washed dishes with it. When it began to rain, they covered their belongings with a tarp. Little Yvonne fell on the slippery path and got covered with mud.

Everyone smeared their faces, legs, and arms with mosquito repellent and went to bed. They wished with all their hearts they had stayed home.

Exercise 3. With books open, take turns answering these questions.

1. How did the campers make a fire?
2. What did they have for supper?
3. How did they wash the dishes?
4. How did they cover their belongings?
5. What happened to Yvonne when she slipped and fell?
6. What did everyone do to their faces, legs, and arms?
7. How did they wish that they stayed at home?

Reading Passage 2. Listen, with books closed.

When the wind stopped blowing, Lily sat with her friends and ate ice cream with the peaches her Uncle Jose had brought with him from the country. They looked through the window with the broken glass.

The yard was strewn with debris. The tree with the swing on it had blown down. A bird with a black cap, chirping with anxiety, was looking for her chicks. Lily's father was working with Uncle Jose, dragging branches off the street with a rope. Her mother was cleaning the porch with a hose.

The children put their dishes in the sink with the rest of the dirty dishes. With the hurricane, the gas had been cut off, so they had no hot water to wash the dishes with. Then they went out to the yard where they had played with each other just yesterday.

Their eyes filled with tears when they saw the mess. The little fountain where the birds had splashed with vigor was broken, their wading pool was filled with mud, the lawn was covered with tiles from their roof, the tool shed was on the ground with a tree on top of it, and the garden, which Lily's mother had just planted with fall flowers, was torn up. The children helped clean up the trash with rakes and shovels. With their help the yard began to look better.

"With all of us working together, we'll soon be back to normal," said her father with a smile.

And he was right. They were.

Now take turns reading the passage, sentence by sentence.

Exercise 4. With books open, take turns answering the questions.

1. What kind of ice cream did Lily and her friends eat?
2. What kind of window did they look through?
3. Describe the yard.
4. What tree had blown down?
5. What kind of bird was looking for her chicks?
6. What were Lily's father and Uncle Jose doing?
7. What were they doing with a rope?
8. Where did the children put their dishes?
9. How did the birds used to splash?
10. Describe the wading pool.
11. Describe the lawn.
12. Describe the tool shed.
13. What was torn up?
14. How would they soon be back to normal?

Turn to Missing Links, page 260.

Lesson 5a. With: in support of, in favor of, (the opposite of *against*)

Practice.

S1: Would you side with a man who was accused of stealing a loaf of bread?

S2: I would certainly sympathize with him. No one would steal a loaf of bread unless he was hungry.

S1: If you were on the jury, would you vote with the members who wanted to set him free?

S2: Yes. I believe he would conform with the law if his family had food.

Example Sentences. With books open, listen to and repeat each sentence as it is read to you.

1. Stefan cooperated with the police in solving the murder.
2. Tamami agreed with the decision.
3. We're in sympathy with the government.
4. The young people were in accord with the liberals.
5. The older people were in accord with the conservatives.
6. The president concurred with his cabinet on taxes.
7. Six people voted with us, and three people voted against us.
8. The city council was in harmony with the mayor.

Now write the *with* phrases.

Exercise 1. With books closed, listen to and repeat each sentence again.

Exercise 2. Choose two of the example sentences and write them. Take turns reading them to the class.

Lesson 5b. With: in opposition to (the opposite of in support of)

Practice.

S1: I disagree strongly with the mayor's plan for providing free bus service for everyone on Saturdays, and I told him so.

S2: Why would you argue with him about such a great idea?

S1: Because it would compete with my taxi service!

S3: I differ with the mayor, too. In order to pay for the free service on Saturdays, he wants to double the fares on all the other days of the week!

Example Sentences. With books open, listen to and repeat each sentence as it is read to you.

1. The pitcher argued with the umpire.
2. She competes with the best swimmers.
3. Quinn disagreed with his employees about salaries.
4. Sue's beliefs conflict with Antonio's.
5. The boys wrestled with each other in the gym.
6. Chikako differs with Becky about how to cook rice.

Exercise 1. With books closed, listen to and repeat each sentence again.

Practice. Write answers in complete sentences using *with* phrases.

1. Who do politicians argue with?
2. Who is it more fun to compete with, a team that is easy to beat, or a team that is hard to beat?
3. Is it possible to disagree with someone and still remain friends with that person?

Now take turns reading your answers to the class. Discuss each other's answers.

> *To Remember:*
> I won't quarrel with my bread and butter.
>
> —Jonathan Swift

Reading Passage 1. Listen, with books closed.

Sally and Nancy, both aged three, began to fight with each other about who could play with the toy stove. Their mothers decided not to side with either one. Then Sally pulled Nancy's hair and wouldn't let go. Sally's mother agreed with Nancy's mother that it was time to stop the fight. They knew that it's natural for children to compete with their friends, but they must also learn to live in harmony with them.

Exercise 2. With books open, take turns answering the questions using *with* phrases.

1. What did Sally and Nancy begin to do?
2. What were they fighting about?
3. What did their mothers decide?
4. What did Sally's mother do?

5. What is natural for children to do?
6. What must they learn to do?

Turn to Missing Links, page 261.

Lesson 6. With: at the same rate or time as something else

Example Sentences. With books open, listen to and repeat each sentence as it is read to you.

1. Does wisdom really come with age?
2. Healing is supposed to come with time.
3. Dad gets up with the sun.
4. Some wines improve with age.
5. With each news report, she worried more.
6. With the passing of time, he grew more restless.

Exercise 1. With books closed, listen to and repeat each sentence again.

Practice. Choose one of the example sentences and write what you think it means. Then volunteer to share your insight with the class.

Reading Passage 1. Listen, with books closed.

Why does wisdom come with age, when we no longer need it as much? Wisdom should come with youth. Just think of all the foolish mistakes that could be avoided if good sense kicked in with the beginning of the teens. We might grow less wise with time, but by then all the big decisions would have been made wisely, and we could just sit back, enjoy the fruits of our good sense, and be as foolish as we pleased.

Turn to Missing Links, page 261.

Lesson 7. With: shows separation from

Example Sentences. With books open, listen to and repeat each sentence as it is read to you.

1. Tricia broke up with her boyfriend.
2. Jason split up with his girlfriend.
3. Eva had a falling out with her sister.
4. The friends parted company with each other in sorrow.
5. Tal broke with the group and formed a new one.

Now write the *with* phrases.

Exercise 1. With books closed, listen to and repeat each sentence again.

Note: In idiomatic speech, *break up* can also mean to lose control or composure, or to convulse with laughter.

Practice. As a class, discuss the difference in meaning between *broke up with* and *broke with*. Then write sentences using both idioms.

Practice. As a class, discuss the meaning of *to part company with* someone, *to split up with* someone, and *to have a falling out with* someone. Which of the three seems most final?

Lesson 8. With: used in comparison and contrast

Example Sentences. With books open, listen to and repeat each sentence as it is read to you.

1. Don't compare yourself with anyone else.
2. They built the garage level with the house.
3. Strong light contrasts with deep shadows in his photographs.
4. This color goes (looks good) with that color.
5. This color clashes (looks bad) with that color.
6. Our team's score is even (tied) with the Cougars'.
7. This course is on a level with an advanced course.
8. Can you compare Paris, Texas, with Paris, France?

Exercise 1. With books closed, listen to and repeat each sentence again.

Practice. Write answers to the questions in complete sentences using *with*.

1. How does a quarter compare with a dollar?
2. What color looks good with orange?
3. What color contrasts most strongly with white?
4. Is comedy on the same level with drama?
5. What does *sea level* mean?

Practice. Discuss what *compare with* means. Think of ways to compare your native country with the United States. Then share them with the class.

Exercise 2. Complete these sentences using *with* phrases.

1. The game is almost over and our team is _____ _____ their team.

2. He always _____ his wife's cooking _____ his mother's.

3. The child's head is _____ _____ the table top.

4. Some colors _____ _____ other colors.

Reading Passage 1. Listen, with books closed.

    Americans have an old saying: "You can't compare apples with oranges." Why not? You can compare roses with daisies, and kittens with puppies, so why can't you compare apples with oranges?

Now discuss as a class.

Reading Passage 2. Listen, with books closed.

First Complainer: Last night our team was tied with the Polar Bears. I was sitting up in the bleachers with the other students. Because the colors of the Bears' uniforms and the colors of our uniforms didn't contrast enough with each other, we couldn't see which team made the winning touchdown. Compared with us, the kids sitting nearest the field could probably see much better.

Second Complainer: The benches that the team sits on are level with the football field. The drill team sits right behind them. It's harder to see the plays from there than it is from the bleachers. Last night we were tied with the Bears. When the final touchdown was made we couldn't tell which team made it. Compared with us, the kids sitting way up in the stands could probably see much better.

Hint to both Complainers: If you would pay attention to the game, instead of visiting with your friends, you would know which goal line your team was trying to cross.

Now take turns reading the passage, sentence by sentence.

Turn to Missing Links, page 261.

Lesson 9a. With: because of, as a result of, under the influence of

---

Example Sentences. With books open, listen to and repeat each sentence as it is read to you.

1. The tree limbs are heavy with snow.
2. The night was bright with moonlight.
3. The furniture was shining with polish.
4. The baby's face was wet with tears.
5. The actor trembled with nervousness as the play began.
6. Bert frowned with annoyance at the poor service.
7. Nat limped with fatigue as he entered the barn.
8. They sighed with relief when the storm was over.

Now write each *with* phrase plus the preceding word.

Exercise 1. With books closed, listen to and repeat each sentence again.

Practice. Using an appropriate verb plus a *with* phrase, tell how you would react if you: were notified that you had won a cruise to the Bahamas; received news that a good friend had died; received a bill for something you hadn't bought; were praised for your good work; heard that a hurricane was heading toward your city; were asked to give a speech before two hundred people.

Exercise 2. Place a link where *with* belongs.

1. The grass sparkled dew.
2. Meta shook fear.
3. The children danced joy when they saw Santa.
4. The sky darkened storm clouds.

5. Georgio groaned pain.
6. The crowd cheered excitement when David hit a home run.

> *To Remember:*
> Most people would succeed in small things if they were not troubled with great ambitions.
>
> —Henry Wadsworth Longfellow, *Driftwood*

Lesson 9b. With: as a result of, thanks to, immediately following

Example Sentences. With books open, listen to and repeat each sentence as it is read to you.

1. With all this rain, the rivers are rising.
2. With a change in jobs, Bill will have less stress.
3. With a move to Arizona, his health should improve.
4. With the death of her father, she became owner of the store.
5. With the children home on vacation, we'll be very busy.

Exercise 1. With books closed, listen to and repeat each sentence again.

Practice. Write endings for these sentences.

1. With all this extra homework _____ .

2. With a new computer _____ .

3. With a raise in pay _____ .

4. With only four hours of sleep _____ .

5. With his acceptance into the university _____ .

Practice. Write endings for these sentences using *with* phrases.

1. No one could hear the speech _____ .

2. The ocean receded from the shore _____ .

3. We have more daylight hours _____ .

4. She seems like a different person _____ .

5. We have to pay more taxes _____ .

Exercise 2. Place a link where *with* belongs.

1. Brad could buy a better car a salary increase.
2. Our air-conditioning bills go down cooler weather.
3. Teresa became president Rob's resignation.
4. They will surely pass the course all their studying.
5. The trees are budding the coming of spring.

Lesson 9c. With: even though, in spite of

Example Sentences. With books open, listen to and repeat each sentence as it is read to you.

1. With all his millions, he's still miserable.
2. With all his talent, he still can't get a job.
3. With all his faults, he's still a good person.
4. With all his education, he still didn't know the answer.
5. With all his intelligence, he still failed the exam.

Exercise 1. With books closed, listen to and repeat each sentence again.

> Note: *In spite of* is often used in place of *with* in these cases. *With* can also be replaced by *even though* plus a noun/pronoun and a verb (i.e., even though he has millions, he's still miserable).

Practice. Write the example sentences, but use *in spite of* instead of *with.*

Practice. Write the sentences again, substituting these beginning phrases for the *with* phrases.

1. Even though he has _____ .

2. Even though he has a lot of _____ .

3. Even though he has many _____ .

4. Even though he is well educated _____ .

5. Even though he is very intelligent _____ .

Exercise 2. Take turns reading your sentences to the class.

Practice. Using the example sentences as models, write a complete sentence of your own telling about someone you know or about an imaginary character.

Lesson 10. With: how someone feels in regard to something or somebody, in reaction or response to

---

Example Sentences. With books open, listen to and repeat each sentence as it is read to you.

1. Daniel is happy with his new job.
2. Clark is content with very little money.
3. The manager was impatient with the new employee.
4. The football coach was patient with the new players.
5. The bus driver was satisfied with his new route.
6. Adelia felt comfortable with her new mother-in-law.

Now write the adjectives plus *with.*

Exercise 1. With books closed, listen to and repeat each sentence again.

Practice. Using words such as pleased, upset, content, delighted, or angry, make up a sentence telling what you are happy with or satisfied with, then make up another sentence telling about something you are not happy with. Then take turns reading those sentences to the class.

Exercise 2. Place a link where *with* belongs.

1. The doctor was pleased the report.
2. My mother was upset me for losing the keys.
3. He didn't want to be bothered junk mail.
4. The professor was impressed Joe's paper.
5. The woman was delighted the flowers.
6. Stan was uncomfortable the new boss.

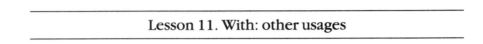

Lesson 11. With: other usages

Example Sentences. With books open, listen to and repeat each sentence as it is read to you.

1. as used to introduce the other person in a relationship or transaction
   a. Romeo was in love with Juliet.
   b. Ed was involved with Edna in a business deal.
   c. Harriet worked with a decorator on her house.
   d. The couple signed a contract with a real estate agent.
   e. Mr. Walz is chatting with his neighbor.
2. as used in exclamations expressing a wish or command
   a. On with the show! (Let the show continue.)
   b. Down with homework! (We don't like homework.)
   c. Off to bed with you! (Go to bed.)
3. in the same direction as
   a. The logs floated south with the current of the river.
   b. They drove toward the suburbs with the afternoon traffic.
   c. A plane flies faster with tail winds.
4. in the membership or employment of
   a. Dr. Tenn is with the university.
   b. Bren is with the electric company now. She used to be with the gas company.
   c. Andy has been with the telephone company for thirty years.

Exercise 1. With books closed, listen to and repeat each sentence again. Then write all of the example sentences from dictation.

Reading Passage 1. Listen, with books closed.

Tommy lives in the house with the red front door. Tammy lives in the house with the white fence. Every weekday morning, Tommy walks to school with Tammy. They carry their books and lunches with them.

One morning Tammy's hat blew off into a ditch filled with water. Tommy fished it out with a stick, but his bag with all his books fell off his shoulder into the ditch. In a minute it filled with muddy water and sank.

That day Tammy shared her books and her lunch with Tommy. She told him that she'd buy him a new book bag and new books with her allowance, but that it would take a long time. With a twinkle in his eyes, he said not to hurry.

"Now we can sit with each other every day and study with each other every night while we share books," he laughed. "I'd rather study with your books than with mine."

Now take turns reading the passage, sentence by sentence.

Reading Passage 2. Listen, with books closed.

All of the students in our class were with Jim. He had been accused of starting a fight with another student, and with breaking a window in the language lab with a chair. We didn't go along with the accusation of the other student. With every hour we grew more upset with the idea that Jim might be punished with suspension.

With his scholastic achievements and his class leadership, we thought the teachers would realize that they were dealing with the wrong person. We knew he was speaking with honesty when he said he had been working with a computer on the other side of the room when the fight started.

With just a few minutes before the end of the school day, the other guy, with courage, I must say, confessed to starting the fight. After school, a bunch of us stood with our arms around Jim and each other and yelled, "Up with the truth!"

Jim shook hands with the other guy, and we all made friends with him. He said that he couldn't have lived with himself if he hadn't confessed. He'll have to pay for the window with his own money. He will also help with younger students in the language lab before school every morning. He smiled with relief when he heard that he wouldn't be suspended.

Now take turns reading the passage, sentence by sentence.

Turn to Missing Links, page 262.

Section B: Without

Lesson 1. Without: not having, lacking

Practice.

S1: Jerry got to the park two hours late without the picnic basket.

S2: What happened?

S1: He found out that a car won't run without gas. He had to walk eight miles without a rest or even a drink of water.

S1: What did you do?

S2: We had a picnic without any food.

Example Sentences. With books open, listen to and repeat each sentence as it is read to you.

1. A school without teachers is not a school.
2. A bird without feathers cannot fly.
3. A cat without claws cannot scratch.

4. A house without a roof will not keep out the rain.
5. A world without laughter would be depressing.
6. A night without a moon is dark.
7. He read the book without interest.
8. They drove two thousand miles without a map.

Exercise 1. With books closed, listen to and repeat each sentence again.

Practice. Using *without,* tell how you would describe: a dark night; a windowless building;a dry lake; a salt-free diet; a diet cola; a bare tree; an empty classroom.

Practice. Write three sentences of your own using *without* to mean *not having* or *lacking*.

Exercise 2. Place a link where *without* belongs.

1. Pizza cheese is not very tasty.
2. A day sunshine is not always gloomy.
3. A car wheels won't go far.
4. An orange seeds is called a seedless orange.
5. Yogurt fat is called fat-free yogurt.
6. A home laughter is not very happy.

> *To Remember:*
> A picture is a poem without words.
>
> —Horace
>
> Learning without thought is labor lost.
>
> —Confucius

Lesson 2. Without: with no or none, used in matters of choice or ability

---

Example Sentences. With books open, listen to and repeat each sentence as it is read to you.

1. We seldom go outside without coats in the winter.
2. The children like to walk in the sand without shoes.
3. Doris likes her coffee without cream.
4. Peter sleeps without a pillow.
5. Boy Scouts can make a fire without a match.
6. Laura can play that sonata without looking at the music.

Now write the *without* phrases.

Exercise 1. With books closed, listen to and repeat each sentence again.

Practice. Answer the following questions using *without* plus these example words (or words of your own): the TV playing, chemicals, a lot of luggage, shoes, without bringing your work along.

1. What's the best way to walk on a sandy beach?
2. What's the best way to plant vegetables?
3. What's the best way to study?
4. What's the best way to spend a vacation?
5. What's the best way to travel?

Exercise 2. Answer these questions in turn, using your written *without* phrases.

1. How does Peter sleep?
2. How does Doris like her coffee?
3. How does Laura play that sonata?
4. How do the children like to walk in the sand?
5. How do we seldom go outside in the winter?
6. How can Boy Scouts make a fire?

Lesson 3. Without: used in matters of omission or freedom from

---

Example Sentences. With books open, listen to and repeat each sentence as it is read to you.

1. He took his father's car without permission.
2. I told the secret without thinking.
3. She took the money without feeling guilty.
4. She cheated on the test without shame.
5. He fights fires without fear.
6. They played loud music without consideration for the people sleeping upstairs.

Now write the *without* phrases.

Exercise 1. With books closed, listen to and repeat each sentence again.

Practice. Write sentences telling about times that you have done something: without thinking, without asking, without fear, without embarrassment.

Exercise 2. Divide the class into two sides. Side A should take turns reading the example sentences up to *without.* Mix up the order. Side B, with books closed, should take turns completing the sentences using your written *without* phrases. Then switch sides and repeat the exercise.

Lesson 4. Without: verbs after *without* always end in *-ing*

Example Sentences. With books open, listen to and repeat each sentence as it is read to you.

1. George got home early without speeding.
2. Gail went the whole day without eating.
3. Gary says he sleeps without dreaming.
4. Ginny can't think of that joke without laughing.

5. Gabe passed the test without studying.
6. Grace watched the sad movie without crying.

Now write the *without* phrases.

Exercise 1. With books closed, listen to and repeat each sentence again.

Practice. Volunteer answers to these questions.

1. How long have you gone without sleeping?
2. Have you ever spent all day trying to do something without succeeding?
3. How long can you type without making a mistake?
4. What have you read or studied without understanding it?

Practice. Write sentences about some of these things you do, or have done, without: worrying, planning, studying, eating, laughing, hurrying, stopping, buying anything, saying anything. Then take turns sharing the sentences with the class.

Exercise 2. Use the written *without* phrases to complete these sentences in writing.

1. Ginny can't think of that joke _____ .

2. George got home early _____ .

3. Gabe passed the test _____ .

4. Grace watched the sad movie _____ .

5. Gary says that he sleeps _____ .

6. Gail went the whole day _____ .

Review

Exercise 1. Place a link where *without* belongs.

1. In December it's too cold to go outside coats.
2. At the beach in July it is too bright to go sunglasses.
3. Children like to walk in the sand shoes.
4. I can't write a pen or pencil.
5. Mikel parachuted out of the plane fear.
6. I like my sandwich mayonnaise.
7. Don't go to bed brushing your teeth.
8. the map we would be lost.
9. Because he was angry, he left the room speaking.
10. Don't start the day eating breakfast.

Lesson 5. With/Without

Example Sentences. With books open, listen to and repeat each sentence as it is read to you.

1. A sky without clouds is clear.
2. A sky with clouds is overcast.
3. A vest is a garment without sleeves.
4. A jacket is a garment with sleeves.
5. A canoe is a boat without a motor.
6. A sloop is a boat with a sail.

Now write the *with* and *without* phrases.

Exercise 1. With books closed, listen to and repeat each sentence again.

Practice. Answer these questions with complete sentences.

1. Do you like fruit with sugar or without sugar?
2. Does a person weigh more with shoes or without shoes?
3. Do you do your homework with help or without help?
4. Do you prefer a classroom with windows or without windows?
5. Do you take car trips with a map or without a map?
6. Do you read with glasses or without glasses?
7. Do you use someone's car with permission or without permission?
8. Would you buy a car with a warranty or without a warranty?

Exercise 2. Complete these sentences in writing.

1. A sky _____ is clear.

2. A sky _____ is overcast.

3. A vest is a garment _____ .

4. A jacket is a garment _____ .

5. A canoe is a boat _____ .

6. A sloop is a boat _____ .

7. A helicopter is an aircraft _____ .

8. A fly is an insect _____ .

Practice. Answer these questions in writing in your own words.

1. Bob likes his hot dog with mustard, but Tom likes his hot dog without mustard. How do you like your hot dog?
2. Tennis is played with a racket, and golf is played with golf clubs. What is basketball played with?
3. Fudge is made with chocolate, and lemonade is made with lemons. What is bread made with?
4. A bucket with water up to the top is full, but a bucket without water is empty. What is a full gas tank? What is an empty gas tank?

Reading Passage 1. Listen, with books closed.

      Carlos came to school without his books. He walked into class without smiling and sat down without saying hello to anybody. The classroom was without heat because the storm had left the school without electricity. The students without sweaters were shivering. Without a doubt, school would be dismissed early.

      The teacher stood in front of the room with her arms filled with papers.

      "Of all of these papers there is only one with an *A+* on it," she said. "By the way, did one of you come to school without your books?"

      "I did," answered Carlos with embarrassment. "I left school without them yesterday, and when I came back to find them, they were gone. They're lost."

      "No, they aren't," said his teacher with a smile. "Without thinking, I put them with the class books in the cabinet yesterday. And by the way, Carlos, this paper with the *A+* on it is yours."

      The classroom was still cold, but Carlos left school that day with a warm feeling in his heart.

Exercise 3. With books open, take turns answering the questions.

1. How did Carlos come to school?
2. How did he walk into the room?
3. Why was the classroom without heat?
4. Who were shivering?
5. What does *without a doubt* mean?
6. Describe the teacher as she stood in front of the room.
7. What did she say?
8. What did she ask?
9. How did Carlos answer?
10. What was his excuse?
11. What does *without thinking* mean?
12. Where had she put his books?
13. Which paper was Carlos's?
14. How did Carlos leave the classroom?

Turn to Missing Links, page 262.

Section C: Through, Throughout

Lesson 1. Through: into at one side and out of the other, from one side of something/someplace to the other side

---

Example Sentences. With books open, listen to and repeat each sentence as it is read to you.

1. The train went through the tunnel.
2. They poured gas into the tank through a funnel.
3. The river rushed through a break in the dam.
4. The firefighter tried to see through the smoke.
5. The needle was too big to go through the cloth.
6. The snake crawled through the hollow log.
7. The actress stepped through the parted curtains to speak to the audience.
8. The drive through Texas from Louisiana to New Mexico is long.

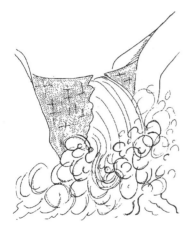

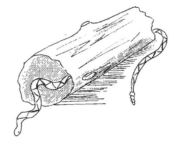

Now write the *through* phrases.

Exercise 1. With books closed, listen to and repeat each sentence again.

Practice. Take turns answering the questions using *through* phrases.

1. How does smoke get out of a fireplace?
2. How does water get from the water tower to the house?
3. If a boy out in his yard bats a ball, and it lands on the floor inside a house, what has he done?
4. If a gopher uses a tunnel to get from one side of a garden to another, what does he do?
5. You are standing at a window with the curtain closed. There is a hole in the curtain, and when you put your eye up to it, you see a bird in a tree. What are you doing?
6. You are in a plane on a cloudy day. Suddenly, the clouds part a little and you see the blue sky. What are you doing?
7. When you walk in the front door and out of the back door of a building, what have you done?

Exercise 2. Using the written *through* phrases, answer these questions in writing.

1. How did they pour the gas?
2. What was the needle too big to do?
3. Where did the train go?
4. Where did the river rush?
5. Where did the snake crawl?
6. Where did the actress walk?
7. How did the firefighter try to see?
8. What drive is long?

> *To Remember:*
> Two men look out through the same bars:
> One sees mud, and one the stars.
>
> — Frederick Langbridge

Lesson 2. Through: by way of, by means of

Example Sentences. With books open, listen to and repeat each sentence as it is read to you.

> *Note:* In sentences 1, 2, and 5, *through* could also be defined as *going in one side and out the other,* but as used here the meaning is more precisely *by way of* or *by means of.*

1. Sandy came into the house through the back door.
2. Molly drank her milk through a straw.
3. We heard the news through the grapevine.
4. Elsa got the hospital job through friends who work there.
5. Tony looked at the birds through binoculars.
6. The French ambassador speaks through a translator.
7. Lang reached his goal through hard work and determination.
8. Mary learned about politics through the newspaper.

Now write the *through* phrases.

Practice. Volunteer answers to these questions.

1. How does a microbiologist examine specimens?
2. How does a photographer see his/her subject?
3. How do we hear about world news?

Exercise 1. With books closed, listen to and repeat each sentence again.

Exercise 2. Use the written *through* phrases to answer these questions.

1. How did Elsa get the hospital job?
2. How did he reach his goal?
3. How did Tony look at the birds?

4. How did the French ambassador speak?
5. How did she come into the house?
6. How did Molly drink her milk?
7. How did she learn about politics?
8. How did she hear the news?

To Remember:
Ideas must work through the brains and arms of good and brave men, or they are no better than dreams.

—Ralph Waldo Emerson

Lesson 3a. Through: past, without stopping

Example Sentences. With books open, listen to and repeat each sentence as it is read to you.

1. Kristin drove through the barricade in the road.
2. Don't go through that intersection without stopping.
3. Go through the green light, not the amber light.
4. The horse ran through the starting gate before the race began.

Exercise 1. With books closed, listen to and repeat each sentence again.

Practice. Discuss what could happen if you drove through a stop sign without stopping. Why would anyone drive through a red light?

Lesson 3b. Through: to or at the end of, past

Example Sentences. With books open, listen to and repeat each sentence as it is read to you.

1. David was glad to have gotten through the training course.
2. Honore got through the interview without any trouble.
3. What a relief to be through paying this year's taxes!
4. It takes a while to go through customs.

Exercise 1. With books closed, listen to and repeat each sentence again.

Exercise 2. Place a link where *through* belongs.

1. Katherine enjoyed going nurses' training.
2. Elmo got his exams without any trouble.
3. He drove the stop sign and got a ticket.
4. He raced the obstacles and won the race.
5. We got customs without any delay.
6. We got the red tape with Paul's help.
7. That woman has gone much suffering.
8. They went the ordeal without complaining.

Lesson 4. Through: because of

Example Sentences. With books open, listen to and repeat each sentence as it is read to you.

1. Through the greed of a few, many suffer.
2. Through bad management, the business failed.
3. We got lost through an error on the map.
4. Through misinformation, we missed our plane.
5. Many have been assisted through that man's generosity.
6. The mistake was made through carelessness.
7. Through a misunderstanding, the meeting started late.
8. The Meals-on-Wheels program has succeeded through the work of volunteers.

Now write the *through* phrases.

Exercise 1. With books closed, listen to and repeat each sentence again.

Practice. Take turns completing the sentences using *through*.

1. If someone gave you a brand new computer, and you were asked how you could afford it, you could

   say: "I got this computer _____ of a friend."

2. If you hurried through a test and failed it, you could say: "I failed that test _____ ."

3. If the manager of a store kept good records, ordered the best stock for the least money, was kind to

   his employees and considerate to his customers, you could say: "That store succeeded

   _____ ."

Exercise 2. Place a link where *through* belongs.

1. They lost the game lack of training.
2. A hospital was built one man's generosity.
3. He was late no fault of his own.
4. The fire started negligence.
5. They employed her an agency.
6. That story was spread gossip.

Lesson 5. Through: from the beginning to the end of

Example Sentences. With books open, listen to and repeat each sentence as it is read to you.

1. Chuck slept through the entire opera.
2. We watched all through the night, but we never saw the meteorite shower.
3. I worried all through class that I would be called on.

4. We thought the baby wouldn't sleep through the flight, but she did.
5. Barbara waited all through the afternoon for the telephone to ring.
6. Evan sat through four tennis matches on TV.

Now write the *through* phrases.

Exercise 1. With books closed, listen to and repeat each sentence again.

Practice. Write your own sentences using *through* phrases of your choice. Here are some examples: through lunch hour; through the whole baseball game; through the morning; through the TV program.

Exercise 2. Use the written *through* phrases to complete these sentences.

1. We thought the baby wouldn't sleep ＿＿＿＿＿＿ but she did.

2. We watched all ＿＿＿＿＿＿ but we never saw the meteorite shower.

3. Evan sat ＿＿＿＿＿＿ and then left.

4. Barbara waited all ＿＿＿＿＿＿ for the telephone to ring.

5. Chuck slept ＿＿＿＿＿＿ .

6. I worried all ＿＿＿＿＿＿ that I would be called on.

Exercise 3. Place a link where *through* belongs.

1. Hanna cared for her aunt all her illness.
2. Agnes heard the sirens all the morning.
3. The baby slept the night.
4. We stayed the first act of the play and then went home.
5. The kids talked the night.
6. Paula didn't say a word all dinner.
7. Her friends remained loyal the whole ordeal.
8. They suffered hunger all the war.

Lesson 6. Through/Throughout: all over, among the parts of, in and around

---

Note: Throughout can also be used in sentences like those in this lesson. It is more emphatic than *through,* but not as commonly used. Used with words about looking for or searching, it means *in all parts of.* Used with words about traveling it means *widely. All through* lends similar emphasis.

Example Sentences. With books open, listen to and repeat each sentence as it is read to you.

1. We drove through New England in September.
2. Portia walked through the garden admiring the roses.
3. The canary's song could be heard all through the house.

4. Their tour took them through Sweden and Denmark.
5. Allen looked through the old suitcase for the journal.
6. The church bells rang through the neighborhood.
7. The police searched through the building for the burglar.

Now write the main verb in each sentence, plus the *through* phrases.

Exercise 1. With books closed, listen to and repeat each sentence again.

Practice. Write complete sentences using *through* and *throughout* telling what you would do in these situations.

1. You put your keys somewhere in the house, but you can't remember where.
2. You have a month of vacation time, you want to see all of Europe, and you're talking to your travel agent.
3. You're having a party at night, and you want the whole house to be bright and festive.

Exercise 2. Use your written *through* phrases to answer these questions.

1. Where did the police search for the burglar?
2. Where did Portia walk?
3. Where did the church bells ring?
4. Where did we drive?
5. Where could the canary's song be heard?
6. Where did Allen look for the journal?
7. Where did the tour take them?

Exercise 3. Substitute *throughout* for *through* in the example sentences. Only one of the sentences does not sound right with *throughout.* Can you find it and explain why?

Lesson 7. Through: up to and including

Example Sentences. With books open, listen to and repeat each sentence as it is read to you.

1. They lived in America from 1989 through 1992.
2. I've read through page 225 in that book.
3. The class will be held from September through November.
4. The TV miniseries will be on from Monday evening through Wednesday evening.

Now write the sentences.

Exercise 1. With books closed, listen to and repeat each sentence again.

Exercise 2. Using the example sentences as models, write some of your own that tell, for example, how long you have lived some place, how much of this book you have studied, when the specials at the grocery store will be, or how long this class will be held. Then take turns reading these sentences to the class.

Review

Reading Passage 1. Listen, with books closed.

On Sunday night, Alisha heard the radio through the wall of her apartment. It was 2:00 A.M. She lay awake through three hours of music and talk. Through will power, she finally fell asleep at 5:00 A.M.

The same thing happened every night throughout the week. On Friday, Alisha got through work early and, through the kindness of her supervisor, left the office at 3:30. As the bus drove through traffic she almost fell asleep. She peered through the bus window at a sign that said, "Get a good night's sleep on a Sleepwell mattress." Alisha thought to herself, "I could sleep through the night on a bed of nails—if there were no radio playing."

That night, the music and voices seemed to sound throughout every corner of her apartment. Alisha could even hear them through the earplugs she had bought. She got through the rest of the night by thinking about how to stop it.

On Saturday, through the help of her landlord, Alisha met the person living in the next apartment. It was Nora, a nice, elderly woman. Nora told Alisha that in the wee hours, when she couldn't sleep, she found companionship through the music and talk on the radio.

That afternoon, Alisha brought the woman a gift. Now Nora listens to her favorite programs all through the night through her new headphones, and Alisha, on her side of the wall, sleeps soundly.

Now take turns reading the passage, sentence by sentence.

Turn to Missing Links, page 263.

Unit 8
Over, Above, Beyond, Across, Under/ Underneath, Below, Beneath

Section A: Over

Lesson 1. Over: in a place that is higher than, directly above
(see *above*)

Example Sentences. With books open, listen to and repeat each sentence as it is read to you.

1. The soap is in the cabinet over the sink.
2. The light is over the pool table.
3. The mother leaned over her sick child.
4. Silas bent over his work table.
5. A single star shone over the church.
6. A little cloud floated over the baseball field.
7. A red and gold banner flew over the park entrance.
8. A mobile turned slowly over the baby's crib.
9. Matt held the mistletoe over Susan's head and kissed her.
10. We saw a rainbow in the distance, but there were dark clouds overhead. (over our heads)

Now write the *over* phrases.

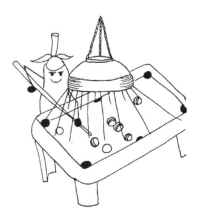

Note: Over plus a pronoun plus *head* often becomes the compound *overhead*, i.e., the overhead light (adj.), or the clouds overhead (adv.).

Exercise 1. With books closed, listen to and repeat each sentence again.

Practice. In groups, discuss the following situations. Use *over* in your discussions.

1. In the classrooms and halls of the school, where are the lights?
2. When it rains on your umbrella, where are the rain clouds?
3. Where is the sun at noon?
4. Are the carry-on compartments in planes on the floor?
5. If you're on a plane and see New York City when you look down, where are you?
6. Where do you often find a medicine cabinet?

Exercise 2. Use your written *over* phrases to answer these questions.

1. Where were the dark clouds?
2. Where did the mobile turn slowly?
3. Where is the light?
4. What flew over the park entrance?
5. Where did Matt hold the mistletoe?
6. Where did the little cloud float?
7. Where does the mother lean?
8. Where is the star?
9. Where is the soap?
10. What did Silas do?

> *To Remember:*
> Over my slumber your loving watch keep -
> Rock me to sleep mother, rock me to sleep.
>
> —Elizabeth Aikers Allen

Lesson 2. Over: from one side to the other side (especially by going up and then going down again)

Example Sentences. With books open, listen to and repeat each sentence as it is read to you.

1. The fox jumped over the fallen log.
2. Clark batted the ball over the fence.
3. Throw the towel over the towel rack.
4. The truck drove over my new hat.
5. The baby climbed over the side of the crib.
6. The scouts hiked over the mountain.
7. Please don't look over my shoulder when I'm working. It makes me nervous.
8. The cat carried her kittens over the wall.

Now write the *over* phrases.

Exercise 1. With books closed, listen to and repeat each sentence again.

Practice. Everyone (except students in the back row) should pass a book to the student sitting behind you. Do not turn around. Use your right hand and pass the book so that it is higher than your left shoulder. What did you do? (Answer in unison.)

Practice. Everyone cross your ankles. What have you done? (Answer in unison.) Put a book on the floor and jump from one side of it to the other. What have you done? (Answer in unison.)

Practice. In groups, discuss these questions. (Use *over* in your answers.)

1. If you were walking down the street and came to a puddle of water, what would you do?
2. If you were on one side of a wall and you wanted to get a rope to your friend on the other side, what would you do?
3. When you climb a mountain from one side to the other, what have you done?
4. You and your friend are planting flowers on either side of a bed of roses. Your friend asks you to hand him the spade. What do you do?
5. You use the back of a chair to hang your jacket. What have you done?

Exercise 2. Use your written *over* phrases to answer these questions.

1. Where did the scouts hike?
2. Where did the fox jump?
3. Where did Clark bat the ball?
4. Where did the cat carry her kittens?
5. Where did the baby climb?
6. Where should you throw the towel?
7. Where shouldn't you look?
8. Where did the truck drive?

Exercise 3. Divide the class into sides. Side A should take turns reading the example sentences up to *over.* Mix up the order. Side B, with books closed, should take turns completing the sentences. Then switch sides and repeat the exercise.

Lesson 3. Over: on the other side of something
horizontally distant

Example Sentences. With books open, listen to and repeat each sentence as it is read to you.

1. Lam's home is over the ocean.
2. Grandmother lives over the river.
3. Don't write over the margin.
4. Life is different over the border.
5. We crossed over the state line.
6. We stepped over the threshold and entered the house.
7. Javier's goal was to skate over the finish line first.
8. Just over the edge of town is a dark forest.

Now write the *over* phrases.

Exercise 1. With books closed, listen to and repeat each sentence again.

Practice. Choose one or more of these questions to discuss as a class. (Use *over* in your discussions.)

1. If John lives in the United States, and Peter lives one mile away in Canada, what is another way you could tell someone where John and Peter live?
2. If you built a house, and your neighbor wanted to tell you that one foot of your new house was on his property, what might he say?
3. You are driving on a two-lane road with a yellow line down the middle. You pass the car in front of you and a policeman stops you and gives you a ticket. Why?

Exercise 2. Use the written *over* phrases to answer these questions.

1. Where shouldn't you write?
2. Where did we step?
3. Where is Lam's home?
4. What was Javier's goal?
5. Where is life different?
6. Where is a dark forest?
7. Where did we cross over?
8. Where does Grandmother live?

Exercise 3. Take turns reading the completed sentences to the class.

Lesson 4a. Over: on the surface of, so as to cover

Practice.

S1: I spilled tea all over the reports on the teacher's desk.
S2: What are you going to do?

S1: I think I'll go home to bed and pull the covers over my head!

    Note: All is often used with *over* when speaking of an entire surface.

Example Sentences. With books open, listen to and repeat each sentence as it is read to you.

1. Hattie spread butter over the toast.
2. She poured syrup over the pancakes.
3. Alma ran cool water over her burned hand.
4. Timmy colored all over his father's checks.
5. Alex wore a coat over his suit.
6. Olga wore an apron over her dress.
7. The king wore a cape over his shoulders.
8. The chair had a sheet over it.

Now write the *over* phrases.

Exercise 1. With books closed, listen to and repeat each sentence again.

Practice. As a class, perform these tasks at the same time and answer the questions in unison.

1. Cover the title of your book with another book. What have you done?
2. Cover your pen with a sheet of paper. What have you done?
3. Write your name on a sheet of paper or on the board. Then cover your name with *x's.* What have you done?
4. Cover one hand with the other. What have you done?

Practice. In groups, choose one or more of these questions to discuss. (Use *over* in your discussions.)

1. What would you do if you were wearing new clothes and you had to go out in the rain?
2. What is a good way to melt the ice on a sidewalk?
3. When you cover an old coat of paint with a fresh one, what do you do?
4. If you make your bed in a hurry, what do you do with the bedspread/comforter?
5. If you are a little cold, but not cold enough to wear your sweater, what might you do with your sweater?

Exercise 2. Divide the class into two sides. Side A should take turns reading the example sentences up to *over.* Mix up the order. Side B, with books closed, should take turns using the written *over* phrases to complete the sentences. Then switch sides and repeat the exercise.

To Remember:
Over the housetops, over the streets,
Over the heads of the people you meet-

—James W. Watson, "Beautiful Snow"

Lesson 4b. Over: so as to close or protect

Practice.

S1: We put storm windows over all our windows to keep out the cold.
S2: Did it work?
S1: No. We forgot to put tiles over the hole in the roof.

Example Sentences. With books open, listen to and repeat each sentence as it is read to you.

1. He put his hands over his ears to shut out the noise.
2. She fit the crust over the pie to keep in the filling.
3. Hold a tissue over your mouth when you cough.
4. Martha sewed a patch over the rip in the jeans.
5. Lee nailed boards over the windows before the storm.
6. Burt hung a blanket over the entrance to the tent.
7. William taped cardboard over the hole in the suitcase.
8. Draperies over the windows help keep out heat and cold.
9. Iris nailed sheetrock over the cracks in the wall.
10. The spider spun a web over the tear in the screen.

Now write the *over* phrases.

Exercise 1. With books closed, listen to and repeat each sentence again.

Practice. In groups, discuss these questions. (Use *over* in your discussions.)

1. You see a man coming out of a doctor's office with a bandage covering his eye. What has the doctor done, and why?
2. You put some leftover soup in a small bowl and cover it with plastic wrap. What have you done, and why?
3. Where do your eyelids go when you blink?
4. If you were taking a box of kittens to your sister's house on the bus, what would you do to keep them from getting out of the box?

Exercise 2. Use your written *over* phrases to answer these questions.

1. Where did Iris nail sheetrock?
2. Where did Burt hang a blanket?
3. Where should you hold a tissue when you cough?
4. Where did the spider spin a web?
5. Where did William tape cardboard?
6. Where should we pull the curtains to keep out the sun?

7. Where did Lee nail boards before the storm?
8. Where did Martha sew a patch?
9. Where did she fit the crust?
10. Where did he hold his hands?

Exercise 3. Place a link where *over* belongs.

1. Susan put a lid the boiling corn.
2. Jack laid boards the top of the old well.
3. They taped cardboard the broken window.
4. Allie put a plastic sheet the hole in the roof.
5. Manuel hung screens the windows in the summer.
6. The plumber put a cap the end of the pipe.
7. The children dragged a branch the mouth of the cave.
8. Estelle held her hand her mouth when she yawned.

Exercise 4. Take turns reading the completed sentences from Exercise 3.

Lesson 5. Over: in many parts of, everywhere in a place

Example Sentences. With books open, listen to and repeat each sentence as it is read to you.

Note: All is often used with *over* when speaking of an entire area.

1. The news was broadcast all over the world.
2. The baby threw her blocks all over the floor.
3. The marbles rolled over the sidewalk.
4. Hundreds of ants crawled over the picnic table.
5. The cattle grazed over miles of grassland.
6. We traveled over Western Canada and Alaska.
7. Gerard drove over the entire city delivering papers.
8. Hundreds of boats bobbed over the bay.
9. Hank walked over every inch of the yard looking for the lost ring.
10. School children ran all over the playground playing tag.

Now write the *over* phrases.

Exercise 1. With books closed, listen to and repeat each sentence again.

Practice. Choose one or more of these situations for discussion. (Use *over* in your discussions.)

1. After playing in the sand at the beach, five children stand on a blanket and brush themselves off. You could describe the blanket by saying, "The blanket has sand all _____
   _____ ."
2. You have misplaced your keys. You look for them in every room in the house. You say, "I've looked all _____ _____ _____ , but I can't find them."
3. On your vacation you traveled through every country in Europe. In describing your vacation you could say, "We traveled all _____ _____ ."

Practice. Write answers to these questions in complete sentences using *over.* Then take turns reading the sentences to the class.

1. Do you know anyone who has traveled all over the world?
2. Do you know anyone who drives all over the city almost every day?
3. Have you ever seen a baby throw its toys all over the floor?
4. Have you ever looked all over the house for something you lost?

Exercise 2. Use the written *over* phrases to answer these questions.

1. Where did Gerard drive?
2. Where did school children run?
3. Where did the baby throw her blocks?
4. Where was the news broadcast?
5. Where did the ants crawl?
6. Where did the marbles roll?
7. Where did Hank walk?
8. Where did boats bob?
9. Where did we travel?
10. Where did the cattle graze?

Lesson 6a. Over: higher than the level or height of

Example Sentences. With books open, listen to and repeat each sentence as it is read to you.

1. The price of the black coat is over my budget.
2. The tree has grown over the rooftop.
3. The new skyscraper towers over the other buildings.
4. This year's rainfall is six inches over last year's.
5. Ten feet from shore, the water is over your head.

Exercise 1. With books closed, listen to and repeat each sentence again.

Note: You could tell someone how deep the water is in a certain place by saying, "It's over my head," without being in the water at the time.

Note: The idiomatic meaning of *in over one's head* is: to be in a situation that one cannot successfully manage.

Lesson 6b. Over: more than

Example Sentences. With books open, listen to and repeat each sentence as it is read to you.

1. Rosa waited over an hour for a taxi.
2. My friend lost over forty pounds in a year.
3. Wendy prefers tennis over golf.
4. Zali flew over fifty thousand miles last year.

5. Sissy read over twenty books this summer.
6. Harry caught three fish over the limit.
7. The vote was over the majority.
8. Over fifty children were at the family reunion.
9. People over fifty-five get lots of discounts.
10. Jinya walks over five miles a day.

Exercise 1. With books closed, listen to and repeat each sentence again.

Practice. Using *over,* answer these questions in writing. Then take turns reading them to the class.

1. You have an appointment for 10:00 A.M. You wait until 11:10 A.M. How long did you wait?
2. If the legal limit for the number of fish you may catch is ten, and you catch twelve, what have you done?

Exercise 2. Read the example sentences again in turn, substituting *more than* for *over.*

Exercise 3. Place a link where *over* belongs. (Note how it changes the meaning of the sentences.)

1. Rosa waited an hour for a taxi.
2. Sissy read twenty books this summer.
3. Zali flew fifty thousand miles last year.
4. Jinya walks five miles a day.
5. People fifty-five get lots of discounts.
6. My friend lost forty pounds in a year.

Lesson 7. Over: from the beginning to the end of a certain period; through the duration of

---

Example Sentences. With books open, listen to and repeat each sentence as it is read to you.

1. Kam stayed with us over the holidays.
2. They had a good talk over dinner.
3. The Browns went to Galveston over the weekend.
4. Kay went to Florida over her vacation.
5. Over the last ten years Ed has learned three languages.
6. Our family always gets together over Christmas.
7. Over the next three months Meg will be in Brazil.
8. Aunt Fran visited with relatives over the summer.

Now write the *over* phrases.

Exercise 1. With books closed, listen to and repeat each sentence again.

Practice. Use any of the *over* phrases you have written to compose a sentence of your own. Then take turns reading the sentences to the class.

Practice. Using *over,* fill in the blanks. Then take turns reading the quotes to the class.

1. If you stay at a friend's home from Friday night to Sunday evening, you could say, "I was at
    _____'s house _____ ."

2. If you need to discuss something with someone, and you're both going to be busy all day, you could
    say, "Let's talk about this _____ ."

3. If you went skiing every day while you were home for the holidays, you could say, "I skied a lot
    _____ ."

Lesson 8. Over: as used with words denoting control

Example Sentences. With books open, listen to and repeat each sentence as it is read to you.

1. The tribal chiefs ruled over the people.
2. The judge presided over the court.
3. Those boys have been a bad influence over my cousin.
4. The owner of the company has control over the stocks.
5. The rebel leader has too much power over his followers.
6. After years of study, Lance gained mastery over the violin.

Now write the *over* phrases.

Exercise 1. With books closed, listen to and repeat each sentence again.

Practice. In groups, discuss these expressions.

1. The meaning of *having too much power over* someone or something. (Give examples.)
2. The meaning of *having influence over* someone. (Name ways a person could be a good or a bad
    influence over someone else.)

Exercise 2. Complete these sentences with your written *over* phrases.

1. The rebel leader has too much power _____ .

2. The owner of the company has _____ .

3. After years of study, Lance gained mastery _____ .

4. The tribal chiefs ruled _____ .

5. Those boys have been a bad influence _____ .

6. The judge presided _____ .

Lesson 9. Over: about, concerning

Example Sentences. With books open, listen to and repeat each sentence as it is read to you.

1. The men argued over money.
2. Mary puzzled over the problem.
3. The boys fought over the baseball mitt.
4. Jerry worried over losing his job.
5. Anita grieved over her husband's death.
6. The parents sighed with relief over the good news.
7. Tommy was in trouble over failing math.
8. Pat is concerned over her medical report.

Now write the *over* phrases.

Exercise 1. With books closed, listen to and repeat each sentence again.

Practice. Name some things that people might argue over, grieve over, get in trouble over, fight over, and puzzle over. Write a complete sentence about each, and then take turns reading your sentences to the class.

Exercise 2. Use the written *over* phrases to complete these sentences. Then take turns reading the completed sentences to the class.

1. Anita grieved _____ .

2. Mary puzzled _____ .

3. Jerry worried _____ .

4. The boys fought _____ .

5. Tommy was in trouble _____ .

6. The parents sighed with relief _____ .

7. The men argued _____ .

8. Pat is concerned _____ .

Exercise 3. Write sentences by using these beginnings and adding *over* phrases of your own.

1. The boys fought _____ .

2. The men argued _____ .

3. Jerry worried _____ .

4. She was concerned _____ .

5. The student puzzled _____ .

Lesson 10. Over: other usages

Example Sentences. With books open, listen to and repeat each sentence as it is read to you.

1. by means of
   a. We listen to music over the car radio.
   b. They exchange gossip over the telephone.
2. so as to protect
   a. The lifeguard watches over the swimmers.
   b. The lioness stood guard over her cubs.
3. because of an obstacle
   a. He tripped over the footstool.
   b. The horse stumbled over the rocks.

Now write the sentences from dictation.

Exercise 1. With books closed, listen to and repeat each sentence again.

Exercise 2. Write complete sentences using: watch over, gossip over, stumble over. Take turns reading them to the class.

Review

Reading Passage 1. Listen, with books closed.

Rosalinda was concerned over her terrible headache. It had started over two days ago, when the feed store where she had worked for over five years had gone out of business. She had made an appointment over the telephone with a doctor in the city.

Rosalinda found the medical building easily, because it towered over the other buildings in the city. She walked over the thick carpet in the lobby to the elevator. The sign over the door said that her doctor was on the fifty-fifth floor. She had never before been in a building over ten stories tall. She stepped over the threshold and pushed a button that read *55*. A light went on over the number and the door slid closed.

Rosalinda closed her eyes and held her hand over her mouth. A strange sensation came over her and her ears popped. In only seconds the ride was over. A nurse handed her a form over the top of a counter. "Don't write over the middle section," the nurse said.

Rosalinda waited for over an hour. She counted the lights in the ceiling over her head. She watched a carpenter nail a piece of plywood over a hole in a wall. She listened to music coming over hidden speakers. She searched over the entire waiting room for something interesting to read.

Many people hurried over the area in front of her. A man with bandages over his hands walked to the elevator. Rosalinda pushed the *down* button for him. A woman on crutches with a cast over her leg dropped her handbag. Its contents scattered over the floor. Rosalinda picked them up for her. A crying child ran down the hallway and fell over a box. Then he started to climb over the counter. Rosalinda calmed him and watched over him until the child's mother came.

A woman in a uniform with a name tag on it walked over to Rosalinda. "You seem to have a calming influence over our patients. We need someone like you to take over the customer relations department. Would you like to talk over the job requirements with me over lunch?"

Rosalinda laughed to herself over this turn of events. Her concern over her terrible headache had disappeared, along with her worry over not having a job. The long trip over the country roads to the city had been worth it. Her visit to the doctor's office had cured her. She would have control over her life again.

Exercise 1. With books open, take turns answering the questions.

1. What was Rosalinda concerned over?
2. How long ago had it started?
3. How long had she worked in the feed store?
4. How had she made the appointment with the doctor?
5. Why could she find the medical building so easily?
6. How did she get to the elevator?
7. Where was the sign?
8. What kind of a building had she never been in before?
9. Where did she step?
10. Where did the light go on?
11. What did Rosalinda do?
12. How did she feel?
13. How did the nurse hand her a form?
14. Where did the nurse tell her not to write?
15. How long did Rosalinda wait?
16. Where were the lights that she counted?
17. Where did the carpenter nail the plywood?
18. Where did she search for something to read?
19. Where did people hurry?
20. Where were the man's bandages?
21. Where was the woman's cast?
22. What happened to the crying child?
23. What did he do next?
24. What did Rosalinda do?
25. What did the woman in uniform say to Rosalinda?
26. What did she say they needed?
27. What did she ask?
28. Why did Rosalinda laugh?
29. What two things had disappeared?
30. What had been worth it?
31. What would she have now?

Turn to Missing Links, page 263.

Section B: Above

Lesson 1. Above: vertically or diagonally up from, higher than
(see *over*)

Note: This usage of *above* is very similar to *over* and the two are often interchangeable. However, *above*, when used in this way, usually implies two things on different levels but with a common base, e.g., the mountain lion stood just above us on the path.

Example Sentences. With books open, listen to and repeat each sentence as it is read to you.

1. The eagle's nest is on a ledge above the waterfall.
2. Our friends live in the apartment above ours.
3. Above the houses on the hill is a row of trees.
4. The harvest moon was just above the horizon.
5. The history books are on the shelf above the geography books.

Now write the *above* phrases.

Exercise 1. With books closed, listen to and repeat each sentence again.

Practice. As a class, discuss whether it would be better to say that the room on the other side of the ceiling is over or above this room.

Practice. Write the example sentences from dictation.

Exercise 2. Use the written *above* phrases, plus any other words necessary, to answer these questions.

1. Where was the harvest moon?
2. Where did our friends live?
3. Where is the eagle's nest?
4. Where are the history books?
5. Where is the row of trees?

Lesson 2. Above: other usages

Example Sentences. With books open, listen to and repeat each sentence as it is read to you.

1. higher in rank or power
   a. A sergeant is above a private.
   b. The mayor is above the councilmen.
2. more than
   a. He values honesty above money.
   b. Selby is six inches above the average height.
3. too good or honorable to
   a. Vincent is above malicious gossip.
   b. Teresa is above cheating.

Exercise 1. With books closed, listen to and repeat each sentence again.

Practice. In groups, discuss the meaning of the example sentences.

Practice. Write complete sentences of your own using *above* phrases as they are used here. Then take turns reading them to the class.

> *To Remember:*
> A peace above all earthly dignities,
> A still and quiet conscience.
>
> —Shakespeare, *King Henry VIII*

Section C: Beyond

Lesson 1. Beyond: on the far side of, on the other side of

Example Sentences. With books open, listen to and repeat each sentence as it is read to you.

1. We live in a village beyond the city.
2. The school is beyond the courthouse.
3. They have never gone beyond the forest.
4. We saw the moon rising beyond the stadium lights.
5. We heard the plane landing beyond the terminal.

Now write the *beyond* phrases.

Exercise 1. With books closed, listen to and repeat each sentence again.

Practice. Write a sentence or two explaining the location of this school in relation to your home. You can use your own reference points or any one of these: the freeway, the business district, the city, the park, a certain street. Be sure to use *beyond* in your directions.

Exercise 2. Use the written *beyond* phrases to complete these sentences.

1. We saw the moon rising _____ .

2. The school is _____ .

3. We live in a village _____ .

4. We heard the plane landing _____ .

5. They have never been _____ .

Lesson 2. Beyond: past the limits of, farther than

Example Sentences. With books open, listen to and repeat each sentence as it is read to you.

1. His behavior was beyond understanding.
2. The bucket of water was beyond his reach.
3. The meeting lasted beyond the dinner hour.
4. I can't see beyond my nose without my glasses.
5. We told them nothing beyond the reported facts.

Now write the *beyond* phrases.

Exercise 1. With books closed, listen to and repeat each sentence again.

Practice. Volunteer answers to these questions.

1. You are at a school meeting. Each person is allowed two minutes to give an opinion about the cafeteria food. One person speaks for five minutes. What has he done?
2. A cat is afraid to climb down from a tree. You get on a ladder and try to reach him, but he is too far away. What do you say to the cat's owner?

Exercise 2. Use the written *beyond* phrases, plus any additional words necessary, to write complete answers to these questions.

1. How long did the meeting last?
2. What did we tell them?
3. How far can I see without my glasses?
4. Where was the bucket of water?

Section D: Across

Lesson 1. Across: moving from one side to the other

Example Sentences. With books open, listen to and repeat each sentence as it is read to you.

1. Jimmy swam across the swimming pool.
2. It took an hour to row across the lake.

3. Columbus sailed across the Atlantic Ocean.
4. The sound of music drifted across the water.
5. Ty drove across the river on the old railroad bridge.
6. Emi walked across the street.

Now write the *across* phrases.

Exercise 1. With books closed, listen to and repeat each sentence again.

Practice. Answer these questions together.

1. If you walk from one side of the room to the other, what have you done?
2. If you reach past the student nearest to you to hand a pencil to the next student, what have you done?
3. If you drive from city limit to city limit of Seattle, what have you done?

Practice. Using the written *across* phrases, make up complete sentences of your own.

Exercise 2. Use the written *across* phrases to answer these questions.

1. What did Columbus do?
2. What did Ty do?
3. Where did Emi walk?
4. Where did Jimmy swim?
5. What did it take five minutes to do?
6. What drifted across the water?

Lesson 2. Across: on the opposite side of

Example Sentences. With books open, listen to and repeat each sentence as it is read to you.

1. Her grandparents lived across the street from her house.
2. The high school is across town from the elementary school.
3. The teacher put the talkers across the room from each other.
4. Daley was sitting across the football field, cheering for our rivals.
5. Becky sat across the aisle from her classmates.

Now write the *across* phrases.

Exercise 1. With books closed, listen to and repeat each sentence again.

Practice. Volunteer answers to these questions.

1. When you're at a football game, where are the fans of the opposing team sitting?
2. You are sitting at the edge of a quiet lake at dusk. On the opposite shore two deer are drinking. Where are the deer in relation to you?

Practice. Make up two complete sentences using *across* meaning *on the opposite side of.* Take turns reading them to the class.

Exercise 2. Use the written *across* phrases to answer these questions.

1. Where did the teacher put the talkers?
2. Where was Daley sitting?
3. Where did her grandparents live?
4. Where did Becky sit?
5. Where is the high school?

Lesson 3. Across: so as to cross through

Example Sentences. With books open, listen to and repeat each sentence as it is read to you.

1. The two roads cut across each other. (intersect)
2. He drew a line across the old price and wrote in a new one.
3. She sliced across the top of the watermelon.
4. They took a short cut across the field.

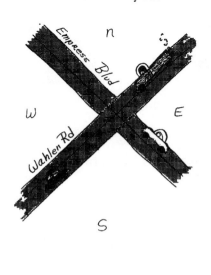

Now write the sentences.

Exercise 1. With books closed, listen to and repeat each sentence again.

Practice. On paper, illustrate the action in the sentences in diagram form. After volunteers draw their diagrams on the board, compare the ones you have drawn with theirs.

Review

Exercise 1. Complete these sentences in writing by supplying the correct prepositions.

   Note: Many of these prepositions are interchangeable.

1. He poured milk _____ his cereal.

2. We heard the news _____ the radio.

3. The balloons floated ＿＿＿＿＿ the children's heads.

4. We lived ＿＿＿＿＿ a candy store.

5. My friend lives ＿＿＿＿＿ the street.

6. The plane flew ＿＿＿＿＿ the storm.

7. He saw the deer ＿＿＿＿＿ the river.

8. James stepped ＿＿＿＿＿ the puddle of rainwater.

9. Throw the wet towel ＿＿＿＿＿ the clothesline.

10. My aunt lives in a town ＿＿＿＿＿ the national park.

11. It's ten degrees ＿＿＿＿＿ freezing and the snowman is melting.

12. She wore a coat ＿＿＿＿＿ her dress.

13. We drove ＿＿＿＿＿ most of the United States.

14. He rolled a rock ＿＿＿＿＿ the entrance to the cave.

15. He was driving ＿＿＿＿＿ the speed limit when he was arrested.

16. Will you please press the button? It's ＿＿＿＿＿ my reach.

17. The medicine cabinet is ＿＿＿＿＿ the bathroom sink.

18. He put a newspaper ＿＿＿＿＿ his face and took a nap.

19. Jinky spread peanut butter ＿＿＿＿＿ her bread.

20. The temperature has been ten degrees ＿＿＿＿＿ average this month.

Exercise 2. Take turns reading your completed sentences to the class. Discuss any questions.

Section E: Under/Underneath

Lesson 1a. Under: in a lower position than

Example Sentences. With books open, listen to and repeat each sentence as it is read to you.

1. The table is under the ceiling fan.
2. The river flowed under the bridge.
3. The campers slept under the stars.
4. Write the date under your name.
5. Huge pipes lie under the streets of the city.
6. The plane flew under the clouds.

Now write the *under* phrases.

Exercise 1. With books closed, listen to and repeat each sentence again.

Exercise 2. Complete these sentences with the written *under* phrases.

1. The plane flew _____ .

2. Huge pipes lie _____ .

3. The table is _____ .

4. Write the date _____ .

5. The river flowed _____ .

6. The campers slept _____ .

> *To Remember:*
> There is nothing new under the sun.
>
> —Ecclesiastes 1:9

Lesson 1b. Under/Underneath: right under something, often covered by something

---

Example Sentences. With books open, listen to and repeat each sentence as it is read to you.

1. He wore a sweater under/underneath his coat.
2. His mother found his socks under/underneath the bed.
3. She hid the scratch under/underneath the tablecloth.
4. The dog buried the bone under/underneath some dirt.
5. The key was hidden under/underneath a flower pot.
6. Under/underneath his calm appearance he was nervous.

Now write the *under/underneath* phrases.

Exercise 1. With books closed, listen to and repeat each sentence again.

Practice. Answer these questions in writing using *under.*

1. If you needed to put a hot dish on a wooden table, what would you do?
2. If you wanted to hide a hundred-dollar bill, where might you put it?
3. If you don't have much closet space, where is a good place to store things?

Practice. Each student should assign a task to the student next to him/her. The task must use *under,* with verbs such as put, hold, or look at (e.g., "Hold your pen under your chin.").

Exercise 2. Write the answers to these questions in complete sentences, using your written *under* phrases.

1. Where did his mother find his socks?
2. Where did he wear a sweater?
3. Where was the key hidden?
4. Where did the dog bury the bone?
5. Where did she hide the scratch?
6. Where was he nervous? (figurative)

Exercise 3. Take turns reading your answers to the class.

Lesson 2. Under: less than

Example Sentences. With books open, listen to and repeat each sentence as it is read to you.

1. We were driving under the speed limit when we hit the deer.
2. No child under five is allowed in the theater.
3. He finished the game with a score of two under par.
4. This shirt cost under five dollars.
5. The class finished the test in under an hour.

Now write the sentences.

Exercise 1. With books closed, listen to and repeat each sentence again.

Practice. Answer these questions in complete sentences using *under.* Then take turns reading the sentences to the class.

1. How much does gas cost?
2. How old must a child be to travel free on a commercial plane?
3. How long does this class last?

Exercise 2. Complete these sentences with any *under* phrase you choose.

1. Bobby was _____ when he learned to read.

2. Felicia finished the book in _____ .

3. That red car cost _____ .

4. He said he was driving _____ when he had the accident.

5. The boys were _____ when they took the car.

Lesson 3a. Under: as used to denote control of or responsibility for someone or something

Example Sentences. With books open, listen to and repeat each sentence as it is read to you.

1. The pharmacy is under new management.
2. Paul has thirty-five people working under him.
3. Our salaries increased under the new policy.
4. The band is under the direction of Mr. Abbott.
5. The baby played under the watchful eye of his mother.
6. Jake worked under the same boss for fifteen years.
7. The team is winning more games under the new coach.
8. The army is under the command of the general.
9. We work under the supervision of the floor nurse.
10. Brenda is under contract to a music publisher.

Now write the *under* phrases.

Exercise 1. With books closed, listen to and repeat each phrase again.

Practice. In groups, complete these sentences with the appropriate *under* phrases in writing. Then compare your version to that of the student next to you.

1. The New City Symphony Orchestra is directed by Josef Musick. An announcement about tonight's

   program might read: "The New City Symphony Orchestra, _____

   _____ Josef Musick, will perform Beethoven's Fifth Symphony."

2. You sign a contract agreeing to work for the Greenfield Landscaping Company. Another company

   asks you to work for them at the same time. You could tell the second company that you're

   _____ to the Greenfield Landscaping

   Company.

3. Your art teacher, Ms. Smith, supervised the project you are submitting to an art contest. In your

   letter you can say that the work was done_____

   _____ of Ms. Smith.

Exercise 2. Use the written *under* phrases to complete these sentences.

1. Where did the baby play?
2. Under whom is the team winning more games?
3. What happened to the pharmacy?
4. For whom did Jake work for fifteen years.
5. What do thirty-five people do for Paul?

Lesson 3b. Under: during the rule of

Example Sentences. With books open, listen to and repeat each sentence as it is read to you.

1. The city has improved under the new mayor.
2. First the people prospered under a kind king, and then they suffered under a cruel one.
3. The Russian people lived under communism for many years.
4. There is not much freedom under a dictatorship.
5. My grandfather lived under fourteen presidents.
6. The university has grown under the new administration.

Now write the *under* phrases.

Exercise 1. With books closed, listen to and repeat each sentence again.

Practice. In groups, discuss the types of government the people of various countries are living under now, or have lived under in the past. Then take turns sharing the information with the rest of the class.

Exercise 2. Use the written *under* phrases to answer these questions.

1. How long did my grandfather live?
2. When did the university grow?
3. When did the city improve?
4. How did the Russian people live for many years?
5. Where is there not much freedom?
6. When did the people prosper, and when did they suffer?

Lesson 4. Under: as used to express a situation, a condition, or a state of mind

Example Sentences. With books open, listen to and repeat each sentence as it is read to you.

1. He's under investigation for tax evasion.
2. The child is under the care of a doctor.
3. I was under the impression that he spoke Spanish.
4. She's under suspicion of stealing.
5. His new plan is still under consideration.
6. The flight can't take off under these weather conditions.
7. The location of the new courthouse is under discussion.
8. When he's under the influence of alcohol, he's a different person.
9. The pyramids were built under great difficulties.
10. The building is under construction.

Now write the *under* phrases.

Exercise 1. With books closed, listen to and repeat each sentence again.

Practice. In groups, discuss the meaning of: under suspicion, under consideration, under the impression, under the influence, under investigation. Then, individually, choose one of those phrases and use it in a sentence. Take turns reading the sentences to the class.

Exercise 2. Use your written *under* phrases to complete these sentences.

1. The child is _____ of a doctor.

2. The pyramids were built _____ .

3. She's _____ of stealing.

4. The location of the new courthouse is _____ .

5. When he's _____ he's a different person.

6. I was _____ that he spoke Spanish.

7. His new plan is still _____ .

8. He's _____ for tax evasion.

9. The flight can't take off _____ .

Lesson 5. Under: in the class of

Example Sentences. With books open, listen to and repeat each sentence as it is read to you.

1. Peas and beans are listed under legumes.
2. Potatoes and carrots are listed under root vegetables.
3. You'll find that store in the yellow pages under *Paint*.
4. Whales come under the heading *Mammals*.
5. Candy is under the *no* heading on my diet.
6. Look under *Physicians and Surgeons* for a doctor.
7. Urdu comes under *Languages* in the curriculum.
8. Tax information is filed under *T.*

Exercise 1. With books closed, listen to and repeat each sentence again.

Practice. Write three complete sentences explaining how various things are listed or filed. Then take turns reading them to the class.

Lesson 6. Under: less than the required amount or degree of

Example Sentences. With books open, listen to and repeat each sentence as it is read to you.

1. Children under the age of seven are not allowed.
2. Alec is under the driving age.
3. Twenty is under the voting age in the United States.

4. He was under the weight requirement of the football team.
5. Those boys were not allowed in the club because they were under the drinking age.

Now write the *under* phrases.

Exercise 1. With books closed, listen to and repeat each sentence again.

Practice. Write sentences about the driving age, the voting age, and the drinking age in your countries. Then take turns reading them to the class.

Section F: Below

Lesson 1. Below: lower than, lesser in degree or rank (sometimes used interchangeably with *under*)

Example Sentences. With books open, listen to and repeat each sentence as it is read to you.

1. Money should always rank below honor.
2. The most fashionable skirts are below the knees.
3. A captain is below a general.
4. It's below freezing; the pond will be frozen soon.
5. The rainfall is below average this year.

Now write the entire sentences.

Exercise 1. With books closed, listen to and repeat each sentence again.

Practice. What do these phrases mean? below freezing, below the boiling point, below average, below the knee. Write complete sentences using each phrase.

> *To Remember:*
> All I ask, — the heaven above
> And the road below me.
>
> —Robert Louis Stevenson, *The Vagabond*

Section G: Beneath

Lesson 1. Beneath: under, below

Example Sentences. With books open, listen to and repeat each sentence as it is read to you.

1. meaning *under* with a space in between
   a. They had a picnic beneath the shade of a tree.
   b. The lake sparkled beneath the starlit sky.

2. meaning close under
   a. Beneath the fallen leaves, green shoots pushed through the dirt.
   b. The mud was hidden beneath the first snowfall.
3. meaning not up to one's standards
   a. Acting silly was beneath the boss's dignity.
   b. Lying to get a job was beneath her.

Now write the *beneath* phrases.

Exercise 1. With books closed, listen to and repeat each sentence again.

Exercise 2. Use the written *beneath* phrases to answer these questions.

1. Where did the lake sparkle?
2. Where was the mud hidden?
3. What was acting silly to the boss?
4. Where did they have a picnic?
5. Where did green shoots push through the dirt.
6. Why wouldn't she lie to get a job?

Exercise 3. Take turns reading the answers to the class.

> *To Remember:*
> Many people have, like uncut diamonds, shining qualities beneath a rough exterior.
> —Juvenal

Review

Exercise 1. Rewrite the sentences with the correct prepositions in the correct places. Then take turns reading the sentences to the class.

> *Note: Under* may be used in all of these sentences, but try to find the few cases in which *underneath, beneath,* or *below* would be more precise.

1. The mouse hid the table while the family ate breakfast.
2. Children two fly free.
3. Benny waited the clock in the train station.
4. The boy found his lunch box his coat.
5. We saw the fish just the surface of the water.
6. Nothing in that store sells for five hundred dollars.
7. The child put his teddy bear his pillow.
8. The office staff is the supervision of Mr. Bentoni.

Reading Passage 1. Listen, with books closed.

Cullen wanted to see what it was like across the border. He walked across the highway to the border patrol station. He could see the lights of Quintero beyond the bridge.

The border guard asked him for his I.D. As he handed it over,* it flew out of his hand, over the guard's head, and into the river. A fishing boat ran over it and it sank below the surface of the water. But as he looked beyond the boat he saw his I.D. card floating quickly across the choppy water. Soon it would be under the bridge!

A sign across the station door said "Traffic Control." An electric bell hung above the sign. The guard rang it. The next boat stopped. The captain looked up at Cullen standing above him on the bridge.

"Could you please try to fish that card out of the water?" yelled Cullen.

The captain reached over the side of the boat with a fishing net and scooped up the card. Cullen ran under the embankment to the water's edge. The captain pulled his little boat over* as far as he could and held the net out toward the shore. Cullen took off his shoes and socks, waded into the river over the soft mud, reached into the net, and got his I.D. card. It was dry beneath its plastic cover.

Thanks to the border guard, the fishing boat captain, and the plastic over his I.D., Cullen got to see what it was like across the border.

*Over when used in this way is an adverb.

Turn to Missing Links, page 264.

Unit 9
Before, After, Behind

Section A: Before

Lesson 1. Before: earlier than, prior to

Example Sentences. With books open, listen to and repeat each sentence as it is read to you.

1. If you arrive before us, please wait.
2. The students finished the test before the last bell.
3. Summer began the day before yesterday.
4. The war was over before her first birthday.
5. Have you ever had sushi before tonight?
6. Before long we'll be living in a new century.
7. Just before sunset, the message arrived.
8. He had never flown in a plane before that day.

Now write the *before* phrases.

Exercise 1. With books closed, listen to and repeat each sentence again.

Practice. Write complete sentences using these *before* phrases. Then take turns reading them to the class.

1. the day before yesterday
2. before our arrival in this country
3. the year before last
4. just before class
5. before lunch

Practice. In groups, discuss how you would answer the following questions using *before.* Then write the answers in complete sentences.

1. This is Monday. What was Saturday?
2. Tonight you are eating musaka for the first time. What might you say to your hostess? (Use "tonight" in your answer.)
3. The store closes at 5 P.M. It is now 4:50. What might you say to your shopping companion?
4. You hurry to beat your opponent to the goal. When you cross the line you see him already there. What could you say about your opponent?

5. May 20 is graduation day. If you are to graduate, you must turn in your report by May 19. When would you say your report was due?
6. You are thinking of calling your friend Tom. Just then the telephone rings and it is Tom calling you. What might you say?

Exercise 2. Use the written *before* phrases to answer these questions.

1. When did summer begin?
2. When did the students finish the test?
3. Had he ever flown in a plane? (Not ＿＿＿＿＿＿)
4. When did the message arrive?
5. When will we be living in a new century?
6. When was the war over?
7. When should you wait?
8. Have you ever had sushi?

> *To Remember:*
> They say fingers were made before forks, and hands before knives.
> —Jonathan Swift, *Polite Conversation*

Lesson 2a. Before: ahead of in place

Example Sentences. With books closed, listen to and repeat each sentence as it is read to you.

1. *A* comes before *B* in the alphabet.
2. Soup is served before the main course.
3. The sophomores walk on stage before the freshmen.
4. The cartoons come before the movie.

Now write the sentences.

Exercise 1. With books closed, listen to and repeat each sentence again.

Practice. Write the answers to these questions in complete sentences.

1. What comes before *L* in the alphabet?
2. Have you ever spoken before you thought?
3. Why do the bridesmaids walk down the aisle before the bride?
4. In your country what is served before the main course?

Practice. Answer these questions in unison.

1. Does April come before May or before March?
2. When you address an envelope, where do you put the street number?
3. What comes before quintillion?

   To Remember:
   Let's go hand in hand, not one before another.

         —Shakespeare, *Comedy of Errors*

Lesson 2b. Before: in front of, in the presence of

Example Sentences. With books open, listen to and repeat each sentence as it is read to you.

1. Jacob gave a speech before the whole school.
2. The teacher stood before the class and lectured.
3. The prisoner appeared before the judge for sentencing.
4. The troublemakers were called before the principal.

Now write the sentences.

Exercise 1. With books closed, listen to and repeat each sentence again.

Practice. Write the answers to the following questions in complete sentences. Then take turns sharing them with the class.

1. Have you ever given a speech before a group of people?
2. Why did the teacher stand before the class to lecture?
3. What does *appear before the judge* mean?
4. Why were the troublemakers called before the principal?

Practice. Complete these sentences with *before* phrases of your own choosing.

1. Andrew was nervous when he sang _____ for the first time.

2. When Carrie got a ticket for speeding, she had to appear _____ .

3. The soldier stood _____ and explained why he had returned to camp late.

4. The student was called _____ to receive a warning about his bad behavior.

Lesson 3. Before: in a more important position than

Example Sentences. With books open, listen to and repeat each sentence as it is read to you.

1. Good health comes before money in order of importance.
2. Ruth always felt that he put his needs before hers.
3. An admiral comes before a captain in rank.
4. Ray put his family before his career.

Now write the sentences.

Exercise 1. With books closed, listen to and repeat each sentence again.

Exercise 2. With books open, answer these questions in complete sentences.

1. What did Ray do?
2. In order of importance, does health or money come first?
3. Who comes first, a captain or an admiral?
4. What did Ruth always feel?

Practice. As a class, discuss what the example sentences mean. Individually, write two sentences of your own using *before* in this way.

Section B: After

Lesson 1. After: following in time, later than

Example Sentences. With books open, listen to and repeat each sentence as it is read to you.

1. Yuri's class starts after lunch.
2. We arrived at the station after the train's departure.
3. They always study after dinner.
4. After the concert they returned to the hotel.
5. Haley didn't think of her early morning exam until after she left the party.

Now write the *after* phrases.

Exercise 1. With books closed, listen to and repeat each sentence again.

Practice. Write the answers to the following questions in complete sentences using *after.* Then take turns reading them to the class.

1. What do you usually do after lunch?
2. What must be done after a snow storm?
3. What happens after graduation from the university?
4. When is dessert usually served?
5. When do you usually brush your teeth?
6. When does the movie begin?

Exercise 2. Use your written *after* phrases to write the answers to these questions.

1. When did they always study?
2. When did Haley think of her early morning exam?
3. When does Yuri's class start?
4. When did they return to the hotel?
5. When did we arrive at the station?

> *To Remember:*
> After crosses and losses, men grow humbler and wiser.
>
> —Benjamin Franklin

Lesson 2. After: behind in place or order

Example Sentences. With books open, listen to and repeat each sentence as it is read to you.

1. *B* is after *A* in the alphabet.
2. Water was listed after juice on the label.
3. The clowns came after the marching band.
4. Abe's name was called after six others.
5. The vice president is seated after the president.

Now write the *after* phrases.

Exercise 1. With books closed, listen to and repeat each sentence again.

Practice. Answer these questions in writing using *after.*

1. In your family, who comes after you in age?
2. In a filing cabinet, where do you file everything that starts with *Z?*
3. If a man and a woman both reach a door at the same time, when does the man usually go through the door?

Exercise 2. Use the written *after* phrases in complete sentences to answer these questions.

1. When is the vice president seated?
2. Where was water listed on the label?

3. Where were the clowns?
4. When was Abe's name called?
5. Where is *B* in the alphabet?

Lesson 3. After: next to or lower than in importance

Example Sentences. With books open, listen to and repeat each sentence as it is read to you.

1. Lieutenants rank after captains.
2. That company is rated after ours in production.
3. Freshmen are after sophomores in seniority.
4. Food is valued after music on Mark's list of priorities.
5. The sophomores placed after the freshmen in the debate.

Now write the verb in each sentence, plus *after.*

Exercise 1. With books closed, listen to and repeat each sentence again.

Practice. In groups, discuss things that are important to you. Then, individually, write your own list in order of importance. Next, share which things come before other things on your list.

Exercise 2. Use the words you have written to complete these sentences.

1. Food _____ music on Mark's list of priorities.

2. Freshmen _____ sophomores in seniority.

3. Lieutenants _____ captains.

4. Our debate team _____ last year's champions.

5. That company _____ ours in production.

Lesson 4. After: with the name of

Example Sentences. With books open, listen to and repeat each sentence as it is read to you.

1. My Aunt Shirley was named after Shirley Temple.
2. The Roscoe Building was named after the man who owned it.
3. The Washington Monument is named after George Washington.
4. The Lincoln Center is named after Abraham Lincoln.
5. Some schools are named after former teachers.

Now write the sentences.

Exercise 1. With books closed, listen to and repeat each sentence again.

Practice. Answer these questions in writing using *after.*

1. Were you named after someone?
2. Do you know of any building or public place that was named after someone or something?
3. What about cars?
4. What does it mean when someone or something is named after someone or something?

Lesson 5a. After: because of

Example Sentences. With books open, listen to and repeat each sentence as it is read to you.

1. After this severe winter, we've decided to move south.
2. After Audrey burned the steaks three times in a row, she now cooks only fish for dinner.
3. After all this rain, we're sure to have a good corn crop.
4. After breaking her ankle twice, she no longer skates professionally.
5. After her rudeness to him, he never called her again.

Now write the *after* phrases.

Exercise 1. With books closed, listen to and repeat each sentence again.

Practice. Think of something that you've done because of something else that happened. Write a sentence about it using the preposition *after.* Then take turns sharing the sentences with the class.

Exercise 2. Use the written *after* phrases to complete these sentences.

1. Audrey now cooks only fish for dinner _____ .

2. She no longer skates professionally _____ .

3. We're sure to have a good corn crop _____ .

4. We've decided to move south _____ .

5. He never called her again _____ .

Lesson 5b. After: despite, regardless of

Example Sentences. With books open, listen to and repeat each sentence as it is read to you.

1. After years of studying English, she never spoke it in conversation.
2. After all their criticism of the house, they bought it.
3. After his great success, he still wanted more.
4. After all the time she spent in her garden, nothing grew.
5. After being told he would always be in a wheelchair, he now walks three miles a day.

Exercise 1. With books closed, listen to and repeat each sentence again.

Practice. Complete these sentences using *after* phrases of your own choosing.

1. _____ , he never became a doctor.

2. _____ , she was not a very good typist.

3. _____ , they finally went on a cruise.

4. _____ , he won the championship.

5. _____ , she still wasn't satisfied.

Lesson 6. After: in search of, so as to get or catch

Example Sentences. With books open, listen to and repeat each sentence as it is read to you.

1. Ed chased after the tennis ball.
2. The miners sought after gold.
3. The tiger crept after the baby zebra.
4. We hurried after the mailman to give him the letter.
5. The police are after the criminal.
6. The archaeologists are after ancient artifacts.
7. The researchers are after a cure for cancer.
8. The journalists are after news.

Now write the *after* phrases.

Exercise 1. With books closed, listen to and repeat each sentence again.

Practice. Answer these questions in unison. What are these people or animals after? competing teams? a dog in a garbage can? shoppers at a sale? researchers in a library? a cat in a spring garden?

Exercise 2. Complete these sentences using your written *after* phrases.

1. The researchers are _____ .

2. Ed chased _____ .

3. The archaeologists are _____ .

4. We hurried _____ .

5. The journalists _____ .

6. The police are _____ .

7. The tiger crept _____ .

8. The miners sought _____ .

Lesson 7. After: following continuously

Example Sentences. With books open, listen to and repeat each sentence as it is read to you.

1. Day after day she waited for her daughter to call.
2. The war went on, year after year.
3. The boring lecture continued, hour after hour.
4. Time after time she missed the ball; finally she hit it.

Now write the phrases containing *after.*

Exercise 1. With books closed, listen to and repeat each sentence again.

Practice. Think of some of the things in your life that happen day after day/year after year/hour after hour. Write about these things in sentences. Then take turns reading them to the class.

Exercise 2. Use the written *after* phrases to answer these questions aloud, in turn.

1. How long did the boring lecture continue?
2. How often did she miss the ball?
3. How long did the war go on?
4. How long did she wait for her daughter to call?

Lesson 8. After (all): in spite of everything

Example Sentences. With books open, listen to and repeat each sentence as it is read to you.

1. Mabel was right about the mistake on the bill after all. (Nobody had believed her.)
2. See! It snowed after all! I said it was going to, but no one believed me.
3. He moved to Arizona after all. (He had always said he wouldn't.)
4. We thought the tree would die after being struck by lightning, but it lived after all.

Exercise 1. With books closed, listen to and repeat each sentence again.

Practice. Write one complete sentence using *after all* as used in the examples. Then take turns reading the sentences to the class.

Lesson 9. After (all): don't forget that

Example Sentences. With books closed, listen to and repeat each sentence as it is read to you.

1. Of course she makes mistakes in grammar; after all, she's only been in this country a short time.
2. It's no surprise that she's nervous about giving a speech; after all, she's never given one before.
3. Yes, I'm sleepy. After all, it's only four o'clock in the morning!
4. Why shouldn't I complain to the manager? After all, the food was terrible!

Exercise 1. With books closed, listen to and repeat each sentence again.

Practice. Write one sentence using *after all* as used in the examples. Then take turns reading the sentences to the class.

Lesson 10. After: past the hour of (See unit 12 for prepositions to use for time.)

Example Sentences. With books open, listen to and repeat each sentence as it is read to you.

1. The bus stops at this corner at twenty after seven.
2. The weather report comes on this station at five after the hour.
3. The fireworks began at one second after midnight.
4. The lunch crowd comes in right after noon.

Now write the sentences.

Exercise 1. With books closed, listen to and repeat each sentence again.
Practice. Make up answers to these questions using *after.*

1. When are you counted late for class?
2. When do you usually have lunch?
3. When does the traffic report come on TV?
4. When do you leave class?

Section C: Behind

Lesson 1. Behind: toward the back of or at

Example Sentences. With books open, listen to and repeat each sentence as it is read to you.

1. The broom is behind the door.
2. Terry hid the letter behind the mirror.
3. Tom heard a car horn honking behind him on the highway.
4. We drove into the country and left our worries behind us.
5. She suspected anger behind his smooth words.

Now write the *behind* phrases.

Exercise 1. With books closed, listen to and repeat each sentence again.

Practice. Answer these questions in complete sentences using *behind*.

1. If you heard footsteps behind you on a dark night, what would you do?
2. You have two posters. You want to keep them both, but you only have room for one. What could you do?
3. What are some things that you could keep behind a door?
4. Why would a family leave their dog behind them when they move to another country?

Exercise 2. Use the written *behind* phrases to answer these questions in complete sentences.

1. Where did we leave our worries?
2. Where did Tom hear the car horn honking?
3. Where did she suspect anger?
4. Where is the broom?
5. Where did Terry hide the letter?

> *To Remember:*
> Lives of great men all remind us
> We can make our lives sublime,
> And, departing, leave behind us
> Footprints in the sands of time.
>
> —Henry Wadsworth Longfellow, "Resignation"

Lesson 2. Behind: later than, less advanced than

Example Sentences. With books open, listen to and repeat each sentence as it is read to you.

1. Our team is behind the Tigers, 7–0.
2. We're three days behind schedule.
3. They are never behind on their rent.
4. I'm behind on my history reading.
5. Valerie was four laps behind the lead runner.

Now write the sentences.

Exercise 1. With books closed, listen to and repeat each sentence again.

Practice. Write a sentence telling about when you have been behind someone, or behind on something. Then take turns reading the sentences to the class.

To Remember:
If Winter comes, can Spring be far behind?

—Percy Bysshe Shelley, "Ode to the West Wind"

Lesson 3. Behind: in support of

Example Sentences. With books open, listen to and repeat each sentence as it is read to you.

1. The employees stood behind their boss when the company president criticized him.
2. Even though our candidate lost the election, we're still behind her.
3. The majority of the people stand behind the government reforms.
4. Marie stood behind her friend when he was in trouble.

Now write the *behind* phrases.

Exercise 1. With books closed, listen to and repeat each sentence again.

Practice. Answer this question in a complete sentence using *behind.* If you believe in someone/something very strongly and want to show your support, what do you do?

Exercise 2. Use the written *behind* phrases in complete sentences to answer these questions.

1. How do the majority of the people feel about government reforms?
2. What did the employees do when the company president criticized their boss?
3. What did Marie do when her friend was in trouble?
4. Even though our candidate lost the election, how do we stand?

Exercise 3. Take turns reading your completed sentences to the class.

Review

Reading Passage 1. Listen, with books closed.

Ned had worked for the Price Company since just before his twenty-second birthday. The company was named after Harold Price, its founder. After all these years, Ned knew he was in trouble. He had been falling behind in his work because he was always late, hungry, and tired. A bad habit was behind his problem.

Ned never had time to eat breakfast because, ever since he had begun watching the late-night talk show on TV, he went back to sleep in the morning after turning off his alarm clock. So day after day he came to the office late and hungry. He was also tired because, after all, the talk show lasted until 1:00 A.M.

One morning he walked into the Price Building (also named after his boss) just before Harold Price himself. Mr. Price called after him. "Ned, I'd like to speak to you after the staff meeting this morning," he said.

Ned felt sick. He sat down behind his desk and put his head in his hands. Before long he was asleep. He had an awful dream. He dreamed about sitting down to a big breakfast of fruit and cereal, ham and English muffins, but before eating even a bite of it, an alarm clock rang and the food disappeared. This happened time after time until he was starving. Then the talk show host began chasing after him, waving his late reports.

When Ned woke up it was a few minutes after nine. He had missed the staff meeting. Dennis, a fellow worker, came out of the meeting room before the rest of the salesmen. Ned had told him about his problem and about his being called before the boss.

"I'll stand behind you if you need me," said Dennis. "Don't worry, everything will be all right." But Ned didn't believe him.

Ned had never been so nervous before that awful time he stood before Mr. Price. Before hearing what Mr. Price had to say, Ned said, "I know I'm behind in my reports, and that everyone else in the office is way ahead of me in sales, but after all, they get plenty of sleep and a good breakfast before coming to work."

"Well, Ned," said Mr. Price, who was holding something behind his back, "I hear you sit in front of the TV set until after 1:00 A.M. every night and skip breakfast because you go back to sleep after turning off your alarm clock."

Ned nodded, sure that he knew what was behind all of this talk: he would be looking for a new job before long.

"I have something to give you, Ned. But before that, I want you to promise me something: never stay up after 11:00 P.M. on work nights. After all, there are times when sleep must come before TV."

"Agreed," said Ned.

Mr. Price held out a package before him. Ned took it and read the directions: "This is a non-stop alarm clock that cannot be turned off before sensing the smell of coffee and toast."

"So you must get up and fix breakfast before it will turn off!" said Mr. Price, laughing instead of being annoyed.

So Dennis had been right, after all. Everything was going to be all right. After this, he would put his bad habits behind him.

Now take turns reading the passage, sentence by sentence.

Turn to Missing Links, page 265.

Unit 10
Between, Among, Around, Along

Section A: Between

Lesson 1. Between: to show that two things are separated

Example Sentences. With books open, listen to and repeat each sentence as it is read to you.

1. Lidia sat between her two children.
2. Ida pressed the flower between two pages of a book.
3. The walls between the rooms were thin.
4. Leann put cheese between two slices of bread.
5. The swing hung between two trees.
6. Jaime hid the quarter between his shoe and his sock.
7. The books between the bookends were very old.
8. The aquarium is between the park and the river.

Now write the *between* phrases.

Exercise 1. With books closed, listen to and repeat each sentence again.

Practice. In groups, discuss situations where these expressions could be used: *between a rock and a hard place* (whatever decision one makes, or whichever way one goes, the result will be difficult); *between the ears; between the covers of a book; between jobs.*

Exercise 2. Use the written *between* phrases to answer these questions.

1. Where did Jaime hide the quarter?
2. Where did Ida press the flower?
3. Where is the aquarium?
4. Where did Lidia sit?
5. Where did the swing hang?
6. Where were the thin walls?
7. Where were the old books?
8. Where did Leann put the cheese?

Practice. Write three sentences using *between* as it is used in the example sentences. Then take turns reading the sentences to the class.

> *To Remember:*
> The meaning of true valor lies between the extremes of cowardice and rashness.
> —Cervantes

Lesson 2. Between: to be shared by, with the cooperation of

Example Sentences. With books open, listen to and repeat each sentence as it is read to you.

1. The mother divided the rice between her two children.
2. Our parents divided the housework between them.
3. Between the pilot and copilot, they made a smooth landing.
4. Between the two of us, we make enough money to live comfortably.
5. Between Judy and Joe, the house will be painted perfectly.
6. We only had seven dollars between us, so we didn't eat out.

Write the *between* phrases.

Exercise 1. With books closed, listen to and repeat each sentence again.

Practice. Using your classroom, your work, or your home as a background, write a sentence using *between* in this way.

Exercise 2. With books closed, use your written *between* phrases to complete these sentences.

1. _____ , they made a smooth landing.

2. _____ , the house will be painted perfectly.

3. Our parents divided the housework _____ .

4. We only had seven dollars _____ , so we didn't eat out.

5. The mother divided the rice _____ .

6. _____ , we make enough money to live comfortably.

Exercise 3. Take turns reading the completed sentences to the class.

Lesson 3. Between: used when choosing or deciding one out of two

---

Example Sentences. With books open, listen to and repeat each sentence as it is read to you.

1. I couldn't decide between chocolate and vanilla ice cream.
2. Elliot had to choose between the red and the white tie.
3. She was offered two jobs and had to decide between them.
4. We have to make a decision between the two schools.
5. It's hard to make a choice between these books. They both look interesting.

Now write the sentences.

Exercise 1. With books closed, listen to and repeat each sentence again.

Practice. Make up questions using *between.* Then, in groups, ask each other the questions and discuss the answers. (An example question is, "If you had to choose between cooking an elegant five-course dinner at home and going to a restaurant for barbequed chicken as someone's guest, which would you choose?)

Exercise 2. Complete these sentences using your own ideas.

1. I couldn't decide between _____ .

2. Jim had to choose between _____ .

3. We had to make a decision between _____ .

4. It's hard to make a choice between _____ .

Exercise 3. Take turns reading the sentences to the class.

Lesson 4. Between: connected in space

Example Sentences. With books open, listen to and repeat each sentence as it is read to you.

1. Clint crossed the yard between their houses.
2. The path between the cottage and the lake was steep.
3. The airline had a shuttle between Orlando and Miami.
4. The hall between the front and back doors was narrow.
5. The silence between them was uncomfortable.
6. There was very little crawl space between the ceiling and the roof.

Now write *between* plus the article and noun preceding it in each sentence.

Exercise 1. With books closed, listen to and repeat each sentence again.

Practice. Discuss these questions in groups.

1. How many feet/yards/meters would you guess are between this building and the next one?
2. Have you ever felt uncomfortable because of a silence between you and another person?
3. If you are separated from your family by a great distance, how could you express this using *between*?

Exercise 2. Use the written articles and nouns plus *between* to complete these sentences.

1. _____ them was uncomfortable.

2. Clint crossed _____ their houses.

3. _____ the front and back doors was narrow.

4. _____ the cottage and the lake was steep.

5. The airline has _____ Orlando and Miami.

6. There was very little crawl space _____ .

Exercise 3. Take turns reading the completed sentences to the class.

Lesson 5. Between: a difference in time, kind, or degree

Example Sentences. With books open, listen to and repeat each sentence as it is read to you.

1. The temperature has been between seventy and eighty degrees all summer.
2. There's a big difference between Italian and Japanese cooking.
3. Between Monday and Thursday they reroofed the house.
4. That dress costs between one and two hundred dollars, depending on where you shop.
5. Between January 1 and December 31, he grew four inches.

Now write the sentences.

Exercise 1. With books closed, listen to and repeat each sentence again.

Practice. Write the answers to these questions. Then take turns sharing them with the class.

1. If you wanted to have your house painted by Friday, and the painter who is painting your house said, "Between now and then I should be able to finish the job," what time frame would he be referring to?
2. Using *between,* write a sentence or two telling how the way you cook and the way Americans cook are different.
3. What is the average winter temperature in your native country? Use a low and a high temperature with *between.*

To Remember:
Between the dark and the daylight,
When the night is beginning to lower,
Comes a pause in the day's occupations,
That is known as the Children's Hour.

—Henry Wadsworth Longfellow, "The Children's Hour"

Lesson 6. Between: privately shared information

Practice.

S1: Just between you and me, I think this art exhibit is terrible!

S2: Unfortunately, your opinion is no longer just between us. The artist is standing right next to you.

Example Sentences. With books open, listen to and repeat each sentence as it is read to you.

1. Remember, this information is just between you and me.
2. They kept the secret between them; no one else knew anything about it.
3. Just between us, I think he's crazy!
4. You have to read between the lines to understand what she's really saying.
5. The two friends had an understanding between them.

Now write the sentences.

Exercise 1. With books closed, listen to and repeat each sentence again.

Practice. Why would you say, "This is just between us," when you tell something to your friend?

Section B: Among

Lesson 1. Among: in the middle of, surrounded by

Example Sentences. With books open, listen to and repeat each sentence as it is read to you.

1. She's like a flower among weeds.
2. He found the letter among his old papers.
3. The baby crawled among his many toys.
4. Dollar bills were scattered among the leaves.
5. The children were lost among the crowd.
6. Grandma sat like a queen among all her grandchildren.

Now write the *among* phrases.

Exercise 1. With books closed, listen to and repeat each sentence again.

Exercise 2. Use the written *among* phrases to complete these sentences.

1. The baby crawled _____ .

2. Grandma sat like a queen _____ .

3. The children were lost _____ .

4. She's like a flower _____ .

5. He found the letter _____ .

6. Dollar bills were scattered _____ .

Exercise 3. Take turns reading the completed sentences to the class.

> *To Remember:*
> Among the changing months, May stands confessed
> The sweetest, and in fairest colors dressed.
>
> —James Thomson, "On May"

Lesson 2. Among: in the group, one of

Example Sentences. With books open, listen to and repeat each sentence as it is read to you.

1. She's among the few astrophysicists in the state.
2. He ranks among the best tennis players of the decade.
3. That plane is among the last of the DC3's still flying.
4. That girl is among the top two percent of her class.
5. Helen Hayes was among the finest of all American actresses.
6. She's just one among many who dislike that TV show.

Now write *among* plus the next two words in the sentences.

Exercise 1. With books closed, listen to and repeat each sentence again.

Practice. In groups, think of the one person among all the people you know who stands out in your mind as being special in some way. Take turns telling the group about that person using this form: Among all the people I know, _____ is/has the _____ .

Exercise 2. Use the written *among* phrases to make up other sentences of your own. Then take turns reading your sentences to the class.

> *To Remember:*
> Among the blind, the one-eyed man is king.
>
> —Anonymous

Lesson 3. Among: when things are shared by more than two

Example Sentences. With books open, listen to and repeat each sentence as it is read to you.

1. Deal the cards among all the players.
2. Distribute the food among the poor families.
3. Divide the money among the five workers.
4. The father apportioned his land evenly among his children.

Now write the *among* phrases.

> *Note: Between* is sometimes used (instead of *among*) when speaking of more than two (i.e., Mary, Allen, and Nita had only seven dollars between them, so they didn't eat out.) This is not really grammatically correct, but it is becoming acceptable.

Exercise 1. With books closed, listen to and repeat each sentence again.

Exercise 2. Divide the class into two sides. Side A should read the sentences up to *among* in any order. Group B, with books closed, should complete the sentences with the written phrases. Then switch sides and repeat the exercise.

Lesson 4. Among: other usages

Example Sentences. With books open, listen to and repeat each sentence as it is read to you.

1. with each other
   a. The children fought among themselves over the toys.
   b. We talked the problem over among ourselves.
2. by cooperating
   a. We should be able to raise the money among us.
   b. Among them, they achieved peace for their nations.
3. with many, with all
   a. That song is popular among teenagers.
   b. Bowing is customary among the Japanese.

Now write the sentences.

> *Note: Amid* is similar in meaning to *among* when defined as: *surrounded by or in the middle of* (e.g., a place of quiet amid the noises of the city). However, it is used in literature more often than in informal speech.

Exercise 1. With books closed, listen to and repeat each sentence again.

Exercise 2. In four of the example sentences *between* would be an acceptable usage. Can you find the two sentences in which it would not? Compare answers as a class.

To Remember:
Falsehoods (lies) not only disagree with truths, but usually quarrel among themselves.
—Daniel Webster

Review

Exercise 1. After filling in the blanks, take turns reading the sentences to the class.

1. The game was _____ the Kangaroos and the Frogs.

2. The Kangaroos were _____ the lowest scorers in the league. The Frogs were not much better.

3. _____ the third and fourth quarters, I walked _____ the fans looking for my friends.

4. I finally found them _____ the people at the concession stand.

5. My friend, Kenji, is very tall, so he was easy to find, even _____ all those people.

6. We only had a little money _____ us, but we were thirsty.

7. We had to choose _____ twelve different kinds of soda.

8. A Cub Scout was standing _____ a group of other scouts.

9. His hot dog slid out from _____ the sides of the bun.

10. It rolled _____ his feet, _____ the slats of the railing, and onto the stands below.

11. An older boy from _____ a group of Frog fans started a fight with a Kangaroo fan.

12. I stepped _____ them and got punched _____ the eyes.

13. Nearby, a young woman was standing _____ two men who were loudly asking her for a date.

14. She couldn't seem to make up her mind _____ them.

15. As the shouting continued _____ them, she tried to disappear _____ the fans, but the crowd was as solid as a brick wall.

16. Kenji and I went to her rescue: _____ us, we helped her escape.

17. When we returned to the game, the referee was holding the whistle _____ his teeth to signal the last play. The final score was 6 to 0.

18. We decided _____ us that the activity _____ the people in the refreshment area had been more exciting than the game.

Section C: Around

Lesson 1a. Around: on the edge or boundary of something (no circular progression)

Example Sentences. With books open, listen to and repeat each sentence as it is read to you.

1. The family sat around the table and talked.
2. The pansies grew around the edge of the flower bed.
3. We saw seventeen cottages around the lake.
4. The desks formed a circle around the classroom.
5. The lace around the hem of Shelly's dress was from France.

Now write the *around* phrases.

Exercise 1. With books closed, listen to and repeat each sentence again.

Practice. Write complete sentences to answer the questions, using *around*.

1. When you are camping out with a group of people, where do you often sit and sing songs after dinner?
2. At a party where someone is playing the piano, where do people stand and sing?

Exercise 2. Use your written *around* phrases to answer these questions in complete sentences.

1. Where did the pansies grow?
2. Where did the desks form a circle?
3. Where did the family sit?
4. Where was the lace?
5. Where were the cottages?

Lesson 1b. Around: so as to enclose or encircle something

Example Sentences. With books open, listen to and repeat each sentence as it is read to you.

1. Billy drew a circle around his name.
2. She wore a ribbon around her neck.
3. Did you see the ring around the moon?
4. The moats around castles were for protection.
5. The fishermen threw a net around the shark.

Now write the *around* phrases.

Exercise 1. With books closed, listen to and repeat each sentence again.

Practice. Answer the questions with complete sentences; using *around.*

1. When you wrap a package, where do you put the string?
2. Where do you wear a belt?
3. If you wanted privacy, where would you build a wall?
4. Where would you put a dog's collar?

Exercise 2. Use your written *around* phrases in complete sentences to answer these questions.

1. Where was the ring?
2. Where did the fishermen throw a net?
3. Where were the moats?
4. Where did Billy draw a circle?
5. Where did she wear a ribbon?

Lesson 1c. Around: encircling a central point (used when expressing movement or progress)

Example Sentences. With books open, listen to and repeat each sentence as it is read to you.

1. The Orfields traveled around the world.
2. The earth revolves around the sun.
3. Spaceships orbit around the earth.
4. The horses galloped around the track.
5. Will walked around the block.

Now write the *around* phrases.

Exercise 1. With books closed, listen to and repeat each sentence again.

Practice. Answer the questions in writing using *around,* and then compare your answers with the student next to you.

1. If you start at the entrance to a park and walk on the outside border of the park grounds until you reach the entrance again, what have you done?
2. What has the minute hand of a clock done when it moves from twelve to twelve?

Exercise 2. Use your written *around* phrases to complete these sentences.

1. Will walked _____ .

2. Spaceships orbit _____ .

3. The Orfields traveled _____ .

4. The horses galloped _____ .

5. The earth revolves _____ .

Exercise 3. Take turns reading the completed sentences to the class.

Lesson 2. Around: here and there, on or to various places
within, near

Example Sentences. With books open, listen to and repeat each sentence as it is read to you.

1. I know my keys are around here somewhere; I had them a minute ago.
2. Bumblebees are buzzing around the garden.
3. Several new houses are being built around the neighborhood.
4. We drove all around town looking for our lost dog.
5. The rumors going around the office aren't true.

Now write the *around* phrases.

Exercise 1. With books closed, listen to and repeat each sentence again.

Practice. Answer the questions in unison.

1. If you walked from your desk to the window, from the window to the door, from the door to the board, from the board to the middle of the room, and from the middle of the room to the teacher's desk, what would you be doing?
2. If you saw a butterfly flying to many different flowers in a garden, what could you say the butterfly was doing?

Practice. Use the *around* phrases to write sentences telling about people or things that are *here and there.* Take turns reading your sentences to the class.

Lesson 3. Around: on or to the farther side of

Example Sentences. With books open, listen to and repeat each sentence as it is read to you.

1. The park is around the next corner.
2. The pilot flew around the storm.
3. The giant tree is around the bend in the road.
4. Around the hill you'll see the river.
5. The garage is around the house to the right.
6. It's faster to take the toll road around the city than to drive through it.

Now write the *around* phrases.

Practice. Answer the questions in unison.

1. What's another way to say *he turned the corner*?
2. If you are driving and see a big box in the middle of the road, what could you do?
3. The moving people are delivering a refrigerator to your house. They come to the front door to tell you that they're there. Since the kitchen is right next to the back door, what would you say?

Exercise 1. With books closed, listen to and repeat each sentence again.

Exercise 2. Use your written *around* phrases to answer these questions. Then take turns reading the answers in complete sentences.

1. Where is the park?
2. Where will we see the river?
3. Where did the plane fly?
4. Where is the giant tree?
5. Where is the garage?
6. What is it faster to do?

Section D: Along

Lesson 1. Along: in a line or at a point next to the length of

Example Sentences. With books open, listen to and repeat each sentence as it is read to you.

1. We walked along the river to the town.
2. She planted flowers along both sides of the driveway.
3. They saw no one along the way to town.
4. Joyce lives in a house along the shore.
5. The signs along the highway were brightly lit.

Now write the *along* phrases.

Exercise 1. With books closed, listen to and repeat each sentence again.

Practice. Write answers in complete sentences using *along*. Then compare your completed sentences with the student next to you.

1. If you wanted to measure a room, where would you place the tape measure?
2. Where do *feeder streets* run?
3. Where are pictures in an art gallery usually hung?
4. If you were walking in the sand following the waterline of the ocean, where would you say you were walking?

Exercise 2. Use your written *along* phrases to answer these questions.

1. Where were the signs brightly lit?
2. Where did we walk?
3. Where did she plant the flowers?
4. Where does Joyce live?
5. Where did they see no one?

Review

Exercise 1. After filling in the blanks, take turns reading the sentences to the class.

1. David put a scarf _____ his neck.

2. Lissa walked _____ the house looking for her skates.

3. The trees _____ the path were heavy with snow.

4. _____ the corner they saw the park.

5. Several squirrels were hopping _____ the trees looking for nuts.

6. A dog was running in circles _____ them.

7. The skating pond had a rope _____ it.

8. Signs _____ the edge of the pond said *Thin Ice.*

9. "That ice can't be thin. The weatherman said it's _____ 10 and 20 degrees," said David.

10. "Mr. Parks, the groundskeeper, must be here somewhere." said Lissa. "He doesn't know how cold it is. Let's try skating _____ the edge."

11. The dog dashed onto the ice and ran _____ two squirrels in the middle of the pond.

12. The ice began to crack all _____ the dog.

13. Mr. Parks appeared _____ the corner of the skating shed.

14. He threw a lasso _____ the dog's neck and dragged him out.

15. Mr. Parks said, "A hot-water pipe _____ the edge of the pond is broken. If you want to get to the other side of the pond, don't go across it, go _____ it."

16. Later, David, Lissa, and Mr. Parks sat _____ the stove in the skating shed and drank hot chocolate. (The dog had a wiener.)

Exercise 2. Write the story, in paragraph form, in your own words.

Unit 11
Like, As, Up, Down

Section A: Like

Lesson 1a. Like: similar to, having the characteristics of

Practice.

S1: Hi, Asumi. Where's Maki?

S2: I'm Maki. Asumi's in class.

S1: You look just like her. You must be twins.

S2: Actually we're triplets. Hiromi looks just like Asumi and me.

Example Sentences. With books open, listen to and repeat each sentence as it is read to you.

1. The 16th of October was like a summer day.
2. That coat looks like real fur, but it's fake.
3. My daughter, Margaret, looks like her grandmother.
4. That rice smells like popcorn.
5. Tuna sometimes tastes like chicken.
6. His voice sounds like Frank's. I get them mixed up on the phone.
7. This fabric feels like silk, but it's rayon.
8. Your computer is just like mine.

Now write the *like* phrases.

Exercise 1. With books closed, listen to and repeat each sentence again.

Practice. Do you know anyone who looks like someone else? Write a complete sentence comparing those persons using the preposition *like*. Take turns reading your sentences to the class.

Practice. In the middle of September, in Tucson, Arizona, the temperature dropped to thirty degrees and snow began to fall. Write a sentence using *like* to describe the day. Then discuss today's weather with your classmates, comparing it to the weather in your own countries. Use *like* in your comparisons.

Practice. Your friend shows you a briefcase she has just bought for twenty-five dollars. You say, "That's a great buy. It looks like real leather." What other things can you buy for less money because they are made of less expensive material? Discuss with your classmates. Use *like* in your comparisons.

Practice. Write sentences about other things you can think of that look, smell, taste, feel, or sound like something else.

> *Note:* We often say that someone or something *reminds* us of someone or something else. This is usually because they share similar qualities or characteristics, i.e., they are *alike* in some way.

Exercise 2. Place a link where *like* belongs.

1. That rice smells popcorn.
2. Your computer is just mine.
3. It looks real fur, but it's fake.
4. His voice sounds Frank's.
5. My daughter, Margaret, looks her grandmother.
6. Tuna sometimes tastes chicken.
7. This fabric feels just silk, but it's rayon.
8. The 16th of October was a summer day.

Lesson 1b. Like: as used in similes after action words

Example Sentences. With books open, listen to and repeat each sentence as it is read to you.

1. Karl ate like a starving man.
2. The lights twinkled like fireflies.
3. The tired workers slept like logs.
4. Money slipped through his fingers like sand.
5. Kristina played tennis like a pro (professional).
6. The kitten leaped like a tiger.
7. The children flapped their arms like geese.
8. She walked like a queen.

Now write the *like* phrases.

Exercise 1. With books closed, listen to and repeat each sentence again.

Practice. Write sentences using some of these phrases (or any other action words plus *like* phrases you can think of): run like the wind; spread like wildfire; cry like a baby; grow like weeds.

Practice. If you can think of similar phrases in your native language, write them in English and share them with the class.

Lesson 1c. Like: typical of, in the manner of

Example Sentences. With books open, listen to and repeat each sentence as it is read to you.

1. Like most cats, Pumpkin was quite independent.
2. I'm not surprised at her kindness. It's just like her.
3. Like many Italians, Lucia has a great singing voice.
4. It's not like Dmitri to be so grouchy.
5. Like most beginning skiers, we fell many times.

Now write the *like* phrases.

Exercise 1. With books closed, listen to and repeat each sentence again.

Practice. Write a description of how you felt on your first day of class. Begin the sentence with *like most students.*

Practice. Think of how someone you know often acts. Would you be surprised if you heard that he/she had acted that way again? Write a complete sentence using *like* to tell why not.

Exercise 2. Complete the sentences with the *like* phrases you have written.

1. I'm not surprised at her kindness. It's just _____.
2. _____ , Pumpkin was quite independent.
3. _____ , we fell many times.
4. It's not _____ to be so grouchy.
5. _____ , Lucia has a great singing voice.

Lesson 2. Like: used to show probability of something happening in the future based on available information

Example Sentences. With books open, listen to and repeat each sentence as it is read to you.

1. The first freeze is early; it looks like a long, hard winter ahead.
2. From the crowds in the malls, it looks like a successful sale.
3. We're already flying over the mountains; it looks like an early arrival time for us.
4. The stars are brilliant. It looks like another cloudless night.
5. From the long lines, it looks like at least an hour's wait.

   Note: If a full clause containing a verb follows *like,* it is more acceptable to use *as if* or *as though* instead of *like,* e.g., it looks as though we're going to have a long, hard winter.

Now write the *like* phrases, preceded by *it.*

Exercise 1. With books closed, listen to and repeat each sentence again.

Practice. If someone says, "It looks like a perfect day for the beach," what time of day would it be? If you read in the newspaper that "It looks like another winning season for the Braves," would it be the beginning or the end of the baseball season? Discuss as a class.

Lesson 3. Like: used with *felt;* be in the mood for; be in a certain state of mind (followed by *-ing* words)

Example Sentences. With books open, listen to and repeat each sentence as it is read to you.

1. Patrick felt like sleeping longer, but he had an early class.
2. Shiko felt like taking a vacation.
3. We all felt like cheering, but we had to sit silently.
4. Maybe our teachers feel like going home, too.

Now write the *like* phrases.

Exercise 1. With books closed, listen to and repeat each sentence as it is read to you again.

Practice. Write the answers to these questions and then take turns sharing them with the class.

1. What do you feel like doing when your feet hurt?
2. What do you feel like doing on a hot day in July?
3. What do you feel like doing after you've eaten a big dinner?
4. What do you feel like doing on the last day of school?

Lesson 4. Like: for example

Example Sentences. With books open, listen to and repeat each sentence as it is read to you.

1. The boy kept reptiles, like snakes, lizards, and turtles, for pets.
2. The children visited lots of interesting places, like the Museum of Natural History and the Space Center.
3. Citrus fruits, like oranges and grapefruit, are good sources of vitamin C.
4. Spectator sports, like football and basketball, are his favorite recreation.
5. Some trees, like pines and live oaks, are green all year.

Now write the *like* phrases.

Exercise 1. With books closed, listen to and repeat each sentence again.

Practice. Complete these sentences using *like* plus examples of your choice.

1. Some school courses, like _____ , are more difficult than others.

2. Many games, like _____ , can be played with a deck of cards.

3. In several countries, like _____ , Spanish is the main language.

4. Using different vegetables, like _____ , make a salad more interesting.

Exercise 2. Complete these sentences with the written *like* phrases.

1. Some trees, _____ , are green all year.

2. Citrus fruits, _____ , are good sources of vitamin C.

3. The children visited lots of interesting places, _____ .

4. The boy kept reptiles for pets, _____ .

5. Spectator sports, _____ , are his favorite recreation.

Review

Reading Passage 1. Listen, with books closed.

My teacher says her grandmother looks just like pictures of Martha Washington. That's just like her—she's always saying someone looks like someone else. She told me I look like my mother. I asked lots of people, like my sister and my brother and my best friend, if they thought I look like my mother, and they said no—I look like my father. Since I'm a boy and not very pretty, my mother should be glad about that.

I may look like my father, but I sure can't pitch a baseball like he does. From my record of strikeouts and walks, it looks like years of practice ahead of me. Sometimes I feel like giving up, but my father says that everyone feels like that sometimes, but that if I keep on trying I'll soon be playing like a pro. It's like him to be encouraging, and I believe he's right.

Turn to Missing Links, page 266.

Section B: As

Lesson 1. As

Note: The word *as* is a preposition when it is used to tell in what way someone or something is acting or is used. It means *in the role of.*

Example Sentences. With books open, listen to and repeat as each sentence is read to you.

1. Oleg works as a lifeguard during summer vacations.
2. The Kims use their extra bedroom as a study.
3. Marya volunteers as a tutor twice a week.
4. Brigitta uses her garage as a workshop.
5. Joanne acts as an interpreter at the hospital.

Now write the entire sentences.

Exercise 1. With books closed, listen to and repeat each sentence again.

Practice. In unison tell in what capacity you are here in this class. If you have ever been a volunteer or held a job, write a sentence about it using *as.* In turn, share the sentence with the class.

Exercise 2. Place a link where *as* belongs.

1. Brigitta uses her garage a workshop.
2. Joanne acts an interpreter at the hospital.

3. Oleg works a lifeguard during summer vacation.
4. The Kims use their extra bedroom a study.
5. Marya volunteers a tutor twice a week.

Review

Exercise 1. Fill in the blanks with *like* or *as* and then take turns reading the sentences aloud.

1. She worked _____ an usher in the theater.

2. The perfume smelled _____ roses.

3. Ivan spent the summer _____ a lighthouse keeper.

4. Some delicious foods, _____ ice cream, are high in fat.

5. Your shoes are _____ the ones I saw in the store.

6. The gym is also used _____ an auditorium.

7. He thinks of his students _____ his children.

8. Kurt felt _____ going for a walk.

9. Jinfen volunteered _____ an ambulance driver.

10. The cafeteria was used _____ a voting place.

11. The race car took off _____ lightning.

12. It looks _____ a long, hot summer.

13. It's just _____ Olena to send flowers; she's so thoughtful.

14. After working all night, we felt _____ sleeping all day.

15. Jeanne spends her weekends _____ a clown in a children's hospital.

16. Jari worked _____ a teacher during the day, and _____ a researcher at night.

17. The hail sounded _____ rocks falling on the roof.

18. Jimmy swims _____ a fish.

19. Miriam acts _____ a guide for the museum on Saturdays.

20. The old papers blew over the road _____ fallen leaves.

Section C: Up

Note: Up and *down* are used most often as adverbs or adjectives. The following sentences are examples of how they are used as prepositions.

1. from a lower to (or toward) a higher place
    a. From the first floor, go up the stairs to the third floor.
    b. The boys raced up the hill to the top.
    c. The squirrel left the acorn on the ground and hurried up the tree.
    d. It takes all day to climb up that mountain to the summit.

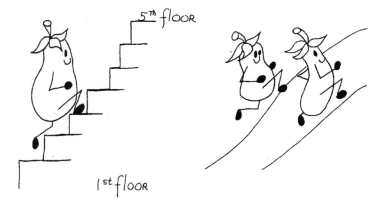

2. to or at a farther point along

    Note: This usage depends on the concept of direction, i.e., north is usually thought of as *up* and south as *down;* the source of something is usually thought of as *up* and its outlet as *down.*

    a. The church is about a mile up the road from here.
    b. If you continue up this path, you'll see the giant tree.
3. toward the beginning or source of
    a. Salmon swim up the Columbia River to spawn.
    b. We traveled up the Mississippi River toward St. Paul.

Exercise 1. Listen to and repeat each sentence. Write the sentences. Take turns reading the sentences to the class.

Section D: Down

1. from a higher to (or toward) a lower place
    a. From the fifth floor, go down the stairs to the second floor.
    b. The boys raced down the hill to the bottom.
    c. It takes all day to climb down the mountain to the foothills.
    d. The rain poured down the spout.

2. to or at a farther point along (See the note at *up.*)
    a. The church is about a mile down the road from here.
    b. If you continue down this path you will see the house.
3. toward the outlet or destination of
    a. The logs floated down the river toward the sea.
    b. They rowed down the creek to the river.

Exercise 1. Listen to and repeat each sentence. Write the sentences. Take turns reading the sentences to the class.

Unit 12
Time: During, Since, Until

Section A: During

Lesson 1. During: all through a period of time, while something else is happening, at some point in a period of time

---

Example Sentences. With books open, listen to and repeat each sentence as it is read to you.

1. I heard it raining during the night.
2. The poinsettia bloomed during the winter months.
3. They rested during the hottest hours of the day.
4. He had slept during class, so he failed the exam.
5. Many people were without jobs during the Depression.
6. The power went off for a minute during the president's speech.
7. She got the hiccups during class and had to leave the room.
8. The baby cried during takeoff, but stopped when his mother gave him a bottle of juice.

Now write the *during* phrases.

Exercise 1. With books closed, listen to and repeat the sentences again.

Practice.

S1: Did you go fishing during vacation?
S2: Yes, during the fourth of July weekend. How about you?
S1: Our family went deep sea fishing for a week during August. We only caught one fish during that whole time.
S2: Very expensive fish dinner!

HARD WORK
During spring we watch baseball,
During summer we're free,
During fall we watch football,
During winter we ski.
Because we're so busy during most of each day
We can't seem to find a minute to play.

232

Exercise 2. Using the written *during* phrases, complete these sentences.

1. Many people were without jobs _____ .

2. The ponsettias bloomed _____ .

3. The power went off for a minute _____ .

4. They rested _____ the hottest hours of the day.

Section B: Since

Lesson 1. Since: for the time following a past time or event up to the present
---

Example Sentences. With books open, listen to and repeat each sentence as it is read to you.

1. I'm hungry. I haven't eaten since breakfast.
2. She has written only one letter since February.
3. He has been unemployed since last year.
4. We haven't seen each other since our aunt's funeral.
5. They haven't been back to school since graduation.

Now write the *since* phrases.

Exercise 1. With books closed, listen to and repeat the sentences again.

Practice.

S1: I haven't seen Bill since early this morning. Where is he?

S2: He hasn't been feeling well since lunchtime. He's lying down in the clinic.

S1: That's funny. That's been happening since last week when he began making his own lunches.

S2: He offered me half of his sandwich—the same kind he's been bringing since Monday—but I declined.

S1: What kind was it, something awful like pepperoni with chocolate sauce?

S2: No, worse. Liver sausage with peanut butter.

Exercise 2. Write three sentences using *since* meaning *during a time in the past up to the present.*

Exercise 3. Complete the following sentences with the written *since* phrases.

1. She has written only one letter _____ .

2. They haven't been back to school _____ .

3. I'm hungry. I haven't eaten _____ .

4. He's been unemployed _____ .

5. We haven't seen each other _____ .

Section C: Until

Lesson 1a. Until: up to the time when, up to as late as

Example Sentences. With books open, listen to and repeat each sentence as it is read to you.

1. She waited until the intermission before she left.
2. They studied until midnight.
3. The students stayed outside until the end of the fire drill.
4. The fields are dry and brown until the rainy season.

Now write the *until* phrases.

Lesson 1b. Until: (as used with negatives) before a certain time

---

Example Sentences. With books open, listen to and repeat each sentence as it is read to you.

1. He didn't laugh until the clown's final appearance.
2. The store doesn't open until ten o'clock.
3. The play won't begin until the arrival of the star.
4. The children may not watch TV until the weekend.

Now write the *until* phrases.

Exercise 1. With books closed, listen to and repeat the sentences again.

Exercise 2. Write four sentences using *until,* two as in the examples from 1a, and two as in the examples from 1b.

Practice.

S1: Where were you? I told you not to go outside until 4 P.M.

S2: I know, but Angelo called and said he couldn't come over until the end of the English tape he had to listen to for homework. I walked over to his house because I was lonely.

S1: Well, because you disobeyed, you can't play with Angelo again until next week.

S2: Well, that's okay. Angelo stopped listening to his English tape and came outside when he saw me. Now he can't play with me until next month!

Exercise 3. Use *until* phrases to complete these sentences.

1. Study this sentence _____ .

2. Wait _____ before you go outside.

3. The store doesn't open _____ .

4. Don't leave _____ .

5. The students stayed at their desks _____ .

6. The play won't begin _____ .

7. They can't watch TV _____ .

Review

Reading Passage 1. Listen, with books closed.

The two sisters had not been back to their grandparents' house since 1991. They had both been working in foreign countries since college days. Both of their grandparents had died during the past year, and now Mary and Therese had come to get the house ready to sell. It had been raining in torrents since their arrival.

"I haven't seen such weather since the hurricane that blew across Mexico last year. Some good will come of it, though. They say it hasn't rained since May," said Mary.

Therese's dog was nervous and restless during the worst part of the storm, especially when the electricity went off.

"Don't worry, Angus," Therese said. "Wait until later and I'll get you something good to eat."

Just then it began to hail. It hailed until bedtime. Mary read by candlelight until almost midnight. Therese listened to her battery-operated radio until sign-off time. Angus waited patiently for his treat until finally giving up and going to sleep.

Sometime during the night the roof began to leak. The next morning, Mary and Therese mopped up puddles until their backs ached. Then they waited until the return of the electricity so they could heat some water for coffee. The telephone didn't work until noon.

The sun came out during the morning, so they spread out all the rugs to dry on the patio. The sisters hadn't spent so much time together since their childhood, and they enjoyed it very much.

During the hours of work, they talked and came to a decision. If it was so much fun being together during a storm, it would be even more fun to be together with their families during pleasant weather. Instead of selling the house, they would keep it. They planned to meet at the house again every year during the summer—but not until the leaky roof was repaired!

Turn to Missing Links, page 267.

Section D: More Time Prepositions

Review: In, At, On, For, From/To, Through, Between, By, About,
Around, Before, After, Over as they relate to time

In	*At*	*On*
in the morning	at dawn	on Monday
in the afternoon	at noon	on January 16
in the evening	at night	on Christmas day
in September	at six o'clock	on his birthday
in 1776	at midnight	

Other *time* expressions using prepositions:

In

in the present (now):	We should live in the present, not in the past.
in the past:	In the past, we seldom ate out. Now we often do.
in the future:	In the future, we will pay more taxes.
in a little while:	In a little while, the bell will ring.
in no time (very soon):	This train is very fast. We'll be in Osaka in no time.

Two expressions with *in* and *on* are used frequently:

in time, by the acceptable time, before it is too late:	We got to the theater just in time for the first act.
on time, at the designated time:	That airline always arrives on time.

At

at the present time (now):	At the present time we're living in Paris.
at one time (once, used to):	At one time I played the piano, but no more.
at that time (then):	She used to read three books a week. At that time she had more free time than she does now.
at this time (now):	I'm not able to help at this time. Call me again next week.
at the same time (simultaneously):	Betty and Bob arrived at the restaurant at the same time.
at no time (never):	At no time will this school allow dancing in the hall.

For

shows length of time:	We studied for five hours last night.
	They haven't been home for three years.

(Also: for a minute, for a second, for the rest of your life, for a little while, for a long time, etc.)

From/To

beginning at a specific time and ending at another:	He works from noon to midnight.
	From nine to ten every weekday we're in a meeting.

Through

without stopping, from beginning to end (similar to *From/To*):	She worked right through her lunch hour, so by evening she was hungry.

Between
used to separate two times (similar in meaning to *From/To*):

The baby usually sleeps between 7:00 P.M. and 7:00 A.M.
Mark sold eight suits between opening and closing time.

By
not later than

He has to have his report done by tomorrow.
By this time next week we'll be in London.

About
not exactly but close to the time of:

I don't have my watch on, but I think it's about nine o'clock.
Father always gets home about seven.

Around
used in the same way as *About,* to mean approximate time:

It was sometime around midnight that she heard the sound.
The mail usually arrives around ten o'clock.

Before
earlier than:

She woke up before dawn.
The day before yesterday was my birthday.

After
later than:

I can't keep my eyes open after 10:00 P.M.
Let's meet for coffee after work.

Over
throughout a period of time:

He wrote the book over a period of three years.
Over the years, he learned to control his temper.

Other Frequently Used Phrases with Time + Prepositions

Out of time
no more time left:

One person talked too long on the TV talk show.
They ran out of time and Harry didn't get to talk at all.
He didn't finish answering the last question on the test because he ran out of time.

Ahead of time
sooner than when something is planned or expected:

The first guests arrived ahead of time and we hadn't even finished setting the table.
She arrived at the concert two hours ahead of time to save good seats for the rest of us who came later.
I wish you had told me about my surprise party ahead of time; I would have at least combed my hair.

Behind time
later than scheduled:

Their flight is behind time because of the weather.
The mail is behind time because of the holidays.

In the nick of time
just in time:

He defused the bomb in the nick of time; a minute later and it would have blown up.

Time after time
again and again: She fell down time after time, but she finally learned to ski well.

From time to time
occasionally, at intervals: From time to time Harry would receive a letter from his old friend.

Against time
getting close to a time limit: The people worked against time to sandbag the levee.

Exercise 1. Write sentences of your own using each of the example sentences as models.

Exercise 2. Take turns telling the class if any of the above time phrases could be translated into your native language. Take turns writing one or more of these phrases on the board opposite the English phrase that means the same thing.

Missing Links

Missing Links Practice. Place a (∧) where the preposition belongs.

Unit 1. Section A: On

Lesson 1

Reading Passage 1 (p. 2)

The snow the ground is white and clean, and the ice the pond is smooth and thick. The woman the park bench has a smile her face. The boots her feet keep her toes warm. The gloves her hands keep her fingers warm. The skaters the pond glide gracefully. The children playing the slide are laughing. The joggers the path seem healthy and happy. What a wonderful day to be living this earth!

Reading Passage 2 (p. 3)

The houses First Street were painted orange. The houses Second Street were painted blue. The houses Third Street were painted yellow. The house the hill was painted purple. The sign the courthouse lawn read: Paintbrush, USA, population 147.

Reading Passage 3 (p. 3)

The cat the windowsill washed itself. It didn't see the mouse the floor. The bell the cat's collar jingled. The mouse saw the cat the windowsill and hurried home.

Lesson 2

Reading Passage 1 (p. 4)

One winter morning, my mother sprinkled powdered sugar a warm cake and went calling our new neighbor. the way it started to snow the rooftops, the trees, the sidewalk, and the cake. The snow looked like powdered sugar so no one knew the difference.

Reading Passage 2 (p. 5)

While my mother was gone, my baby brother poured a whole bottle of maple syrup his cereal. Then he dumped it the floor and was about to sit down it when I grabbed him and threw a towel the mess. My sister said I was a hero.

Lesson 3

Reading Passage 1 (p. 6)

The house the beach was empty. The gas station the highway was closed. The bait house the river was boarded up. No wonder, it was thirty-five degrees below zero!

Lesson 4

Reading Passage 1 (p. 8)

Most college freshmen complain that they gain weight dorm food so they boycott the dining hall. Of course they soon get hungry and fill up junk food.

Our daughter, Marcy, wrote: "It's impossible to stay a diet here, so a group of us decided to get some exercise. We pedaled to the park our bicycles and then explored the woods foot because there are no roads."

"That night we dined pizza, fried chicken, and hot fudge sundaes because we were starving after all that exercise. When we weighed ourselves the restaurant scale we didn't believe what it registered! It must have been out of order."

Lesson 5

Reading Passage 1 (p. 9)

Most boys' discussions center sports; some girls' discussions center people; the majority of ecologists' discussions center the environment; a lot of doctors' discussions center medicine; many artists' discussions center art; *all* dieters' discussions center food!

Lesson 6

Reading Passage 1 (p. 10)

Your business is the brink of bankruptcy. Your treasurer is trial for embezzling company funds; the workers the payroll have not been paid for three months; the chairman of the board is extended vacation; your vice president is sick leave; the bank has put your credit hold and told you to go a strict budget. This is no time to go a spending spree.

Reading Passage 2 (p. 10)

The weatherman said it was the worst storm record. The city workers were all emergency standby. The doctors call at the hospital were exhausted. But the mailman delivered the mail schedule.

Lesson 7

Reading Passage 1 (p. 11)

Sara is the refreshment committee. She has to plan an appreciation dinner for the teachers the faculty. She's a reporter the school paper, and she's also the yearbook staff. She's the dean's list, too. What a busy person!

Lesson 8

Reading Passage 1 (p. 12)

The Spanish explorers sailed westward the premise that India was west of Europe. They charted their course the calculations of the map makers. Depending their imperfect knowledge, they became lost.

After several weeks, the sailors continued acting orders even though they were discouraged. seeing land, they were relieved and thankful.

Lesson 10

Reading Passage 1 (p. 14)

We have to be at the bus stop time school days. Last week a rainy morning, our alarm clock didn't go off and we woke up late.

The buses run strictly schedule weekdays. When our bus didn't come time, we thought we had missed it. Then we remembered: it was July fourth. holidays we don't have to be schedule for anything. We went back to bed.

Lesson 11

Reading Passage 1 (p. 15)

a summer day ten years ago, June 15th to be exact, I contacted my cousins their fax machine. Since we were all vacation I asked if they would meet me Saturday to go fishing Lake Bluegill. They agreed.

One of my cousins worked a shrimp boat weekends and the other cousin worked a newspaper as fishing editor. They were both up water sports and fishing. I was relying their knowledge to help us get a good catch.

their advice I bought a book fishing. I read it the train the way to the river town. My fishing poles, which I had bought sale because I'm a budget, were the floor my left. My bait box was the floor my right. There was no room for anyone to sit the seat next to me because my picnic basket was it. I was surrounded all sides.

As I got off the train loaded down with all my gear, I bumped my head the door frame. I was very dizzy and I couldn't remember why I was standing a bait shop porch. Then I saw a big houseboat the water. It had a sign it: For Sale. impulse, I found the owner and bought the boat.

Just then my cousins rowed up in a little rowboat and I remembered what I was there for. It was too late to return the houseboat and my budget was ruined, but we've gone fishing trips it hundreds of times since then. I'm glad I bumped my head the train that summer day ten years ago.

Unit 1. Section B: Combined usages of On and Off

Review

Reading Passage 1 (p. 18)

While we were driving a mountain road several miles the main highway, our car suddenly slid the road and landed its side. Fortunately we had our seatbelts so we weren't hurt.

We tried to push a boulder that had fallen the door but we couldn't. It was getting dark, so I turned the emergency lights and turned the radio so I could make a call for help the car phone the dashboard.

Soon we saw lights the treetops above us. Someone had turned the road and was the incline leading to our car. They had heard our SOS!

Unit 2. Section A: In

Lesson 1

Reading Passage 1 (p. 21)

When Monica arrived Houston she rented a small apartment an old neighborhood and found a job a doctor's office. She was very happy except for one thing: her piano was back home Mexico. She was the only one the family who had learned to play it and it had been very important her life.

One day a truck with her piano it pulled up the driveway. She knew her heart that her family had pooled their money and sent it. Now she could play it her new country.

But there was a problem: the piano didn't fit her little living room. After trying for an hour to get it, the movers put it down the middle of the lobby and left. Monica sat on the piano bench with tears her eyes. Her family should have left the piano their home!

Her landlady said, "Why don't you leave it here the lobby? We would all be glad to have some real music our lives." Monica was very relieved. Now every evening she plays beautiful music for all the other tenants the building to enjoy.

Lesson 2b

Reading Passage 1 (p. 23)

The robber was full view of the hidden camera when he robbed the bank. The teller screamed panic. The robber dropped the money confusion as he ran out the door. No one was danger because the gun he brandished desperation was fake.

Lesson 3

Reading Passage 1 (p. 24)

The woman's portrait had been painted oils by a famous artist, but she preferred the one her little son had drawn colored chalk. She had it framed silver and hung on a wall covered silk. The other portrait was draped old rags so no one could compare it to her son's picture. The famous artist never painted oils again.

Reading Passage 2 (p. 24)

The menu was written Japanese, the waiter spoke Spanish, and I could only understand English. So we communicated sign language.

Lesson 4

Reading Passage 1 (p. 25)

The actress who plays Annie Warbucks the musical *Annie* doesn't look like the Annie the comic strip. the role of Annie, the young actress gives warmth and life to the character the cartoon.

Lesson 5

Reading Passage 1 (p. 26)

The woman white is the bride. The man the tuxedo is the groom. The other guys tuxes are groomsmen. They look very uncomfortable. The girls the pretty dresses are the bridesmaids. The kids cowboy outfits are a calf-roping contest.

Lesson 7

Reading Passage 1 (p. 28)

The teenaged fans went up to the stage groups of ten. They stood around the singer a semicircle while he autographed his photographs, which were stacked piles on the table.

Lesson 8

Reading Passage 1 (p. 29)

The president arrived a helicopter and was whisked away a black limousine. Three hours later he was flying to Antarctica Air Force One. He would have preferred sitting his little fishing boat at home, but he had no choice the matter.

Lesson 9

Reading Passage 1 (p. 30)

I wonder why Bob is coming to see us the middle of winter. He usually comes June when the weather is nicer. His plane will land an hour. We'd better leave for the airport a few minutes because the traffic is always heavy the morning. If we had a helicopter we could be there no time, but we'll be lucky to get there forty-five minutes by car.

Review

Reading Passage 1 (p. 31)

Her name was _____ the class chart. It was "Meelia." She looked like a girl _____ the cover

of a book _____ the school library, but that girl was smiling. I had never seen Meelia with a smile

_____ her face. She sat _____ the left side of the room _____ the back corner.

_____ October we were _____ the middle of a test when a gust of wind blew _____ the

window and carried my paper up _____ the air. It landed _____ Meelia's desk. When she

looked at it, her eyes opened wide _____ disbelief. And then a big smile appeared _____ her

face.

I had drawn kittens _____ all the margins, because our teacher had just told us about a kitten

she had found _____ her mailbox. _____ that day Meelia and I became friends. Her smile made

her even prettier than the girl _____ the book cover.

Reading Passage 2 (p. 31)

It happened _____ April _____ a Sunday afternoon. She was sitting _____ the front porch

_____ her rocking chair. Her baby was _____ her lap. The sun shone _____ the grass and

_____ the flowers _____ the garden.

Suddenly she heard music _____ the distance. Was it _____ someone's radio? Then,

_____ amazement she realized the music was _____ her head. _____ the night before, she had attended a symphony concert _____ the Music Bowl _____ the city. She had read a book _____ the composer and listened to a tape of one of his concertos when she returned home. _____ her dreams she had heard the music. And now, _____ the silence of a sleepy spring afternoon, the music played on _____ her inner ear.

Unit 2. Section D: Inside/Outside

Review

Reading Passage 1 (p. 36)

When we got _____ the bus _____ Denver it was cold. When we got _____ the bus _____ Houston it was warm. We took our bags _____ the bus and went into the bus station, where we put a quarter _____ the telephone slot to call our grandmother.

"Get _____ a taxi and hurry out here," she said. "I just put a pie _____ the oven. Be sure to turn _____ the highway _____ Pine Street."

When we got _____ of the taxi, Grandma was _____ the house looking _____ of the window. Then she came _____ and told us to come _____ the house and take _____ our coats. We put our bags _____ the guest room, showered, and put _____ clean clothes. We brushed the dust _____ our shoes and shook the wrinkles _____ of our clothes before we hung them _____ the closet.

Grandma got _____ her best crystal glasses, which her mother had bought _____ England _____ 1900, and poured iced tea _____ them. Then she took the apple pie _____ of the oven and put it _____ the dining room table. She took _____ her apron, cut the pie, and said, "Now be sure to clean every crumb _____ the plate." We were glad to be _____ Grandma's house again.

Unit 3. Section A: At

Lesson 1a

Reading Passage 1 (p. 38)

Professor Think lives 405 Ogden Street, but he spends most of his time his desk the university. One day last week while he was driving to work he forgot to stop a red light. Now he's spending most of his time in the whirlpool the rehabilitation hospital and his car is in the shop the garage.

Lesson 2

Reading Passage 1 (p. 40)

Randy has been the University of Texas all year but he's home now for the summer. He and his friends are the beach this afternoon, and tonight they'll be a party. I'm glad he's having fun today, because tomorrow he'll be the dentist's having a root canal.

Reading Passage 2 (p. 41)

My brother is archery practice; my sister is gymnastics; I'm the opening of the new water park; my mother is a garage sale; my father is his wit's end wondering how he'll pay the bills. He shouldn't worry, because my grandmother's church praying for us all.

Lesson 4

Reading Passage 1 (p. 42)

The baby stared the kitten. The kitten stared the baby. The baby threw a toy the kitten. The kitten clawed the baby. The dog growled the kitten. The kitten scratched the dog. The mother yelled the kitten. The kitten ran away.

Reading Passage 2 (p. 42)

Our family spent Sunday afternoon the zoo. The elephants sprayed water us, the monkeys threw bananas us, the lions roared us, the snakes hissed us, and the goats nibbled our clothes. We decided to go home and watch *Wild Kingdom* on TV.

Reading Passage 3 (p. 43)

When Jim was a little boy, his father taught him never to direct insults anyone, unless he would enjoy having insults directed him. Years later, that advice kept him from jeering a young man who would later stand his side in time of trouble, and who would later still become his best friend.

Lesson 6

Reading Passage 1 (p. 45)

Marta's better math than she is history. Jack's better history than he is math. They're both good explaining things, so they help each other with their homework, even though they're brother and sister.

Reading Passage 2 (p. 45)

My father is lucky fishing, my mother is great cooking fish, and my sister and I are expert eating fish. This is a great way to practice ecology.

Review

Reading Passage 1 (p. 48)

This story happened last Christmas Eve seven o'clock night my grandparent's house. They live 128 Cedar Street, the edge of town.

My sister and I were the kitchen window looking out the first snowfall, and the rest of the family was sitting the kitchen table, talking. Suddenly we heard someone knocking loudly the front door. the same time, my little brother, who was standing the top of the stairs, shouted us. He was looking down and pointing the door.

We all crowded into the hall once. When my father opened the door we were shocked what we saw. Santa Claus! His sleigh stood the curb, with his reindeer pawing the loose gravel. Santa was yelling someone or something, "Come back, you toy thief!"

My mother's great tennis and my father's pretty good running; my grandmother's super Ping-Pong and my grandfather's a star badminton. Everything they needed was hand, so they were prepared.

As they ran down the driveway after the toy thief, my mother aimed a tennis ball the middle of his back, my father threw a jogging shoe his legs, my grandmother fired a Ping-Pong ball his head, and my grandfather pitched his badminton racket the bag of toys he was dragging away.

The thermometer was thirty degrees, and ice had formed the end of the driveway. The thief skidded and dropped the bag of toys. We laughed him as he ran into the woods the side of the house. Santa was relieved the outcome, and so were we. What would a raccoon do with all those toys, anyway?

Reading Passage 2 (p. 48)

six o'clock last evening, my family was home except for my father, who was still work. My brother, sister, and I were the kitchen table doing our homework. Suddenly our mother yelled us: "Look the stove! It's on fire!"

that moment, the fire alarm went off. My brother grabbed a bag of flour that was right the edge of the counter, and threw the flour the flames. We were amazed how quickly he acted. He was good knowing what to do times like this. The fire went out once, and we all cheered the same time: "Hurray, John!"

Unit 3. Section B: By

Lesson 2

Reading Passage 1 (p. 52)

I said to my teenage son: "Thomas Edison patented over twelve hundred inventions using his brains and working hard; Hannibal crossed the Alps determination and perseverance; Lincoln educated himself studying candlelight; your father got his law degree going to night school. Do you think you're going to raise your grades playing video games?"

Lesson 3

Reading Passage 1 (p. 53)

When Stephen was ten years old, he was urged his father to take piano lessons. He was advised all his friends to play baseball instead. He was almost persuaded them to forget about music. Then he read a story about a great pianist who was inspired Bach's concertos to study music.

Stephen was impressed the story and was motivated them to begin lessons.

Sometimes we can be influenced more what we read than what we hear.

Review

Reading Passage 1 (p. 57)

The boy, who was patient nature, stood the door all himself. The door was ten feet six feet and the boy looked very small comparison. Suddenly, a big black dog ran. The boy grabbed it the collar and held it force. He called the dog name: "Toby! Toby! Sit down and stay here me."

Just then several people, who had arrived car, walked the boy, two two. The child knew they were actors like his mother because they were saying lines from a play Shakespeare. that time, his mother had appeared as if magic.

"I'm afraid you've all come here mistake," she said. "I know we agreed to meet for rehearsal at four o'clock so we would be through ten, but we planned to meet the stage door. Don't you remember? You've overshot the mark two miles."

Toby, who had become famous singing *Down the Old Mill Stream* began to howl it out. The actors quickly moved away. the time Toby had finished the song, they were standing the four cars parked the curb. One had hurried away another route.

"With the boy and his mother there are twenty of you," said the head driver, just as Toby began tuning up for another song. "Twenty divided four equals five. That means five in each car. the way, we charge the mile, so if we drive you back we've undercharged you twenty dollars."

"That's better far than staying here!" someone cried. "Let's leave the quickest route possible!" And they did.

Unit 3. Section C: At, By, On, In, Off, Out of, Inside, Outside

Reading Passage 1 (p. 58)

When Jennifer and Sarah shopped _____ the mall, they always walked _____ the pet shop

to look _____ the animals. _____ closing time one afternoon, they were horrified _____ what

they saw. Five puppies were crowded together in a cage about four feet _____ four feet. A spotted puppy was huddled _____ itself _____ the far side. A small boy was poking a stick

_____ it. The girls were angered _____ his behavior and frowned _____ him as they told him

to stop.

The two sisters, who were compassionate _____ nature, looked _____ each other and

knew what they must do. They asked the girl standing _____ the desk how much the spotted

puppy cost. She pointed _____ a sign _____ the cage. It read, "$200.00 each. Payment By Cash

Only." Jennifer said, "_____ that price we may as well forget it." And Sarah replied, "You're right.

_____ the time we earn $200.00 the puppy will be gone."

As they left the shop they saw another sign leaning _____ an angle _____ the side of the

counter: "Two Helpers Needed." They looked _____ each other again, and this time they smiled.

_____ noon the next day the girls were being trained _____ a veterinarian, and _____ the

next morning they were working _____ the grooming table. They discovered that they were

both very good _____ handling animals.

_____ working hard, Jennifer and Sarah paid for the puppy all _____ themselves, and now

it lives _____ their house. They also made a doghouse _____ following the directions in a book

_____ a famous woodworker. _____ the end of the summer they'd been motivated _____

their work _____ the pet shop to become veterinarians. Their lives were changed _____ that

day _____ the mall. And the pet shop was changed _____ the sisters. _____ their insistence,

the cages were enlarged and the customers are now closely watched _____ the employees.

Review

Reading Passage 1 (p. 59)

_____ Monday morning, Letty drove _____ the oriental rug shop _____ her way to work.

She glanced _____ the rugs _____ the window _____ fascination.

Monday evening she parked _____ the curb _____ the front of the shop, got _____ her

car and stood looking _____ the rugs _____ the window. She was amazed _____ their beauty.

Letty was interested _____ old oriental rugs because she was thinking about starting a

business of her own. She was now quite good _____ appraising their value because she had

spent many hours _____ the library studying books _____ experts _____ the subject, as well

as examining rugs _____ galleries. But she was _____ a small budget and had to be _____ her

guard about spending too much.

It was after five o'clock and no one seemed to be _____ the shop. _____ the chance it was still open, she knocked _____ the door. The owner, with an anxious look _____ his face, welcomed her _____ the showroom.

The rugs were heaped _____ piles _____ the floor. By 6:00 P.M. he had shown her many of them, one _____ a time, lifting each one _____ the floor so she could inspect it more closely. But she had her eye _____ one _____ the corner.

It was an antique, woven _____ the last century _____ what used to be Persia, _____ people who were weavers _____ tradition. They learned to weave _____ an early age and continued _____ their craft _____ old age. This rug had a Tree of Life design _____ the center, and stylized flowers _____ either side woven _____ rich colors.

She decided _____ once that this rug was quite valuable, but when she looked _____ the price tag she was shocked. She had estimated it _____ much less, even though it would rate high _____ the appraisal list.

The man knew _____ her expression that she was shocked, and _____ a weary voice he offered the rug to her _____ twenty-five percent off. _____ this point she almost decided to buy it, but first she called her business partner _____ the phone to ask his opinion. He advised her to think _____ it.

_____ hearing her decision to wait, the owner offered her seventy-five percent off.

She answered, "Maybe I'll come _____ again some other time."

As she stepped _____ , she smiled _____ relief. She had almost put her money _____ a bad investment. Her guess about the value of the rug had been wrong. She got _____ her car and drove to the library to take out more books _____ oriental rugs.

Unit 4. Section A: To

Lesson 1

Reading Passage 1 (p. 62)

When our father was transferred Washington, D.C., we kids wanted to stay in Omaha. We didn't want to move a new city where we couldn't walk the corner and meet our best friend. We didn't want to go a school where we wouldn't feel at home. But of course we did move the new city, and after a few weeks, we were walking the corner to meet our *new* best friend and attending a new school where we felt very much at home.

Lesson 2a

Reading Passage 1 (p. 63)

When people from Europe migrated America one hundred and fifty years ago, the ocean voyage the shores of the "New World" was long and rough. Now a flight Europe takes just hours. How long do you think a trip Europe will take one hundred years from now? How about the other planets?

Lesson 2b

Reading Passage 1 (p. 64)

Our class went on a field trip Space City last week. We were there from early morning to late afternoon. The guide took us Mission Control.

That night, when I went to sleep, I had a dream. We were in a spaceship on our way Saturn. The space ship started vibrating, so we radioed Earth to come our rescue. our right and our left alien ships were attacking us! The trip Saturn was over; my mother was shaking me awake and saying, "It's time to go school!"

Lesson 4

Reading Passage 1 (p. 67)

Polar bears, who were starved a frenzy, attacked the explorers at their camp at the North Pole. The ragged crew drove the bears away, but not before some of the men had been slashed ribbons. The men who could still move ripped their tents pieces to make stretchers for the wounded.

They walked for two days and were almost frozen death. They had gotten the limit of their endurance and believed they were walking their doom when they heard a sound. It was a plane. They were saved!

Lesson 5

Reading Passage 1 (p. 68)

Most of the animals reverted their wild states after they were released. They adapted their natural environments as though they'd never left them. One thing was certain: they all preferred the jungle the cage.

The experiment demonstrated the conservationists that they should devote more time assessing cruelty animals in captivity.

Lesson 11

Reading Passage 1 (p. 74)

Ellen knew her job was important her family's independence. The food, clothing, and shelter that it paid for were essential their well-being. But she was shy, and shyness was a barrier communication. Would it be an obstacle her chance to succeed?

Unit 4. Section B: Toward

Lesson 2

Reading Passage 1 (p. 76)

Soon after the early settlers migrated _____ America, they continued their trek _____ the West in covered wagons. They were often crowded several _____ a wagon.

As they moved _____ the interior of the country, the rough trails _____ each new campsite ground the horses' shoes down _____ their hooves and the wagon wheels _____ filings.

Progress _____ their destination was slow, but everyone contributed their labor, expertise, and emotional support _____ the rest of the settlers. Children adapted _____ the hard life and shouted _____ each other from dawn _____ dusk. Babies slept _____ the rhythm of the turning wheels and the clopping hooves.

_____ evening, families passed travel information _____ each other as they rested _____ the eerie howls of the coyotes. The covers _____ the wagons provided a bit of shelter and privacy as the weary families slept.

Severe winters were threats _____ their lives but not an obstacle _____ their determination. Some almost starved _____ death, and others succumbed _____ illness, but they were never abandoned _____ the elements by their companions.

These people were committed _____ a dream, and they remained faithful _____ that commitment.

Unit 4. Section C: From

Lesson 4

Reading Passage 1 (p. 80)

When Charles arrived at the University his home town, he had to borrow money his new roommate to buy a soft drink the machine in the cafeteria. His brains may have come his genes, but his money came summer jobs that hadn't paid very much.

Even with the extra income he had earned selling fishing poles he made willow trees, he was several hundred dollars away the total of his book bill. He was exhausted all the nights spent worrying over finances.

The next day he took some good advice his roommate and applied for a job at the student union, which was only one block his dormitory. He got the job. He works 4:00 to 8:00 P.M. Monday to Friday, and 10:00 A.M. to 4:00 P.M. on Saturday. At last he's free financial worries. Now his headaches come his studies instead.

Unit 4. Section D: From/To

Lesson 1

Reading Passage 1 (p. 81)

_____ July 1st _____ July 14th every summer, I take the train

_____ Chicago _____ a little town in Colorado to visit my cousin Jerry. Last

summer he received two free tickets _____ the county fair. They came _____ a

friend who had some connection _____ the rodeo.

We went _____ bed early the night before the fair, and _____ dawn the next

morning we started out _____ town. We rode _____ the ranch _____

the fairgrounds on horseback and when we got there, Jerry tied the horses _____ a post

not far _____ the main tent. A sign _____ the side of the gate said the show was

_____ 2:00 P.M. _____ 3:00 P.M., so we went in and stood close _____

the stage. It was crowded. There were about two people _____ every seat, but we

intended to stay _____ the beginning _____ the end, even though we had to

stand shoulder _____ shoulder with the crowd.

The tent was at least a block long _____ one end _____ the other. A big

band was playing, and the crowd swayed from side _____ side with the music. Rodeo

riders _____ all over the Southwest were in the crowd, waiting for their special events.

Coming _____ a big city, I wasn't accustomed _____ this kind of entertainment

and I was thrilled _____ the core.

Suddenly a back door _____ the stage opened and a masked man walked

_____ the back _____ the front of the stage. He grabbed a handful of souvenirs

_____ a table and threw them _____ the audience. Then he began to juggle

glass balls _____ one hand _____ the other. _____ his appearance you

would have thought he was pretty old, but _____ his agility he seemed young. He was

the introduction _____ the main act.

Just then a voice came over the loud speaker. _____ our astonishment we heard: "Two horses are pulling down the tent! They're trying to break away _____ a tent post close _____ the entrance. They're a danger _____ the crowd. Whoever owns them, hurry and stop them, They're too wild even for the cowboys!"

Our reaction _____ this announcement was to run _____ the tent with great speed. When we got outside, the horses were heading _____ the ranch. Some men were retying the ropes _____ the post to keep the tent _____ caving in. We shamefacedly followed the horses down the road _____ home. We'll never know what the main act was.

Unit 5. Section A: For

Lesson 1

Reading Passage 1 (p. 84)

Grandma cooked dinner my brother and me last night. We brought our guitars to play her while she was cooking. She had left a message our cousin on his mother's answering machine inviting him, too. He was busy writing an article the school newspaper so he didn't come. That was okay—we shared the food meant him.

Grandma keeps a cheerful home Grandpa and herself—and us to visit. She always picks flowers the table, and she makes sure there are plenty of games us to play and books us to read. We supply music and company her, and she provides food and attention us. A good trade us all.

Lesson 2

Reading Passage 1 (p. 86)

In my suitcase I packed a skating outfit skating, a swimming suit the pool, nice clothes dining and dancing, ski clothes skiing, boots hiking, and plenty of casual clothes.

At the lodge, the restaurant was closed remodeling, so meals guests were served in the kitchen. The power the ski lift was cut off, so there was no skiing. It was forty degrees so there was no ice skating. The guide our hikes and tours quit, and the pump the indoor pool was broken. It poured every day.

Thank goodness I had gone to the library a good book the day I left home. It had fourteen hundred pages, just enough a week's read. By the way, do you know anyone who needs some very nice secondhand resort clothes?

Lesson 3a

Reading Passage 1 (p. 87)

The shipwrecked people on the island used bamboo mats roofs and floors, seashells cups and spoons, and coconut shells bowls. They used fish bones needles, seaweed thread, and vines rope. They ate fish breakfast, lunch, and dinner. They even ate it snacks.

Lesson 4

Reading Passage 1 (p. 89)

The Parents

"We had a family meeting to get support our plan dividing the housework. We put up a good defense equal work each member of the family. We spoke strongly the idea of *work in exchange privilege!*"

The Children

Fran: "Since I play soccer the school team, I should be excused from chores."
Nan: "Since I'm working hard the debate team, I don't have time chores."
Van: "Since I'm busy campaigning student council president, I'm not home enough chores."
Dan: "We stand together: no chores children."

The Parents

"Since there's no enthusiasm our ideas, we made a new rule: only those over the age of twenty-one may vote. We vote equality in household chores. Mothers and fathers must stand up their rights, too."

Lesson 5

Reading Passage 1 (p. 91)

Every morning at 6:15, my wife leaves the hospital where she's a nurse. At 7:30, the children get on the bus school. At 8:00, I take off the university where I teach.

At 3:00 P.M., my wife leaves the hospital the parking lot where she parks her car. At 3:30, the children leave school home. At 2:50, I leave my last class the bus station, where I catch a bus our street. We all arrive at home together and head the refrigerator a cold drink.

Review

Reading Passage 1 (p. 101)

1. Grandma baked cookies us every Saturday.

2. She had a red tin the cookies.

3. She was tired last Saturday, so we washed dishes her.

4. She worked a living five days a week.

5. She had fought independence and won.

6. This Saturday she headed the mountains.

7. We waited her to answer her door.

8. We had the key her house, so we went in.

9. Inside she had left a note us. "Aloha!" it said.

10. *Aloha* is Hawaiian *until later.*

11. Our tin of cookies was there, so we ate them breakfast.

12. Then we went out and walked about an hour.

13. We bought four bananas twenty-five cents.

14. Lunch was planned noon, so we only ate one each.

15. When we got home we were scolded being late.

16. When we didn't eat our vegetables, our father said, "Broccoli is good you!"

17. It was warm March, so after lunch we invited all our friends over to play.

18. My mother said, "Where can I go some peace and quiet?"

19. Then she left, and she may be at the North Pole all we know.

20. If it weren't our father making us cut the grass, we would have left the movies.

Unit 5. Section B: Against

Lesson 5

Reading Passage 1 (p. 106)

Joe could hear the crash of the falls the rocks just behind him. He had acted the guide's advice, and his own better judgment, when he had taken the kayak out on the river alone. He had worn a life jacket as a safety measure overturning, and he was glad he had.

He put his shoulder the boat and pushed it with all his might. His feet slipped the slick stones. It was almost impossible to make headway the current. He inched slowly the spray of the rapids. The reflection of the sun the water was blinding, but the wind his face was freezing. He was struggling the elements.

Unit 6. Section A: Of

Review

Reading Passage 1 (p. 113)

The flashlights the searchers dotted the side the hill. Someone cried out: "I've found a button a coat! Maybe it's Gary's! It was lying at the bottom a fork this tree. A strip a handkerchief was tied to the top a twig and stuck in the crevice. Some petals a red flower were scattered on top it, but I used the sleeve my sweater to brush them off. The button was lying on the bottom the crevice!"

The mother the missing boy was elated. "I recognize the shape and color the button. It's Gary's! Now I understand the value his scouting lessons. He left a kind clue for us."

The mood the searchers lifted. As the light the moon grew brighter, it reflected on the surface the pond. Now they could see more clearly into the dark places the forest.

Suddenly they heard a rustling leaves. The little boy stood at the edge the pond, with the collar his coat pulled up around his ears, and the brim his hat pulled down over his eyes.

"Here I am!" he cried. The long search the weary townspeople was over.

Lesson 5c

Reading Passage 1 (p. 123)

Margaret is a teacher English at the school adult education at the University the North. In her class is the pastor a Lutheran church who is from Germany, a professor Russian from Moscow, a doctor orthopedics Korean descent, and two members the Japanese-American Society. The rest the class is made up college students many different language backgrounds, including Thai, Chinese, and French, plus seven natives Mexico, and three Central America.

Before the beginning class, Margaret asks each student to greet the class and to announce the date and time in the language his/her native country. Margaret sometimes feels as if she's been sent to the Tower Babel biblical times, to get everyone speaking in one language again.

Lesson 6c

Reading Passage 1 (p. 125)

The drama department the University Oldhall invited the graduates our school to attend a play. We were told that we would see one the historical plays Shakespeare, but we didn't. The title the play was "Puzzles," and it was the creation the president the university's son.

In an account the play in the program, the background the playwright seemed hazy. The list characters was exceedingly long, and the members the cast numbered one hundred and thirty.

The designer the sets was a genius; the lighting the stage was brilliant; the star the evening was talented; the director the production had done his best; but the meaning the play was unclear, and the words the actors made no sense. Worst all, the number scenes was eighteen. We had to sit through six acts three scenes each! Our sighs boredom and loud yawns weariness were noisier than the voices the cast.

The ending the play was abrupt, because the members the audience were suddenly awakened by the bright lights the theater, which came on after the curtain closed. There was no sound clapping.

We were sure one thing: this was not a play Shakespeare's!

Lesson 7b

Reading Passage 1 (p. 128)

Dr. Jean Taline's face wore a smile contentment. She had just written a report her team's research work and had asked her assistant, Barbara, to make a copy it. Now she was enjoying the feeling satisfaction a year accomplishment.

Suddenly a cry alarm came from the area the animal cages. A squeal protest soon followed. Dr. Taline hurried to check on the source the noise. She soon found it.

Primo, the chimp Africa, and Barbara, the research assistant Ohio, were having a tug-of-war, with Dr. Taline's report as the prize! With grunts effort, Primo tugged at one end the report, and Barbara tugged at the other.

One word command and a frown disapproval from the boss stopped the contest. Dr. Taline retrieved the pages the tattered report and said a prayer thanks. It was still readable and, though full rips and tears, could be copied.

Primo uttered a squeak embarrassment, and Barbara gave a speech apology. She had stopped to feed the chimp a snack, holding the report in one hand and the cracker in the other. the two, Primo had preferred the report and grabbed it.

The stress the moment was replaced by a laugh amusement as Primo, full shame, draped a piece newspaper over his head. All was forgiven.

Lesson 9

Reading Passage 1 (p. 130)

As the moment her marriage drew near, Jane was not sure she could live through the next twelve hours pageantry. She was a woman composure and gentleness, while her husband-to-be, Ken, was a man restless energy and charm. Jane would have preferred a quiet ceremony attended by family and close friends, but Ken had insisted on a wedding great size and expense.

Jane's mother was a person sensitivity; she had seen the aura unhappiness surrounding her daughter. On the evening the rehearsal, she drew Jane aside. In the stillness the Chapel Prayer, she said, "Jane, now is the moment truth. Do you want a life glamour and excitement, or a life peace and serenity? This is your time decision."

Jane finally realized that Ken's need excitement and her need tranquillity would result in a marriage misery. She told Ken her concerns, and he, being a man understanding, agreed to a plan.

The morning the expected nuptials, the guests were asked to stay for a reception without a wedding. They toasted two wise people, who had spared themselves a lifetime unhappiness.

Lesson 11b

Reading Passage 1 (p. 133)

It was five minutes four, on the afternoon the sixth July, when Timmy let go his kite. It had been a day strange happenings, but what happened next was the strangest them all.

A blue heron, a bird placid disposition, flapped its wings and followed the flight the kite. As we watched, the heron caught the kite in the grip its long bill. Little Timmy cried for his lost kite.

All us who were gathered on the beach watched in amazement. This bird the seashore circled overhead and then swooped within feet the spot where Timmy stood sobbing. The heron's release the kite was a miracle accuracy, and the glow joy on Timmy's face was as bright as the sunlight on the bird's wings.

We'll always remember that day our family reunion as a symbol the wonders and mysteries the world nature.

Unit 6. Section B: About

Review

Reading Passage 1 (p. 142)

On the first _____ October _____ my twenty-third year, my trip

_____ the Orient turned _____ dreams into reality. _____ the time I

was a child, I had loved stories _____ travel and especially _____ the countries

_____ Asia. Every night when I went _____ bed I would look forward

_____ my dreams. They were _____ far-off places.

_____ years I saved my pennies _____ a trip. I worked _____ my

father _____ _____ a dollar an hour, removing brush _____ our land

and dragging fallen trees _____ the clearing _____ firewood _____

the winter. A farm is never short _____ jobs. When I got _____ college, I

worked part _____ the time as a waiter, and _____ _____ a year in the

library _____ the school _____ engineering.

After years _____ planning, the day _____ departure finally arrived. I

worried _____ being late _____ my flight and got _____ the airport

_____ two hours early. My carry-on bag was full _____ maps _____

Asian cities and, of course, my camera and film. I planned on taking many pictures _____

these lands _____ mystery, and thought _____ writing a book _____

them. The plane took off _____ San Francisco and headed west _____ the East!

The first stop _____ the trip was Japan. The memory _____ that day is one

_____ the clearest _____ my life. I sat in the front _____ the plane and

pressed my forehead _____ the window as we came in sight _____ the Tokyo

airport. It was the end _____ a long flight and the beginning _____ a wonderful

adventure.

Unit 7. Section A: With

Lesson 1c

Reading Passage 1 (p. 145)

The Johnsons like to listen to music their dessert. Joanne sits at one end of the table Robert, their tape recorder playing classical music. Philip sits at the other end of the table Elise, the CD playing opera arias. Combined that is the sound of the VCR in the next room playing reggae music.

When I spent the week them last summer, I always took a walk my dog at dessert time, even when they served my favorite — ice cream chocolate sauce — because my dog liked to howl along the music.

The next time I visit the Johnsons, I'm going to bring some earplugs me and leave my dog a friend.

Lesson 2b

Reading Passage 1 (p. 147)

My sister and I went to meet our aunt at the train station. Aunt Ella said she'd be the one the flower in her lapel. At least thirty people carnations on their coats got off the train. It was Memorial Day, which we celebrate parades — and by wearing red or white carnations!

We finally found Aunt Ella in spite of all the people flowers. She was the only one a yellow rose in her lapel. We yelled at her excitement and we hugged each other relief. As she rode home us in the taxi, she said she would have found us, even though we hadn't seen each other in years. We were the only twins bright red hair in the station!

Lesson 4

Reading Passage 1 (p. 150)

The campers made a fire kindling and lit it matches. Their supper was a can of beans, flavored tomato sauce, and some hot dogs, covered mustard and onions.

After supper they filled a pot creek water, heated it over the fire, and washed dishes it. When it began to rain, they covered their belongings a tarp. Little Yvonne fell on the slippery path and got covered mud.

Everyone smeared their faces, legs, and arms mosquito repellent and went to bed. They wished all their hearts they had stayed home.

Reading Passage 2 (p. 150)

When the wind stopped blowing, Lily sat her friends and ate ice cream the peaches her Uncle Jose had brought him from the country. They looked through the window the broken glass.

The yard was strewn debris. The tree the swing on it had blown down. A bird a black cap, chirping anxiety, was looking for her chicks. Lily's father was working Uncle Jose, dragging branches off the street a rope. Her mother was cleaning the porch a hose.

The children put their dishes in the sink the rest of the dirty dishes. the hurricane, the gas had been cut off, so they had no hot water to wash the dishes. Then they went out to the yard where they had played each other just yesterday.

Their eyes filled tears when they saw the mess. The little fountain where the birds had splashed vigor was broken, their wading pool was filled mud, the lawn was covered tiles from their roof, the tool shed was on the ground a tree on top of it, and the garden, which Lily's mother had just planted fall flowers, was torn up. The children helped clean up the trash rakes and shovels. their help the yard began to look better.

"all of us working together, we'll soon be back to normal," said her father a smile.

And he was right. They were.

Lesson 5b

Reading Passage 1 (p. 152)

Sally and Nancy, both aged three, began to fight each other about who could play the toy stove. Their mothers decided not to side either one. Then Sally pulled Nancy's hair and wouldn't let go. Sally's mother agreed Nancy's mother that it was time to stop the fight. They knew that it's natural for children to compete their friends, but they must also learn to live in harmony them.

Lesson 6

Reading Passage 1 (p. 153)

Why does wisdom come age, when we no longer need it as much? Wisdom should come youth. Just think of all the foolish mistakes that could be avoided if good sense kicked in the beginning of the teens. We might grow less wise time, but by then all the big decisions would have been made wisely, and we could just sit back, enjoy the fruits of our good sense, and be as foolish as we pleased.

Lesson 8

Reading Passage 2 (p. 155)

First Complainer: Last night our team was tied the Polar Bears. I was sitting up in the bleachers the other students. Because the colors of the Bears' uniforms and the colors of our uniforms didn't contrast enough each other, we couldn't see which team made the winning touchdown. Compared us, the kids sitting nearest the field could probably see much better.

Second Complainer: The benches that the team sits on are level the football field. The drill team sits right behind them. It's harder to see the plays from there than it is from the bleachers. Last night we were tied the Bears. When the final touchdown was made we couldn't tell which team made it. Compared with us, the kids sitting way up in the stands could probably see much better.

Hint to both Complainers: If you would pay attention to the game, instead of visiting your friends, you would know which goal line your team was trying to cross.

Lesson 11

Reading Passage 1 (p. 158)

Tommy lives in the house the red front door. Tammy lives in the house the white fence. Every weekday morning, Tommy walks to school Tammy. They carry their books and lunches them.

One morning Tammy's hat blew off into a ditch filled water. Tommy fished it out a stick, but his bag all his books fell off his shoulder into the ditch. In a minute it filled muddy water and sank.

That day Tammy shared her books and her lunch Tommy. She told him that she'd buy him a new book bag and new books her allowance, but that it would take a long time. a twinkle in his eyes, he said not to hurry.

"Now we can sit each other every day and study each other every night while we share books," he laughed. "I'd rather study your books than with mine."

Reading Passage 2 (p. 159)

All of the students in our class were Jim. He had been accused of starting a fight another student, and breaking a window in the language lab a chair. We didn't go along the accusation of the other student. every hour we grew more upset the idea that Jim might be punished suspension.

his scholastic achievements and his class leadership, we thought the teachers would realize that they were dealing the wrong person. We knew he was speaking honesty when he said he had been working a computer on the other side of the room when the fight started.

just a few minutes left before the end of the school day, another guy, courage, I must say, confessed to starting the fight. After school, a bunch of us stood our arms around Jim and each other and yelled, "Up the truth!"

Jim shook hands the other guy, and we all made friends him. He said that he couldn't have lived himself if he hadn't confessed. He'll have to pay for the window his own money. He will also help younger students in the language lab before school every morning. He smiled relief when he heard that he wouldn't be suspended.

Unit 7. Section B: Without

Lesson 5

Reading Passage 1 (p. 164)

Carlos came to school _____ his books. He walked into class _____ smiling and sat down _____ saying hello to anybody. The classroom was _____ heat because the storm had left the school _____ electricity. The students _____ sweaters were shivering. _____ a doubt, school would be dismissed early.

The teacher stood in front of the room _____ her arms filled _____ papers.

"Of all of these papers there is only one _____ an *A+* on it," she said. "By the way, did one of you come to school _____ your books?"

"I did," answered Carlos _____ embarrassment. "I left school_____ them yesterday, and when I came back to find them, they were gone. They're lost."

"No they aren't," said his teacher _____ a smile. " _____ thinking, I put them _____ the class books in the cabinet yesterday. And by the way, Carlos, this paper _____ the *A*+ on it is yours."

The classroom was still cold, but Carlos left school that day _____ a warm feeling in his heart.

Unit 7. Section C: Through, Throughout

Review

Reading Passage 1 (p. 171)

On Sunday night, Alisha heard the radio the wall of her apartment. It was 2:00 A.M. She lay awake three hours of music and talk. will power, she finally fell asleep at 5:00 A.M.

The same thing happened every night the week. On Friday, Alisha got work early and, the kindness of her supervisor, left the office at 3:30. As the bus drove traffic she almost fell asleep. She peered the bus window at a sign that said, "Get a good night's sleep on a Sleepwell mattress." Alisha thought to herself, "I could sleep the night on a bed of nails — if there were no radio playing."

That night, the music and voices seemed to sound every corner of her apartment. Alisha could even hear them the earplugs she had bought. She got the rest of the night by thinking about how to stop it.

On Saturday, the help of her landlord, Alisha met the person living in the next apartment. It was Nora, a nice, elderly woman. Nora told Alisha that in the wee hours, when she couldn't sleep, she found companionship the music and talk on the radio.

That afternoon, Alisha brought the woman a gift. Now Nora listens to her favorite programs all the night her new headphones, and Alisha, on her side of the wall, sleeps soundly.

Unit 8. Section A: Over

Review

Reading Passage 1 (p. 183)

Rosalinda was concerned her terrible headache. It had started two days ago, when the feed store where she had worked for five years had gone out of business. She had made an appointment the telephone with a doctor in the city.

Rosalinda found the medical building easily, because it towered the other buildings in the city. She walked the thick carpet in the lobby to the elevator. The sign the door said that her doctor was on the fifty-fifth floor. She had never before been in a building ten stories tall. She stepped the threshold and pushed a button that read *55*. A light went on the number and the door slid closed.

Rosalinda closed her eyes and held her hand her mouth. A strange sensation came her and her ears popped. In only seconds the ride was over. A nurse handed her a form the top of a counter. "Don't write the middle section," the nurse said.

Rosalinda waited for an hour. She counted the lights in the ceiling her head. She watched a carpenter nail a piece of plywood a hole in a wall. She listened to music coming hidden speakers. She searched the entire waiting room for something interesting to read.

Many people hurried the area in front of her. A man with bandages his hands walked to the elevator. Rosalinda pushed the *down* button for him. A woman on crutches with a cast her leg dropped her handbag. Its contents scattered the floor. Rosalinda picked them up for her. A crying child ran down the hallway and fell a box. Then he started to climb the counter. Rosalinda calmed him and watched him until the child's mother came.

A woman in a uniform with a name tag on it walked to Rosalinda. "You seem to have a calming influence our patients. We need someone like you to take the customer relations department. Would you like to talk the job requirements with me lunch?"

Rosalinda laughed to herself this turn of events. Her concern her terrible headache had disappeared, along with her worry not having a job. The long trip the country roads to the city had been worth it. Her visit to the doctor's office had cured her. She would have control her life again.

Unit 8. Section G: Beneath

Review

Reading Passage 1 (p. 197)

Cullen wanted to see what it was like _____ the border. He walked _____ the highway to the border patrol station. He could see the lights of Quintero _____ the bridge.

The border guard asked for his I.D. As he handed it _____ , it flew out of his hand, _____ the guard's head, and into the river. A fishing boat ran _____ it and it sank _____ the surface of the water. But as he looked _____ the boat, he saw his I.D. card floating quickly _____ the choppy water. Soon it would be _____ the bridge.

A sign _____ the station door said, "Traffic Control." An electric bell hung _____ the sign. The guard rang it. The next boat stopped. The captain looked up at Cullen standing _____ him on the bridge.

"Could you please try to fish that card out of the water?" yelled Cullen.

The captain reached _____ the side of the boat with a fishing net and scooped up the card. Cullen ran _____ the embankment to the water's edge. The captain pulled his little boat _____ as far as he could and held the net out toward the shore. Cullen took off his shoes and socks, waded into the river _____ the soft mud, reached into the net, and got

his I.D. card. It was dry _____ its plastic cover.

Thanks to the border guard, the fishing boat captain, and the plastic _____ his I.D.,

Cullen got to see what it was like _____ the border.

Unit 9. Section C: Behind

Review

Reading Passage 1 (p. 210)

Ned had worked for the Price Company since just _____ his twenty-second birthday.

The company was named _____ Harold Price, its founder. _____ all these years,

Ned knew he was in trouble. He had been falling _____ in his work because he was

always late, hungry, and tired. A bad habit was _____ his problem.

Ned never had time to eat breakfast because, ever since he had begun watching the late-night

talk show on TV, he went back to sleep in the morning _____ turning off his alarm clock.

So day _____ day he came to the office late and hungry. He was also tired because,

_____ all, the talk show lasted until 1:00 A.M.

One morning, he walked into the Price Building (also named _____ his boss) just

before Harold Price himself. Mr. Price called _____ him. "Ned, I'd like to speak to you

_____ the staff meeting this morning," he said.

Ned felt sick. He sat down _____ his desk and put his head in his hands. Before long

he was asleep. He had an awful dream. He dreamed about sitting down to a big breakfast of fruit

and cereal, ham and English muffins, but _____ eating even a bite of it, an alarm clock

rang and the food disappeared. This happened time _____ time until he was starving.

Then the talk show host began chasing _____ him, waving his late reports.

When Ned woke up it was a few minutes _____ nine. He had missed the staff

meeting. Dennis, a fellow worker, came out of the meeting room _____ the rest of the

salesmen. Ned had told him about his problem and about his being called _____ the

boss.

"I'll stand _____ you if you need me," said Dennis. "Don't worry, everything will be all right." But Ned didn't believe him.

Ned had never been so nervous _____ that awful time he stood _____ Mr. Price. _____ hearing what Mr. Price had to say, Ned said, "I know I'm _____ in my reports, and that everyone else in the office is way _____ of me in sales, but after all, they get plenty of sleep and a good breakfast _____ work."

"Well, Ned," said Mr. Price, who was holding something behind his back, "I hear you sit in front of the TV set until _____ 1:00 A.M. every night and skip breakfast because you go back to sleep _____ turning off your alarm clock."

Ned nodded, sure that he knew what was _____ all of this talk: he would be looking for a new job _____ long.

"I have something to give you, Ned. But _____ that, I want you to promise me something: never stay up _____ 11:00 P.M. on work nights. _____ all, there are times when sleep must come _____ TV."

"Agreed," said Ned.

Mr. Price held out a package _____ him. Ned took it and read the directions: "This is a nonstop alarm clock that cannot be turned off _____ sensing the smell of coffee and toast."

"So you must get up and fix breakfast _____ it will turn off!" said Mr. Price, laughing instead of being annoyed.

So Dennis had been right, _____ all. Everything was going to be all right.

_____ this, Ned would put his bad habits _____ him.

Unit 11. Section A: Like

Review

Reading Passage 1 (p. 229)

My teacher says her grandmother looks just pictures of Martha Washington. That's just her— she's always saying someone looks someone else. She told me I look my mother. I asked lots of people, my sister and my brother and my best friend, if they thought I look my mother, and they said no—I look my father. Since I'm a boy and not very pretty, my mother should be glad about that.

I may look my father, but I sure can't pitch a baseball he does. From my record of strikeouts and walks, it looks years of practice ahead of me. Sometimes I feel giving up, but my father says that everyone feels that sometimes, but that if I keep on trying I'll soon be playing a pro. It's him to be encouraging, and I believe he's right.

Unit 12. Section C: Until

Review

Reading Passage 1 (p. 235)

The two sisters had not been back to their grandparents' house _____ 1991. They had both been working in foreign countries _____ college days. Both of their grandparents had died _____ the past year, and now Mary and Therese had come to get the house ready to sell. It had been raining in torrents _____ their arrival.

"I haven't seen such weather _____ the hurricane that blew across Mexico last year. Some good will come of it, though. They say it hasn't rained _____ May," said Mary.

Therese's dog was nervous and restless _____ the worst part of the storm, especially when the electricity went off.

"Don't worry, Angus," Therese said. "Wait _____ later and I'll get you something good to eat."

Just then it began to hail. It hailed _____ bedtime. Mary read by candlelight _____ almost midnight. Therese listened to her battery-operated radio _____ sign-off time. Angus waited patiently for his treat _____ finally giving up and going to sleep.

Sometime _____ the night the roof began to leak. The next morning, Mary and Therese mopped up puddles _____ their backs ached. Then they waited _____ the return of the electricity so they could heat some water for coffee. The telephone didn't work _____ noon.

The sun came out _____ the morning, so they spread out all the rugs to dry on the patio. The sisters hadn't spent so much time together _____ their childhood, and they enjoyed it very much.

_____ the hours of work, they talked and came to a decision. If it was so much fun

being together _____ a storm, it would be even more fun to be together with their

families _____ pleasant weather. Instead of selling the house, they would keep it. They

planned to meet at the house again every year _____ the summer—but not

_____ the leaky roof was repaired!

Phrasal Verbs: On, Off, In, Out, Through, Over, Up, Down

Learners of English often hesitate to use the informal structures of the language and instead use the single Latinate word, resulting in stilted speech. A mastery of phrasal verbs is essential to the mastery of natural, conversational speech.

A phrasal verb is a verb followed by a particle. A particle is a word that looks like a preposition or an adverb. The combination of particles with certain verbs creates word forms with new meanings. These are called phrasal verbs, or two-part verbs. They are among the most unpredictable forms in the language.

The English learner finds these idiomatic word forms especially difficult to master because of the lack of rules telling when and how to use them. There is no way to decide through reason which verb should combine with which particle to produce an exact meaning. To add to the confusion, many identical phrasal verbs have different meanings.

Another difficulty lies in knowing when the verb and its particle may be separated by a noun or pronoun and when they may not. In this book, an arc connects the verb with its particle in instances where they must not be separated. If separable, and the object is a pronoun, the object must always come between the verb and its particle. In most other cases where separation is permissible, whether to separate or not is optional. Learning by rote and by listening to native English speakers is the safest guide to natural sounding usages.

Only a fraction of all idiomatic phrasal verbs are included in this book, but they are among the most commonly used.

Phrasal Verbs with On

add on	make larger: They added on a bedroom and bath to their house.
bank on	to depend on: We're banking on him to get us the information we need.
bring on	cause: Her headaches are brought on by stress.
call on	ask to answer (in school): Why does the professor always call on me?
call on	pay a visit: When Sarah called on her new neighbors, she brought them a plate of cookies.
carry on	complain loudly: The child carried on because he couldn't have a piece of candy.

carry on	continue: The daughter carried on the family tradition.
carry_on	continue under stress: He carried on with a smile, even though he was unhappy.
catch_on	to understand: He caught on to how the magician did the disappearing trick.
count_on	depend on: You can always count on a true friend to be there when you need him.
drag_on	went slowly: The afternoon dragged on as they waited for the mail carrier.
draw_on	used: They drew on their experience to guide them.
egg on	to incite; urge: The boys egged him on to throw the rock through the window.
gain_on	to increase: Their team is gaining on our team. The score was six to ten and now it's ten to eleven.
get_on	to board: He got on the train and waved goodbye.
go_on	continue talking: The salesman went on and on about how wonderful the car is.
grow_on	accept and like with time: No one likes his paintings at first, but they grow on you.
had on	wear: He had on the brightest necktie she had ever seen.
hang_on	wait: Hang on! We'll be there in a minute!
hold_on	wait: Hold on, please. I'll see if she's in.
jump_on	criticize or scold: The boss jumped on them for losing sales.
keep_on	continue: Ed's going to keep on studying English until he can speak it well.
lead on	fool; mislead: She led him on to think she really liked him.
let_on	divulge; allow something to be known: Terry never let on how she helped the poor.
live_on	subsist: How can that family live on so little money?
look_on	observe: The student nurses looked on while the surgery was performed.
pass on	pass along to others: Please pass the information on to the rest of the hospital staff.
pass_on	die: Maria, who has been ill for so long, passed on this morning.
pick_on	continually criticize; nag: The woman picked on her husband about not doing the yard work.
settle_on	agree; decide: After discussing it for hours, they finally settled on a price for the house.
sit_on	think about before making a decision: He's going to sit on it for a while before deciding what to do.
slip on	put on; don: She slipped on her robe and slippers.
switch on	change from *off* to *on:* He switched on the light/TV/radio, etc.
take on	assume responsibility: In order to keep his job he had to take on many extra duties.
tell_on	tattle: When Sadie broke the vase, Sissy said she was going to tell on her.
touch_on	mention: The professor had only touched on the subject, but he expected us to know all about it.
try on	wear to check for size, etc.: She tried on the hats and made us laugh.
turn on	change from *off* to *on:* He turned on the light/ TV/radio, etc.
turn_on	change from friend to enemy: The dog seemed friendly, but he turned on us and growled.
wait_on	serve: Emma waited on many famous people when she worked at that restaurant.

Some phrasal verbs are followed by another preposition. Here are a few of them with *on:*

bear down on	put pressure on: The manager really bore down on them to finish their reports.
brush up on	review; restudy: We're going to Mexico, so I'm going to brush up on my Spanish.
burst in on	come in abruptly: We were having breakfast when our neighbor burst in on us.
go on with	continue: They went on with the party even though the weather was terrible.
hang on to	keep: She hung on to her money so she could buy a house.
hold on to	grasp tightly: The little girl held on to her mother on the first day of school.
look in on	check to see if everything is all right: The doctor looked in on the old man every day.
walk out on	to leave abruptly: His secretary walked out on him without warning.
walk out on	abandon: That man walked out on his family when his children were still young.

Phrasal Verbs with Off

call off	cancel: The meeting was called off because the chairman resigned.
call off	give orders to stop: The owner called off his dog when it started to jump on the children.
carry off	successfully accomplish: She carried off her role as Queen Victoria with style.
check off	indicate completion: Check off all the things on the list that you have already done.
cool off	become less angry or upset: He gave his wife time to cool off before he apologized.
cross off	remove by putting a line through: Cross off the names of the people on the list who are not going to attend the wedding.
die off	slowly disappear: Some wild animals are dying off naturally; others are being killed.
drop off	decrease: Sales of homes are dropping off.
drop off	deliver: He dropped off a package for you.
drop off	fall asleep: She dropped off during the lecture.
get off	leave a public vehicle: She got off the bus at fifth and Edison.
get off	receive better treatment than expected: He got off without paying taxes this year.
get off (with)	escape harsh punishment: He got off with only two years parole.
give off	emit: That refinery gives off bad smells.
go off	explode: A bomb went off in the empty building.
go off	ring or sound: The alarm clock went off at six.
head off	divert: They headed off the speeding car with barriers.
hold off	wait; delay: They held off writing until they were sure of his address.
hold off	keep from approaching: They held off their creditors until they borrowed money to pay them.
keep off	refrain from stepping on: The sign read *Keep Off the Grass.*
keep off	refrain from touching: Mother told us to keep our hands off the cooky jar.
kick off	start a game or special event: They kicked off the campaign with a dinner.
lay off	dismiss from a job; fire: Many employees were laid off from their jobs at the oil company.
laugh off	not take seriously: She laughed off their threats because she didn't believe them.

let off	allow someone to exit a vehicle: On the way home, she asked if he would let her off at the bakery.
let off	allow to go without difficulty: The judge let them off without punishment because it was their first offense.
pull off	succeed: I didn't think he could pull it off when he said he was going to buy that company, but he did.
put off	delay: It's easy to put off doing unpleasant things.
rip off	to cheat: Thousands of people were ripped off by that scam.
see off	be at the point of departure when someone is leaving on a trip: We all went to the airport to see off our friends when they left for Europe.
set off	activate: The kids set off the fireworks with their fathers helping them.
shove off	leave: It was time to shove off, so we said goodbye.
show off	call attention to oneself: He liked to show off by driving his new car too fast.
shrug off	act as if something is not important: He shrugged off his responsibilities.
shut off	disconnect: The electric company shut off their power because they didn't pay their bill.
sign off	ending a program or communique: The announcer signs off station KUHF at midnight.
skim off	take from the top: He had been skimming off the profits for years.
sound off	be vocal about: That woman really sounded off about the bad service in this store.
swear off	determine to quit a bad habit: That couple both swore off smoking.
take off	remove (clothing or accessories): She took off her coat and hat, glasses, and jewelry.
take off	remove: Take the books off the desk.
take off	leave the ground: The plane took off on time.
wear off	erode; become less obvious: The names on the old tombstones were almost worn off.
write off	cancel: He wrote off all their debts because he knew they would never pay them.

Phrasal Verbs with In

break in	interrupt: The operator broke in while we were talking long distance.
break in	enter illegally: While we were out of town, someone broke in and stole our VCR.
check in	register: We checked in as soon as we arrived at the hotel.
chip in	Contribute money: The staff chipped in for a farewell gift for their boss.
close in	approach in order to surround: As the police closed in, the murderer grew desperate.
come in	enter: She told us to come in and make ourselves comfortable.
come in	arrive: The fall fashions have already come in and it's only June.
dig in (slang)	eat heartily: When we sat down to eat, Uncle Bill told us to dig in.
dig in (slang)	begin to work earnestly: There's a great deal of work to do. Let's dig in and get it done.
dig in	prepare for an extended period of time in a protected place: The frontier families dug in for the winter.
drop in	come for an unannounced visit: We were having breakfast when Aunt Molly dropped in.

fill in	put information in or color in blank spaces: Be sure to fill in the blanks on the test.
fill in (on)	furnish information: We filled him in on all the news he missed while he was on vacation.
fit in	be compatible: That quiet secretary doesn't seem to fit in with this noisy office staff.
get in	arrive: His plane finally got in two hours late.
get in	arrive home: They didn't get in from the party until midnight.
give in	yield to pressure: The kids begged to go to the circus for days, and their parents finally gave in.
hand in	submit: The students handed in their homework.
join in	become part of: The neighbors were invited to join in the celebration.
lay in	store supplies: The farmers laid in food and firewood for the long winter.
let in	allow to enter: Don't ever let a stranger in when you're home alone.
let in (on)	tell in confidence: They let him in on the secret plans because they needed his help.
pile in	crowd into a small space: The family piled into the truck and drove away.
pitch in	contribute help: Everyone pitched in and did something, so the work was finished quickly.
plug in	connect to an electric outlet: When we plugged in the toaster, the fuse blew.
pull in	drive to a place off the road: Let's pull in here and ask directions.
put in	devote time/energy: How many hours have you put in at work this week?
rub in	keep reminding about something; tease: He feels bad enough about his goof without his friends rubbing it in.
sign in	register: He signed in at the registration table.
sink in	become part of one's consciousness: He read the letter three times before the truth finally sunk in.
sink in	be learned/understood through repetition: The teacher explained the math problem to the class over and over until it finally sank in.
slip in	enter quietly: They slipped in during the middle of the speech and sat in the back of the room.
stop in	come for a brief visit: If you're ever in this part of town, stop in and say hello.
take in	observe; absorb: Disney World is so huge you can't possibly take it all in in one day.
take in	give shelter: That family often takes in people who have no place else to stay.
take in	furnish housing: The university students my aunt takes in as boarders like her comfortable rooms and good meals.
take in	collect: The club took in three hundred dollars from the pancake breakfast.
throw in	include without extra charge: The butcher threw in some bones for the dog with our purchase.
trade in	to exchange and use as partial payment: He traded in his old car for a newer one.
tune in	turn on to listen: He tunes in the same station every evening at six to hear the news.
tune in	be aware: They were all tuned in to the seriousness of the situation.
turn in	go to bed: It's eleven o'clock; time to turn in.
turn in	take back: Your library books are overdue. You'd must turn them in today.

Phrasal Verbs with Out

ask out	to invite on a date: He asked her out to dinner and a show.
back out	go in reverse: He backed out of the driveway and drove into the ditch.
back_out	break a promise; fail to honor a contract or commitment: He told us he would lend them the money but he backed out at the last minute.
be_out	not home: Mother doesn't answer her phone. She must be out.
be_out	be unconscious: After he was hit on the head, he was out for almost an hour.
blow out	extinguish: Philip blew out all the candles on his birthday cake.
break_out	become covered with: The children broke out with a rash.
break_out	erupt: A fight broke out among the wrestling fans.
break_out	escape: The criminal who broke out of jail was captured.
bring out	cause to appear: That teacher brings out the best in her students.
burn out	destroyed by fire: The inside of the house was completely burned out.
burn_out	stop burning: It's cold; the fire in the fireplace burned out.
burn_out	be exhausted mentally from over-concentration on a job or situation: She'll be burned out soon if she doesn't take some time off.
carry out	complete: The plans were carried out perfectly.
check_out	leave; pay the bill: He checked out of the hotel while the family waited in the car.
check out	examine; find out about: We will check out that rumor to see if there's any truth to it.
come_out	be made known: He didn't want anything about his illness to come out until after he had retired.
come_out	be on the market: The new medicine came out just in time to save his life.
cross out	draw a line through: Cross out the incorrect addresses and put in the correct ones.
cut out	stop: Cut out that noise! You're waking the baby.
drag out	extend: She dragged out the story until we were all bored.
drop_out	quit: He dropped out of school when he was only fourteen.
figure out	work out a solution: We finally figured out how to fix the broken blinds.
find out	learn new information: They found out that they were cousins.
fish out	pull from the inside: She fished a handkerchief out of her handbag.
get_out (of)	leave: He got out of the car and walked.
get_out (of)	become free of something undesirable: She got out of washing the dishes by saying she had homework.
get out	remove: She scrubbed and scrubbed but she couldn't get out the stain.
get out	take from an enclosed place: She got out some cheese and crackers for a snack.
hang_out	spend idle time: He hung out with kids his parents disapproved of.
iron out	make a situation smoother: They ironed out their problems by discussing them honestly.
knock out	render unconscious: The ball hit him in the head and knocked him out.
leave_out	ignored; not a part of: The child felt left out because no one asked her to play.
leave out	omit: She left out the most important answer on the test.
let out	allow to leave: School let out early today. She let out the cat every night.
make out	see what something is or says; discern: The fog was so thick she could hardly make out the street sign.
pass out	distribute: The ushers passed out the programs.

pass out	faint: She passed out from lack of oxygen.
pick out	select: The teacher picked out the best papers and put them on the board.
point out	draw attention to: The engineer pointed out the weaknesses in the design.
put out	be irked: The patient was put out because she had to wait to see the doctor.
put out	work hard for: Those employees really put out for their boss.
rule out	omit from consideration: You can rule out George as the thief. He's absolutely honest.
run out (of)	deplete: Time has run out; the game is over. We've run out of tea; we'll drink coffee instead.
run out (on)	abandon: That man ran out on his wife and children.
set out	begin a journey: The bicyclers set out at dawn on their two-hundred-mile ride.
slip out	leave quietly: They were all so busy talking that no one noticed her slip out.
snap out (of)	break away from a negative condition: She snapped out of her depression when she heard the good news.
sound out	try to determine by listening: Father sounded out my boyfriend to see how he felt about marriage.
spell out	be specific: The director spelled out exactly what he expected of them.
stand out	be noticeable: She always stood out in a crowd because of her height and her silver hair.
stick out	extend: The nurse told the child to stick out her tongue.
straighten out	improve: That boy has been in a lot of trouble, but now he's trying to straighten out his life.
take out	remove: It's my son's job to take out the trash.
thin out	make less dense: The tree man thinned out the branches.
throw out	dispose of: Restaurants throw out a lot of food.
try out	sample by experience: We tried out the new coffeemaker, but we didn't like it.
turn out	end: I didn't finish the book, so I don't know how it turned out.
wear out	use until no longer functional: The washing machine finally wore out after twenty years.
weed out	select items to discard: They spent all day in the attic weeding out the junk.
wipe out	demolish: The village was wiped out by the earthquake.
work out	exercise: They work out at the gym every day.
work out	solve problems: They're trying to work out their problems by talking.

Phrasal Verbs with Through

be through	be finished: He worked for weeks on the project, but now he's finally through.
carry through	continue to completion: The father relied on his sons to carry through his last wishes.
carry through	have sufficient means or support: The money from his parents will carry him through the semester.
come through	fulfill expectations; achieve in spite of difficulties: We knew Dulce would come through for us when we needed her. She is always dependable.
fall through	fail to materialize: The plans for the new airport fell through because of lack of funds.
follow through	complete something already begun; implement: Bill initiated the project, and his staff followed through on it.

get through	be understood: We talked for an hour, but I still couldn't get my idea through to him.
go_through	endure; experience hardship or sorrow: Lin has gone through so much suffering already, I hate to give him more bad news.
go_through	search: She went through all her desk drawers looking for her keys.
live_through	experience: At age ninety, she has lived through many changes.
live_through	endure; survive: Those people have lived through years of war and hardship.
put through	connect: The operator in Africa put me through to my husband in ten minutes.
put through	be subjected to: The doctor put him through many tests before he diagnosed his illness.
ran through	read quickly: We only had time to run through our notes once before the exam began.
ran_through	rehearse: The cast ran through the last scene of the play several times.
ran_through	use up; deplete: The print shop runs through tons of paper in a week.
see through	stay with something until it is completed: She is determined to see her plans through to the end.
see_through	detect the real meaning behind a false front: She saw through his charm to his greed.

Phrasal Verbs with Over

ask over	invite: She asked her friend over to play after school.
blow_over	disappear: It took a few days for the bad feelings caused by the quarrel to blow over.
blow_over	move on: The storm blew over during the night and now the sun is shining.
carry over	continue later: Because it was so late, the meeting was carried over to Monday.
get_over	recover: She finally got over her cold and is feeling much better.
get_over	be surprised: She can't get over how huge this country is.
go_over	examine: The lawyer told them to go over the contract carefully before signing it.
go_over	review: The professor told the class to go over the last three chapters before the exam.
go_over	gain approval: His bad manners didn't go over well with her parents.
hand over	give to someone immediately: The guy with the gun said, "Hand over the money!"
have over	invite to one's home: They had eight people over for dinner.
hold over	stay longer than planned: That movie is so popular it's being held over for a week.
lay_over	stop on a trip: Our plane had to lay over in Boston because of the snow storm.
leave_over	surplus; extra: Three ears of corn were left over from dinner.
look over	examine; inspect: We looked over the neighborhood before we bought the house.
make over	redo: Tallie is going to make over her mother's wedding dress for her own wedding.
pass over	ignore; skip: He was very disappointed that he was passed over for the promotion.
pull over	go to the side: The policeman signaled the speeder to pull over to the curb.
put over	succeed through deception: That crook put one over on my uncle. He sold him some bad stocks.

run_over	exceed: We ran over our budget this month; we'll have to spend more carefully next month.
run_over	overflow: The heavy rains caused the river to run over its banks.
skim_over	read superficially: She only had time to skim over the long letter, so she missed the most important part.
skip_over	omit: He skipped over the boring parts of the book and just read the interesting parts.
smooth over	improve a troubled situation: He smoothed over the misunderstanding with tact.
take over	assume responsibility or control: The new nanny took over the household as if it were her own.
talk over	discuss: They talked over their problems instead of quarreling about them.
think over	consider carefully; ponder: I don't know whether I will or won't. Just give me time to think it over.
throw over	leave for someone else: Allie was shocked when her boyfriend threw her over for her best friend.
tide over	sustain temporarily: These groceries should tide us over until next week.
tip over	tilt and fall: The child ran into the Japanese screen and tipped it over.
turn over	relinquish: The former mayor turned over his office to the new mayor.
win over	persuade to be on one's side: The man won over the jury with his sincerity, and he was acquitted of the crime.

Phrasal Verbs with Up

back up	go in reverse: We had driven too far so we backed up a few feet.
back up	stand behind; confirm: The car dealership said they would back up the claim in their ads.
blow up	enlarge: The photographer blew up the snapshot so we could see the details.
blow up	exaggerate: The newspapers blew up the story to make it more interesting.
blow_up	explode in anger: She suddenly blew up and screamed at everyone in the room.
break_up	end a partnership or relationship: She and her boyfriend broke up after two years together.
bring up	mention: Don't bring up that subject; it makes her feel sad.
bring up	raise a child: Her aunt brought her up because her parents died in an accident.
burn up	be angry: He was really burned up about the lies she had told him.
call up	reach by telephone: She called up her mother, but the line was busy.
call up	select for military service: Even men with families were called up to fight.
catch_up	reach the same place or level: If we walk faster, we'll soon catch up with them.
cheer up	feel happier: Aunt Irene cheered everyone up with her optimism.
clear up	dispel information: He called us together to clear up the rumors going around the office.
come_up	be mentioned: His name came up several times while we were talking.
draw up	compose a document: The man drew up his will and left all his money to a charity hospital.
dress up	wear especially nice clothes: It's fun to dress up and go to a party once in a while.
dry up	deplete: Their source of information had dried up.
fix up	improve: They fixed up that old house and sold it at a good price.

get up	put together; organize: We're trying to get up a party to celebrate her birthday.
give up	abstain: He gave up cigarettes last year.
give up	sacrifice: She gave up her weekend to help her brother.
give_up	surrender: He tried for three days to solve the puzzle, but he finally gave up.
hang up	replace the telephone receiver: She hung up when she heard his voice.
hold up	delay: The parade held up traffic for a mile.
hold up	rob: A policeman in plain clothes was held up last night. He caught the robbers and arrested them.
keep up	maintain; continue as before: If he keeps up the good work, he will graduate with honors.
let_up	ease; abate: The storm let up toward daybreak.
lighten_up	take life less seriously: If he doesn't lighten up a bit, he's going to get sick from worry.
look_up	improve: The job market is looking up.
look up	seek information from books or records: If you don't understand what a word means, look it up in the dictionary.
make up	create through imagination: Eulalia could always make up wonderful stories.
make up	assemble; put together: We made up a list of volunteers.
make up	apply cosmetics: She takes special care making up her face if she's going to a party.
make_up	become friends after a quarrel: Let's make up and be friends.
make_up	complete what is lacking: His insurance will make up the difference between the charges and his payments.
make up	come to a decision (with *mind*): Mother made up her mind to move to Ireland.
measure_up	meet certain standards: The actress says she will never measure up to what she expects of herself.
mess up	make disorderly: He just got the desk in order when she came in and messed it up again.
mess up	spoil: Our travel plans were messed up by the bad weather.
mess up	bungle; do a bad job of: I really messed up the job interview.
pick up	make neat: They picked up all of the litter on their street.
put up	accommodate: They put us up for the night because we couldn't get hotel reservations.
show_up	appear: They showed up two hours late.
show_up	expose: Their lack of training showed up in their work.
stay_up	not go to bed: We stayed up until after midnight.
suit up	put on a sports uniform: The players suited up for the game.
take up	begin a new activity: He was seventy when he took up oil painting.
tear up	rip into pieces: I tore up the old checks.
throw_up	vomit; regurgitate: Fortunately, he threw up the spoiled food.
tie up	keep from going ahead: We got tied up in the five o'clock traffic and were late for the meeting.
turn_up	appear unexpectedly: They turned up at the party without an invitation.
use up	deplete: They used up all of their vacation days on weekend trips.
wake up	waken from sleep: She woke up early this morning.

wash up	come to dry land by the movement of water: The remains of the ship were washed up onto the shore.
wind up	end: They finally wound up the meeting at midnight.

Some verb phrases have an extra preposition. Here are a few using *up.*

come up with	think of: After thinking for hours, they came up with a good idea.
face up to	accept reality: He faced up to the fact that he didn't know how to do the work.
keep up with	stay even: He kept up with his studies, even though he was in the hospital.
live up to:	meet expectations; fulfill: The mayor is living up to his promises.
look up to	hold in esteem: She looked up to her mother and used her as a model for her own life.
put up with	tolerate: Most teachers won't put up with talking in class.
speak up for	express one's viewpoint: She's not afraid to speak up for the things she believes in.
stand up for	be strong in what one believes: Even though everyone disagreed, he stood up for his beliefs.
stick up for	defend; support: Stick up for your rights.
wait up for	be awake when someone comes home late: Her parents always wait up for her when she's out at night.

Phrasal Verbs with Down

boil down	condense: All that talk boils down to this: they don't want to go.
break down	analyze: They broke the problem down into its many parts in order to get an answer.
break down	lose control emotionally: He broke down and cried when he heard of his father's death.
break down	fail: The old car broke down on the freeway.
buckle down	get to work: We'd better buckle down and study; the final exam is next week.
calm down	become quiet or less agitated: She calmed down when she knew her child was safe.
die down	lessen: The cheers of the fans died down when their team lost.
flag down	signal to stop: The guard flagged us down as we approached the border.
let down	disappoint: I hate to let him down by telling him he didn't get the job.
mark down	put a lower price on: The shoes were marked down during the sale.
narrow down	make smaller, leaving the most important: The police narrowed down the suspects to three.
pin down	demand an answer: When the reporter pinned him down, he finally told the truth.
pipe down	be quiet: Pipe down! We can't hear the speaker!
put down	criticize; humiliate: That interviewer always puts down anyone who doesn't agree with him.
run down	become unwound: The alarm clock ran down during the night.
run down	to speak badly about someone: If he runs them down like that, he probably runs us down too.

simmer_down	relax; become calmer: The father told his angry son to simmer down and listen.
turn down	reject: The bank turned him down when he asked for a loan.
turn down	fold over: The hotel maid turned down the covers on the bed.
weigh down	be overburdened with: He was weighed down with worry about the war.

Some phrasal verbs are followed by a preposition. Here are a few with *down* + preposition.

back down on	retreat; yield: He backed down on his story when confronted by the facts.
crack down on	become strict: The police are cracking down on drug offenders.
cut down on	not use as much: We should all cut down on fat in our diets.
get down to:	begin something seriously: Let's get down to business; we've wasted too much time already.
go down in	be recorded: This date will go down in history as the first day of world peace.
look down on	feel superior to: People who look down on others are snobs.
talk down to	speak condescendingly: People who talk down to others are intellectual snobs.